Sea Island Roots:
African Presence in the Carolinas and Georgia

Edited by
Mary A. Twining & Keith E. Baird

With a Foreword by
John Henrik Clarke

Africa World Press, Inc.
P.O. Box 1892
Trenton, New Jersey 08607

To
Thomas and Timothy
and
Diana, Marcia, and Carmen

Africa World Press, Inc.
P.O. Box 1892
Trenton, NJ 08638

©1991
Mary A. Twining & Keith E. Baird

Cover Design by Ife Nii Owoo

Cover Illustration by Rosetta Williams

Typeset by TypeHouse of Pennington, Inc.

Library of Congress Catalog Card Number: 88-70201

ISBN: 0-86543-068-3   Cloth
      0-86543-069-1   Paper

Contents

Foreword

The aftermath of the African Independence explosion that started with the Gold Coast, now Ghana, in 1957, the Civil Rights Movement, and the student demand for Afro-American Studies, gave birth to a new renaissance of interest in African history and culture. At first, this interest was too broad to be effective. Now that the ceremony of self-discovery no longer consumes the time and attention it did during the early phase of this movement, serious scholars are calling attention to neglected areas of African history and culture, in what is called the "New World." This book is about one of the neglected areas of culture and folk history.

The Sea Islands of Georgia and the Carolinas, like most islands, are cultural incubators and containers. The contributors to this book examined the many dimensions of the culture and its manifestation, in time, and under pressure. A consistent theme runs through most of the articles in this book— cultural continuity and survival—in spite of pressure.

In human societies as a rule, it is in and through the family that the survival of the group is effected and cultural continuity assured and maintained. The survival of African people away from their ancestral home is one of the great acts of human endurance in the history of the world. In the United States, a nation of immigrants, we Africans were the immigrants against our will, the only immigrants who were "invited" here. We brought African cultures that refused to die. Some of the elements in these cultures helped to create what is distinctively American culture.

The culture of the Africans in the United States varied from one part of the country to the other but remained the same, basically. The culture of the Sea Islands is a special case. The lack of contact with the mainland helped to preserve some of the important features of their African culture. Because the Africans that were brought to these islands were not sold and resold as often as those on the mainland, some of their ancestral family patterns remain to this day.

This book is about the different dimensions of the culture of the African people who live on the Sea Islands. A book of this nature is urgently needed and long overdue.

John Henrik Clarke
Professor Emeritus of African History
Department of Black and
Puerto Rican Studies
Hunter College of the City
University of New York

Preface

S ome of this volume comes out of individual experience; some of the selections are by people whose lives were affected by their contact with the people of the Sea Islands. The compilers have tried to cover as many areas of significance as possible without putting together an encyclopedia. Other scholars such as Billingsley (1968), Staples (1978), McAdoo (1981), Stack (1974), Bambara, Ladner (1972), and Gutman (1976) have made valuable contributions to this history and sociology of the African American family. Their works are reliable and authoritative sources especially since they move toward an African-centered framework and assert the cultural autonomy of African American family and culture.

Among the Afro-American groups in North America, the culture of the Sea Islands is that most closely related to certain African cultures. On the Sea Islands, moreover, there are family and culture patterns that relate to areas along the African cultural continuum between Africa and the Americas, including Afro-North American, Afro-Caribbean and Afro-South American, as well as continental African societies.

The Sea Islands are a showcase in North America for the concept of creolization. This idea stemmed from the linguists' study of creole languages formed from the melding of languages in contact, and moved to the notion of creolization as a process not only in the formation of language but of society as well. At its simplest, creolization is a mixture of elements from different cultural sources. Like the Caribbean Island societies which have strong African components, the Sea Island families and culture constitute a mixture of African and European cultural elements which supply variety to the modes of life and expression of the people.

This culture complete with its own creole language, folklore and social institutions, is predominantly oral/aural in its communication. Its expressions are spoken and heard in an intensely sociable atmosphere as the Island dwellers carry on their lives in many face-to-face contacts every day.

The family is the single most important organizing principle in the Sea Islands as in other African and Afro-American communities. It is the intimate core from which everything else radiates. The memberships of voluntary associations such as the churches, the burial societies, the savings clubs, and the craft units are often predetermined through kinship and family connections. The organization of such social entities into a community, however, is in accordance with a different principle—that of binding together people not otherwise obligated to help each other as in the family grouping.

This collection of articles presents mainly the work of authors asked to contribute to this book. A few pieces were written and in some cases published some time ago. The late William Bascom and Simon Ottenberg are better known for their work on continental African cultures. Recognizing, however, the connection of the Sea Islands to other segments of the African world, they wrote papers on certain aspects of Sea Island society. In the light of such perceptions of trans-Atlantic African cultural relationships, Edisto Island, S.C., was the site of a linguistics field school conducted by Jack Berry for Northwestern University graduate students whose eventual aim was to do research in African societies.

Many of the matters Paul Salter writes about, such as the difficulties in control of water flow because of uneven field levels and the problems of drainage, are still a vital part of the agricultural situation on the Islands. Bascom's article on the folk beliefs surrounding children was written many years ago; since that time midwifery, which features in the article, has been outlawed in South Carolina. Conscious of their vulnerability and apprehensive of the law, present day midwives in the area are, understandably, not readily forthcoming with testimony; therefore it is difficult to elicit information on this subject from the elderly ladies who once practiced these vital skills. The influence and authority of these practitioners is bright in the memory of the culture of the Islanders, however, and many stories are told of the delivery of this or that child through the use of the material devices and ancillary beliefs cited by Bascom. African Americans now bear names which are more or less indistinguishable from those of European Americans, especially those of Anglo-Saxon origin. At an earlier period, however, and even presently in the intimacy of the family circle, Americans of African descent have borne names that relate them to their ancestral origins. Baird and Twining in their essay on naming practices discuss names used among Sea Islanders and show that naming customs followed patterns and served specific functions that originated in the cognitive equipment brought to the Americas by transplanted Africans.

Some interesting comparisons are made by Bamidele Agbasegbe Demerson among family units in the Sea Islands, Haiti, and Yoruba speakers in Nigeria. He makes clear the distinction between African and European attitudes toward marriage and children, and points out that the concept of illegitimate children is simply not present on the Sea Islands in the same degree as on the mainland.

In the essay on world view, Twining shows, in the words of the Islanders themselves, their feelings about the world in which they live. In the 1960s, when Civil Rights "struggles for radical change, true freedom and lasting justice" were in full vigor, this was a time of history in the making, and while there was a certain amount of "radical change," it became sadly apparent that "true freedom and lasting justice" would take a little longer. Throughout Twining's sojourn on the Islands, her sense of the world view of the people grew as it was revealed both in the maelstrom of social change and in the calmer currents of the traditional culture.

George Starks's article on song in the Sea Islands of necessity touches on other significant aspects of the folklife of the religion, such as dance and the movement associated with the sung music. The body percussion which marks the rhythm of otherwise unaccompanied singing is widespread in children's games, secular dances and religious music.

The "shout" referred to by Starks is still practiced today, though not as much as formerly. The "ring shout" has almost completely died out but still exists in the memory culture of the older residents. It is occasionally performed by the Sea Island Singers of St. Simons Island, Georgia.

One of the editors (Mary A. Twining) witnessed the returning home of a young man who had left the Islands and become a successful football star. His return was occasioned by an injury he had sustained. As he sat in church, immobile, an old lady of the choir tenderly inquired "What's the matter, son, couldn't you shout?" By that question she signified her concern for both his physical and spiritual well-being, since she knew that there had to be something wrong with a person unable to "shout."

Moore's account of her own "conversion" to a sense of her culture's Africanity is a human story which is in itself an illustrative vignette of the Afro-American experience. From an attitude of doubt and embarrassment she came, with the willing assistance of continental Africans with whom she was attending the Theological Seminary at Atlanta, to the realization that many of the practices and notions maintained by her archipelagan community were similar to and at times even identical with those of her classmates from Africa.

Inspired and guided by these insights, and aided by study of the works of Melville Herskovits, Lorenzo D. Turner, J.S. Mbiti, and others, Moore examined with the empathy of one from within the culture various aspects of the Sea Island way of life, including language, healing practices and burial observances. She discovered that what the Euro-American community regarded as "superstitions" were in fact part of a belief system that fitted into an African cultural continuum. This new understanding had for her the nature of a personal revelation.

William "Bill" Saunders grew up on Johns Island, South Carolina. He was a member of a dedicated and daring group who during the 1960s worked together under the leadership of Esau Jenkins to bring civil rights and social progress to their Island home. Today, as family man and outstanding community leader, he furthers the beneficial activity begun during those troubled, yet exciting times. In his informal, chatty essay, Bill Saunders discourses with candor and affection, communicating his and his fellow Islanders' pride in the recollection of their self-sufficiency in the past, and their sense of hopeful concern in the face of an uncertain but challenging future.

Saunders talks about his childhood days on the Island and some of the radical changes which have taken place since those times. He mentions many aspects of the folklife enjoyed by the Islanders, and their relationship with the environment. While recognizing the inevitability of progress, he laments the damage to the culture and the natural environment which seems to be the price exacted for the dubious benefits of change. At this point in the 1980s, Saunders feels there may be a resurgence of interest in the Island culture and an increase in the appreciation of its value for the national African American community.

Simon Ottenberg's descriptive analysis of leadership and change treats the area in its character of a small isolated Southern community—isolated as a consequence of racial exclusivity as well as geography, language and social custom. Little work has been done on leadership in Afro-American communities and many of the patterns of behavior he reported are still extant in the Sea Islands. The deacons of the church and the hierarchy of the other voluntary associations are found, particularly among the older and traditionally-oriented segments of the population. Patterns of authority are not readily apparent to the outsider and are never revealed to the supercilious European Americans in the communities if doing so can be avoided. The traditional patterns in these remote areas of the South are influenced by Civil Rights Movements, increased communication with the mainland, the advent of television and upward mobility. Ottenberg's "Shrimp Creek" however was typical of the old South where, for African Americans, some measure of safety lay in isolation and concealment. It is not surprising or insignificant that the three co-authors of the article, "Sea Islands as a Research Area," are all involved in a research project dealing with the historical roots and socio-cultural implications of the Afro-American experience. A notable feature of this piece is that the writers not only present the results of their study, but also express a profound concern regarding those traditions and lifeways they are investigating. The senior scholar, J. Herman Blake, himself a Sea Islander, exemplifies that happy combination of academic objectivity and person-in-the-culture sensibility which is suggested as desirable in this kind of research.

Their article can serve as a valuable guide for persons seriously interested in learning about cultures too long exploited as merely "fascinating" or "exotic." The cautionary remarks on the ethical responsibility of scholars investigating the Sea Islands are not to be lightly dismissed. For it is still too possible for irresponsible persons interested in the quick book and the "fast buck," like archeological pot hunters, to simply take what they want without regard for the effect on subsequent serious research or concern for the people whose lives they disrupt, and so to spoil the field for serious and ethical scholarship.

CHAPTER ONE

Sea Island Culture:
Matrix of the African American Family
Mary Arnold Twining and Keith E. Baird

I. THE SEA ISLAND FAMILY

It is possible to see the Sea Islands as a matrix of African American family traditions since it is the historical presence of Africans in isolated circumstances which insured the survival of families-in-the-culture. Thus, for instance, because of the retention in the Sea Islands of some West African attitudes toward family and children, young people left orphaned by the Civil War were absorbed into friendly households in accordance with an African cultural pattern which institutionalized the "gifting" of children (Herskovits, 1941). The Sea Island "extended" families retained many features which reflect the African heritage as well as the adjustments made to the slavery experience.

African American families have customs which are reminiscent of the various areas of Africa from which they came, and continuing research is expected to reveal much vital information in this regard. Thus Alex Haley (1970) was able to trace a branch of his family back to the Mandinka people of the Gambia in West Africa. Cultural clues from the material and non-material culture, including familial and voluntary association patterns, can be added to historical research into the past to identify and locate the precise ethnic groups from which some African Americans came.

Lorenzo Dow Turner in his important study, *Africanisms in the Gullah Dialect* (1949), traced lexical and grammatical features of Sea Island speech back to specific African languages. Melville J. Herskovits (1941) studied the cultures of African peoples both on the ancestral continent and transplanted in the Americas. He concluded that not only were there patent continuities between African and Afro-American cultural traits, but also that the Sea Islands, by reason of their relative isolation from the mainland, constituted a distinctive region the inhabitants of which exhibited the highest number of African cultural retentions to be found in the United States.

Thus, data concerning language usage, folktales, religious practices and polygynous mating can all be utilized to assemble a corpus of information concerning the African American past. This body of knowledge, some portions often retrieved from the oldest living members of the community, can be drawn upon to further the investigations into family history. While many of these culture traits have been more abundantly in evidence in the Sea Islands than elsewhere in the U.S.A., we can see similarities between other isolated neo-African populations (often rural) and the Sea Island culture that let us know that the case of the Sea Islands is not an atypical phenomenon. What we observe, as evidence accumulates, are cultural patterns common to the entire African World, whose characteristic features may have been modified but definitely were not erased by the European contact and interaction.

On Wadmalaw Island, for instance, one family gathers for conferences called by the mother which take place on or near the grave of a family forebear. This relates to an analogous custom among the Yoruba who bury certain ancestors under portions of the house. Meetings of a serious nature are held with the eldest person in the family conducting it from a seated vantage point on that grave. Another example is the persistence of polygynous marriages in which a man will have more than one wife with children for whom he is and feels responsible. Clearly this custom, useful in the agricultural economy of West Africa, was transferred to the similar situation in the Sea Islands. Other Africanisms include the naming of children according to circumstances existing at the time of their birth or relating to physical features; the Africanized Christianity which is practiced in the praise houses and churches; the singing styles, the carrying of head loads, the hair tying (preceding the modern return to corn rowing), the layered clothing and many other customs known but in the present state of scholarship not yet definitely associated with specific African societies.

The patterns of family membership, conjugal pairing customs, child rearing practices, and other family related aspects of Sea Island culture can accordingly be seen in the positive framework of the continuity of African precedents. They should also be understood in the context of the life of a people, taken unwillingly from their own homeland, who consciously and unconsciously passed on to their progeny elements of their traditional way of life which made at least survival possible in the new, alien and oppressive situation in which they found themselves. Enslaved Africans tended to structure their lives according to patterns inculcated early in whichever culture area of Africa they might have originated.

These various cultures, while characterized by differences in language and custom, were not incompatible and mutually exclusive; rather, they represented variations on a fundamental African cultural unity and integrity which structured their universe for them (Diop 1978). The most immediate evidence at once of origins and continuity was the family. The three systems of tracing descent—matrilineal, patrilineal and double—recognized by Billingsley (1968) are found both in West Africa and the United States (e.g., Ottenberg 1968). The Africanity at the core of the transplanted African family was a central organizing force that throughout the centuries sustained Africans in the Americas.

The Sea Islands is an area where these ancestral patterns have been seen possibly more clearly than in other Afro-American populations and therefore constitute a useful showcase of culture through the study of which a fuller understanding of the definite autonomy of African World culture may be obtained. More particularly we can appreciate the lasting vigor, and the value for group survival, of the African American family.

II. THE AFRICAN FAMILY IN TRANSPLANTATION

The cultural, societal and family behavior of Africans forcibly transplanted in the United States through the institution of slavery was, inevitably, profoundly disrupted by the violent impact of that experience. Their modes of conduct, their moral and aesthetic values, and their sense of psychosocial integrity were not, however, completely extinguished. On the contrary, the Africans reacted to the life situations imposed upon them in America by taking recourse to their ancestral patterns of social and cultural conduct to the extent that these modes of behavior could be re-enacted in the new environment.

Gutman (1976) has shown that enslaved Africans, even when separated and sold away from their spouses and children, endeavored to maintain communication with their loved ones and to preserve as much as they could of their familial attachment and mutual concern. Expressive behavior such as music and dance, religious beliefs and practices, and such arts and skills as basketry and fishing-net making, important as they are in the assessment of ancestral retentions, do not displace the marriage and family association patterns of transplanted Africans as the primary means of reaffirming the cultural ways of their continental homeland.

The study of the African American family is bedeviled to some degree by the fact that the notion "family" conjures up quite different images for

European Americans from those it does for members of the African World Community. Thus, what European American scholars refer to as "the extended family" is for African peoples "the family," and is therefore more typical for the African World situation than the European and European American "nuclear family." Any family unit, African, European, or otherwise, has shifting membership from time to time, so that it is difficult and even unwise to align a given family with a particular definition for all time. On the whole, however, African families, both autochthonous and diasporic, tend to be more inclusive of personnel while European American families are usually more exclusive.

Family size and composition may vary in African groups as custom or circumstance may dictate. Each family may consist of several households depending on whether the man in the patrilocal society has several wives and whether each of his brothers is also polygynous.

Billingsley (1968) has devised a classificatory scheme to order our knowledge about African-American families. While his tripartite classification into nuclear, extended and augmented families may be useful in guiding our thinking from a Euro-American perspective, it is more appropriate for our purposes to look at an Afrocentric scheme of how the family is structured. John Mbiti (1969) considers the family in terms of two dimensions—time and space. He gives the example, in such groups as the Basuto and Ngoni, of a request being forwarded to the Supreme Deity through the hierarchy of brothers, then fathers, then back to the deceased ancestors. The ancestral intercessors are regarded just as much a part of the family as the living members. The excarnate members of the family are clearly valued, especially the recently departed, some of whom are thought likely to reappear in the flesh in the persons of the newborn arriving in the family. (The name Babatunde in Yoruba means "father has returned.") The unborn stock of family members are also counted in as an integral, though unnamed, group of individuals.

Among traditional African Americans in South Carolina, there are domiciliary complexes or "compounds" consisting of several households assembled on the basis of kinship and economic constraints. Organized around the oldest progenitorial couple, often around the senior surviving female progenitor—since women tend generally to outlive men—such a complex of households encompasses brothers and sisters and their families all living in houses close by. A good example of this arrangement may be observed in the traditional Sea Island families in Mount Pleasant, who live in enclaves where several generations occupy houses situated in close proximity with a common open area in the midst as a kind of courtyard. This residence pattern closely approximates its African counterparts, adjustments being made to allow for the differences in climates. Members of the family sit in groups under the trees making baskets, joking, and generally enjoying one another's company. There is a high degree of communication and interdependence within these groups just as there is in their African prototypes. In both the African and the American setting, cooperative work patterns foster familial interaction and material productivity in the traditional mold.

The African custom of polygamy is still practiced. Needless to say, it is on a *de facto* basis as United States law makes no allowance for this mode of societal conduct, which it regards as deviant. As in Africa, polygamy in the Sea Islands might be more narrowly designated as polygyny, since it is the males who have multiple spouses. Polygynous families thus have not been unusual on the Sea Islands, and housing was adapted to the families' needs. Sometimes one wife and her offspring would live on one floor of the house, and another wife on the other. In other cases there might be a wall, with no door through, separating one wife's section of the dwelling from another's.

In addition, family sub-units, each consisting of a wife and her children, might be scattered throughout the community housed independently or living with her parents. These seemingly matrifocal residential enclaves, which are actually parts of polygynous marriages, are not readily observable to the casual or scientific observer from the mainstream culture. Varying degrees of acculturation on the part of African Americans and incomprehension of the part of European Americans may combine to mask the reality of the situation.

Interestingly enough, the involvement of enslaved Africans in polygynous marriages, related though it may have been to their African cultural traditions, was actively promoted by the European American slave-owners who encouraged, even compelled, the breeding of many children to increase the labor force. Historically, the economics of agriculture has required numerous personnel, whether kin or peons, chattel slaves or migrant workers. In treatment of African American polygamy, discussion has tended to center on the man's having several wives. It should be recognized, as part of the record relating to multiple marriages, that during slavery women also found themselves with more than one husband, either simultaneously or serially, to whom they were bound emotionally. Marital unions were broken and families were disrupted through the selling away and remarriage of one of the partners of an enslaved African marriage. A man might thus find himself with ties to two or more families, with a wife and children in each case; similarly a woman may have been married two or more times with children from each union, and emotional attachments to each of her husbands from whom she was involuntarily separated. When after emancipation men and women sought or were sought after to be reunited with prior spouses and families, complex situations resulted, calling for solomonic wisdom to resolve.

Elizabeth Botume (1893), a northern schoolteacher in the Sea Islands, told of four distinct situations in which Africans, through the harsh vicissitudes of their enslavement, found themselves embroiled in marital complexities. In one case, a woman had two sons by her first husband and a daughter by the second. Both husbands returned, each took his offspring and departed, leaving the woman with neither spouse nor children. Another woman remarried after the protracted absence of her first husband. He returned, and rejecting her efforts to resume their marriage, himself remarried and took his daughter away with him. In the third case, a formerly enslaved African returned to claim his wife who was by that time married to another man. The woman, who had borne children to neither man, decided to spend a few weeks with each husband and then make her choice. She elected to stay with her second husband. In the fourth situation, the husband was sold away after the couple had had a child. The woman did not expect her first husband to be able to return, and remarried. She explained to her second husband, however, that if her first husband did manage to come back that he (the first) would be her husband above all others. The first husband did return. The wife had a letter dispatched to the second husband who was at that time in the federal army, reminding him of what she had said at the time of their marriage. Responding to a question put to her on her decision, she explained: "Martin is my husband . . . and the father of my child; and Ferguson is a man." (Gutman 1976, 421-422)

The African background, or memories of it, was no doubt a steadying influence in the changeable socioeconomic atmosphere of the prewar South. In human communities, culture systems provide structure which maintains some consistency and a certain amount of predictability around which to build lives. In the hostile and insecure environment of the American slave system, where alien and repugnant values were urged upon the enslaved Africans, the ancient certainties from Africa filled in the sociocultural spaces for which the dominant group provided no substitutable concepts or institutions.

The female elders called "Mammys" or "Mommas" functioned as such matriarchs had in Africa, teaching to yard and house children alike communal proprieties, familial lore and basic survival strategies—a heritage the South still enjoys today. The West African societies who contributed to the population of the Sea Island communities would find their descendants and diasporic relatives as well-spoken and respectful as their ancestors and contemporaries were in West Africa.

The customs of child rearing have also been carried over from the African background. The sometimes acrimonious debate on illegitimacy is merely a reflection of the patrilineal, male-dominated mainstream society whose ethnocentric notions on the subject seem beyond question. In most West African societies children are regarded as legitimate whatever the parentage, since the children belong not only to their biological parents, but to all the adults in the community. Families everywhere organize themselves within a societal context to insure the raising of children within a stable social and economic unit. Families also provide mutual support and refuge for their members, or at least a standard by which to measure a society's capability to cope with life's vicissitudes. The Afro-American family shares universal characteristics with all other families. However, it has a special distinction as a group institution which has survived unusual emotional and physical hardships. Brought to America in extremely adverse circumstances, not only did the Africans adapt to the exclusively monogamous Christian marriage form of the Euro-Americans, but they also maintained their African polygynous customs where feasible and possible. The isolation of the Sea Islands provided a perfect situation for the transplanted Africans to re-create their ancient culture, because the polygynous family functioned well in the agricultural economies of both West Africa and the Southeast coastal United States.

Viewed from the conventional perspective of the dominant Euro-American society, polygyny still looks like deviant behavior. The practice, however, emanated from an authentic socio-economic imperative and had its own cultural validity, even though understanding and appreciation of its societal value has been obstructed by Eurocentric prejudice and puritanical misinterpretation.

In Africa polygyny was a means of extending and strengthening the kinship network, since marriage was not a simple dyadic union, but a relationship established between the families of the married couple. The complex interlinking of families created an intricate web of communal interactions and interdependencies which bound people together in a closely knit society, cemented by mutual concerns, common values and reverend sanctions. In America, Africans forced into involuntary polygynous arrangements, drawing on their cultural heritage, strove—to the extent that it was possible—to maintain their ties of familial affection and to establish kinship networks of assistance and support, emotional and otherwise, for their children. The sense of kinship and community thus engendered was not only a creative response to the shared negative experience of slavery, but also a practical means of ensuring the survival of the African American people.

There are a variety of systems in various African societies to structure the family and cope with problems of inheritance. One attitude in particular seems to have been retained in the African American Sea Islands population: the notion that no children are in fact illegitimate. The issue of legitimacy of birth relates to the importance of property and the establishment of primacy in the order of inheritance. Legitimacy is a matter of importance in patriarchal societies that need to insure the control and passing on of property through the male.

There are some African groups whose mores require that a pregnant daughter or sister be immediately married off, because the child at birth would otherwise be literally nameless and therefore non-existent without its agnatic kinsfolk from the male progenitor's family. In many West African traditional societies, however, children are welcomed without overstrict regard for questions of "legitimacy," because they add to the total familial entourage, the size of which signifies fertility and well-being.

Such an attitude has received positive reinforcement from the fact that in America, slave owners had but small respect, if any, for the conjugal bonds or any other family ties of the Africans they controlled. All African children were thus from a Euro-American standpoint orphans, either actual or potential—or, to put it differently, of equally precarious exclusive parental attachment. There was no tangible, transferrable property to be inherited either through the male or female line. However, from the standpoint of the enslaved Africans, because of values and attitudes deriving from the traditional African kinship network, reinforced by imposed conditions of polygamy and polygyny, all African children were considered as belonging to the community at large, and were brought up to regard and to respect every African adult as a parent. Legitimacy, with its notions of exclusivity in connection with inheritance, was therefore irrelevant. What was relevant for the enslaved Africans was the bond of common origin, common status, common suffering, and common inclusive affectional regard and group concern for all the children—the community's main evidence of and hope for the possibility of perpetuity.

III. INTRODUCTION TO SEA ISLAND FOLKLIFE

The Sea Islands of the United States are located along the coasts of South Carolina and Georgia, extending almost four hundred miles from the southern border of North Carolina to the northern border of Florida. The Islands themselves, actually a part of the coastal plain, are readily accessible by the sea through the streams, riverine waterways and brackish marshes which separate them from the mainland. Some of the Islands are located far enough out in the ocean to require boats for transportation, while others are now connected (since the 1930s) to the mainland by bridges or causeways, making access possible by car or bus. The continuing inaccessibility of some rural Islands such as Sapelo and Daufuskie, a key factor in their economic and social life, perpetuates the isolation that has so significantly operated to preserve the folklore and culture of the Sea Island area. These Islands have been written about as a source of interesting cultural phenomena since before the days of the American Revolution (Jones 1960; Wood 1974). Often the accounts in the nineteenth and early twentieth centuries tended to stress the exotic nature of the customs of the people, and that attitude survives today in some of the literature. This is not entirely surprising since the Sea Islanders, although native to the United States of America, actually manifest in their speech, customs, and general manner of life, features which show greater affinities with the Afro-Caribbean populations and continental African peoples than with other Americans of African origin.

The Sea Island area has a long history of European exploration and appreciation; writers have recorded the climate and vegetation and general atmosphere of the place since the coming of Spanish explorers such as Lucas Vásquez, who came to Florida and Saint Helena Island (Santa Elena) in the 1520s. French Huguenots were not far behind the Spanish adventurers, as they arrived in Port Royal in the 1560s in order to escape the persecutions at home, much as the English did in the following century (Jones 1960; Wood 1974).

The first European arrivals were explorers and adventurers for the most part. Later, however, plantation owners from Barbados and other Caribbean areas disembarked, bringing with them their households and enslaved Africans to settle in the Ashley River area and other parts of South Carolina in the seventeenth century. These families formed the nucleus of what is still a very Anglophilic society. Their arrival and settlement is documented both in Barbados and South Carolina, and is easily seen in the similar family names borne by both African Americans and Euro-Americans in both places (Chandler 1946). Their historically-documented presence gives us a key to the cultural similarities found between the Caribbean and Sea Islands.

Military service in the Second World War dramatically broadened the experience and raised the expectations of many Sea Islanders. War veterans expressed their feelings regarding the need for change. However, improvement was long in coming and is still in process. As a result, as late as the mid-1960s, some veritable peonage conditions remained among the farming population in spite of their efforts toward the amelioration of social and economic inequities.

The Civil Rights Movement of the 1960s helped to raise the social awareness of the Islanders, and effected some few alterations in their lifestyle designed to better their way of life through increased economic opportunity. Improvement projects achieved varying degrees of success. For example, it was expected that through well-intentioned government teams such as "Catch Up" and "Speed Up," educational gaps would be eliminated and positive social and economic changes would result. In the Sea Islands, however, the "grassroots" movement of the 1960s, which emanated from the people themselves, was more successful than any of the government teams. The late Esau Jenkins of Johns Island actually began an adult literacy campaign with the help of the Voter Education Project and Highlander Folk School (Carawan 1966). The idea was his own and it spread from Johns Island across the South from its small beginnings in one of Mr. Jenkins' buses.

Thus change and progressive attainment of some mainland socioeconomic norms have resulted not merely from passive acculturation, but from active participation by the Islanders themselves. The acquisition of a new and different lifestyle almost inevitably involves some loss of old habits and values. Indeed, the greater the extent of acculturation, the higher is the degree of erosion of original distinctive features. By the same token, cultural retentions are precisely those folkways which have significantly and obstinately resisted or escaped acculturation pressures. Parameters of acculturation may serve, therefore, by a reversal of emphasis, as measures of cultural survival.

Increased transportation and communication between the mainland and the Islands, together with socioeconomic progress resulting from the Civil Rights Movement, have tended to mitigate the Islands' isolation. These mitigative factors, however, have not yet (by 1985) been strong enough to extinguish completely the Islanders' distinctiveness in such cultural modes as language, oral lore, social and economic organization, and some aspects of material production. As a result, there persist within the population certain behaviors and attitudes, moral values and aesthetic preferences, creative arts and useful crafts, which are quite alien to European cultural traditions; on the contrary, these traits can be traced back to African origins. These cultural retentions, deeply rooted as they are in ancestral African folkways, are of considerable importance in the study of Sea Island family life. For although they exist in syncretistic form, these survivals are still eminently functional in the society; and at the same time, consciously and unconsciously, Sea Islanders clearly derive from them a reassuring sense of cultural and historical continuity.

Four features have been proposed as indices which may be useful in thinking about cultural retentions in population enclaves: language, education, religion, and demography (Gilbert 1953). We shall remark on each one of these four features in relation to the people of the Sea Islands as we indicate the degree and nature of African continuities in both their societal structure and familial functioning.

In the Sea Islands, the local creole language, Gullah, is spoken mainly by the older people and the children, who are primarily monolingual.[1] The group between the two age extremes is upwardly mobile, and actively strives to assimilate to the dominant national culture with a view to procuring the resultant socioeconomic advantages. The attendant linguistic division is reinforced by the fact that the old people care for the very young while the parents go off to the mainland to work. Sometimes they work at locations which permit their daily return home, and sometimes they work further off and see their children less frequently.

Some members of this mobile group become bilingual; they acquire the proficiency in English necessary for success in their off-island endeavors, but have recourse to Gullah when they meet other Islanders and when they return home to the family elders and to their own children.

Lorenzo Dow Turner (1949) has shown that the Sea Island speech in its vocabulary (including personal names) as well as in its phonetics, morphology and syntax, exhibits elements directly traceable to their origins in West African languages. Since, as we have noted, the children spend their early years in the care of their grandparents, it is in the course of this relationship that the young acquire Gullah as their first language.

In sum then, we have a situation in which a significant portion of the Afro-American Sea Island population, possibly as high as sixty percent, is at all times retentive of the creole. Another, perhaps slightly less numerous group, is at least partially retentive, even though subject to the influence of contact with the dominant Euro-American language habits.

There has been some difference of opinion as to the degree of continuing use of Gullah in the Sea Islands. Johnson (1972) maintains that returning to St. Helena Island in 1965 for the first time in thirty-five years he did not hear a single phrase of "the old-time Gullah." He concluded that on St. Helena and possibly on Edisto and other easily accessible islands, Gullah had all but disappeared. The present editors took a group of Atlanta University graduate students on a field trip to Johns Island in the summer of 1974 and heard Gullah spoken by Islanders of all ages. Baird (1980) suggests that the reason Johnson did not hear Gullah is that his presence as a European American might have caused the Sea Islanders to code-switch from Gullah to English. Jones-Jackson (1983) has compiled a description of some of the persistent features of "contemporary Gullah." She comments that while some linguists are of the opinion that the language is dead or dying, residents of the Islands, teachers, and administrators with a high concentration of Island students will surely disagree. Jones-Jackson (1983) clarifies her use of the expression "contemporary Gullah":

> I use the term "contemporary Gullah" to describe the language as it now exists on the Sea Islands. It is being influenced by outside motivational forces such as better transportation and better educational facilities. These forces, however, are not yet strong enough to influence the language to the extent that it has become indistinguishable from Black dialect or standard English.

There are some interesting implications here for the origin, nature and development of what Dillard (1972) has so strongly vindicated as a language in its own right, and called "Black English." One of the present editors (Baird) prefers to refer to the language resulting from the African-English language contact as "Afrish" (cp. English, Spanish, Polish, etc.), since the term clearly indicates the connection with African-originated speakers and avoids the gratuitous employment of the reference to English as in "Black English." Thus it is emphasized that the creole speech formed as a result of the language contact between speakers of African languages and speakers of English is a linguistic continuum that embraces the United States variety (U.S. or American Afrish), the Caribbean variety (Caribbean Afrish), as well as that of Sierra Leone (where the Afrish spoken has for years been called Krio, that is "creole"). Gullah is mutually intelligible with the Caribbean Afrish of Barbados and Jamaica, for example, and shares with them an origin in the proto-Afrish of the early days of the slave trade. The persistence among the Sea Islanders of Gullah to the degree noted is a significant indication not only of the extent of linguistic retention, but also of the nature of the familial interaction which has been a factor in the transmission and preservation of the language.

Closely related to language as an index of cultural retention is education: how many children are enrolled in school? In discussing a parallel situation among the enslaved Africans in the quite sizable Caribbean island of Jamaica, Curtin (1955) stated that they were left to their own devices in educating their children. As a result, Curtin says, " . . . there developed a new culture compounded of the diverse elements of the African heritage and some European elements." A similar situation obtained in the Sea Islands,, where geographical isolation from the dominant metropolitan culture, though not as marked as Jamaica, also definitely influenced the acquisition of formal learning among the African American population.

Two additional factors served to put a brake on the acculturation of Sea Islanders. The first, curiously enough, was an unexpected consequence of civil rights legislation. The percentage of enrollment decreased in South Carolina when school attendance became voluntary rather than mandatory following the 1954 Supreme Court decision concerning school desegregation. Consequently, though children may have been registered in school, attendance was not compulsory according to state law and many did not always attend.

The second additional factor retarding the process of acculturation was the predominantly agricultural basis of the Sea Islands' economy, and this factor became linked with the first. As a result of the change in attendance requirements, young people of school age could make themselves available to work in the fields and with their meager earnings contribute to their families' support, thus reinforcing family solidarity. In return, the young people derived from their elders a prolonged period of cultural indoctrination and social initiation into Sea Island folkways, undistracted by the acculturative inducements to mainstream American values and conduct which public schooling normally provides. For many youthful Sea Islanders, then, school did not intrude significantly upon their living habits; and consequently their cultural traditions were left relatively undisturbed, and their family allegiances were enhanced and confirmed.

The third index of cultural retention is religion: what percentage of the group practices traditional religion? As compared with Euro-American forms, a singular situation arises in the Christian church of the Sea Islanders, whose syncretistic practices relate as much to West African ceremonial as to Euro-American Christianity. The syncretized Christianity of the Islands bears resemblance to the Africanized religious forms and ceremonials of Cuba, Haiti, and Brazil, where Santería, Voodoo and Umbunda all have a strong admixture of European and African elements. The African aspects are more obvious in Brazilian and Afro-Cuban groups; viewed on the surface, the European contribution is more apparent in the Sea Islands, but a certain amount of syncretism is present. A so-called Methodist service in the Islands closely resembles what one finds in Herskovits's description of a West African Legba cult ceremonial. Here we recognize an Afro-European religious syncretism and can classify this particular variety of Christianity as the traditional religion of the African-descended Islanders. The religiosity of African peoples is well-known, and conjointly with African family traditions, both in concepts and practice, it has been a source of psychological reassurance and a motivation toward survival, for religious gathering is a primary institution of socialization in the Sea Island culture. It was in the praise house that the families traditionally assembled to celebrate their joy in being together and to reaffirm their faith, albeit attired in the habiliments of Christianity, that they could, and would somehow, survive.

The fourth parameter of cultural retention is the demographic index: what percentage of the group is African American? The population of Johns Island (ten miles from Charleston, S.C.) is fifty percent African American. As one proceeds further from the urban center among the Islands, the African American demographic proportion increases until one reaches Edisto Island at the other end of Charleston County, where the African American population is eighty-five percent to European American fifteen percent. The Sea Island population may accordingly be estimated as close to seventy percent African American. Taken together with the implications for the family of the linguistic, educational, and religious factors, the significance of the. numerical preponderance of African Americans is readily apparent; for this factor definitely provides a basis for, and an indication of, the relative viability of African cultural retentions and the strength of familial connections.

In light of the four indices of retention discussed above as applied to the Sea Island case, it is clear that the erosive influence of mainstream culture, even though undeniably operative, has nevertheless left a considerable residue of Island folklife relatively intact. Moreover, in addition to the physical separation from the continent and the comparative lack, until recently, of easy communication with the greater mainland area, historical factors attendant on slavery have limited the opportunity for wide-ranging social and cultural contacts and thus have favored African retentions.

The agricultural history of the Islands has moved through various one-crop economies including indigo, rice, cotton, potatoes and truck gardening. Indigo was grown before the American Revolution and was a government-subsidized crop; the Revolution put an end to the price supports from Britain, and the cultivation of indigo ceased. Rice, a crop as capricious as indigo, became the big seller and continued until replaced by cotton, though both rice and cotton were grown simultaneously by owners who had more than one plantation. Cotton was enormously successful, but its growers experienced serious labor problems which have been well discussed in *A Woman Rice Planter* (1913). Elizabeth Allston Pringle (1913) and Frances Butler Leigh (1883) encountered similar difficulties and found the system with which they had grown up to be neither economically viable nor workable. After the Civil War, the members of the old planter class made the painful discovery that they could not run the plantation by relying on the old obligations without the old coercions to make the ex-slaves work.

The Africans had ceased to be chattel. Plantation owners could no longer at their convenience sell away members of African American families. They failed to recognize that the African American family, freed from the manipulative power of the former slave-owner, was in fact a social and economic entity possessing its own values and following its own existential imperatives. The lack of understanding of this fundamental fact of the changed relationship between African Americans and European Americans led the planters to attempt to conduct their business on the basis of the assumptions which had operated in the old situation, with disastrous economic consequences.

Other factors contributed to the planters' economic downfall, including the fierce storm in 1915 which destroyed the cotton crop and ruined the soil for further agriculture of that type. The great days of Sea Island cotton yielded to those of vegetable gardening, now the favored agriculture. Sea Island potatoes dominated the crop list for a while, but in the last ten years, emphasis has shifted to tomatoes. Cabbages and other vegetables are now also grown on a large scale (Johnson 1930).

European Americans controlled the land before the Civil War, and even though some of the Southerners lost their property during that upheaval, European Americans from the North came down to buy the land at the cheap prices. By replacing the older Southern owners, they effectively perpetuated the peonage system. Some owners tried to continue the outmoded pattern of mutual paternalistic obligations through sharecropping, but found it unsuccessful. As a system of agricultural economics, it could no longer function without either the coercion of slavery or the reward of money. Land was made available for purchase to the African Americans under the aegis of the Freedman's Bureau, and many preferred to work for themselves. Their former association with the land was continued under altered circumstances and a kind of peasantry came into being.

Although many of the African Americans acquired land during the time of the Freedman's Bureau immediately following the Civil War, they have since had much of this land systematically taken from them by legal and extralegal means (Rose 1960). When the Sea Island veterans came back after the Second World War, they had seen how some of the rest of the world lived and they felt the injustice of the peonage based on racial segregation under which they had existed. The landowners had let a lot of arable land go back to swamp and trees during the Second World War so that less labor would be needed to maintain the farms. The European American farmers further retaliated to demands for increased wages and decent working conditions by bringing in foreign contract laborers from Florida, many of whom were Caribbean. As a result, more people on the Islands had to look for jobs elsewhere and many were shipped off to

Northern fruit orchards in trucks as contract laborers themselves. Through migrant work, the people could earn enough money to come back home to the Islands to live. This migrant labor had a divisive impact on the family similar to that of the selling off of its members during slavery times.

The only economic opportunities for many are still off the Islands. Kiser (1932) shows the conflicts in the lives of the St. Helena Islanders whose strong desire to stay with their families and community competes with their desire to make money. The closely knit, broadly-based families, and the voluntary association which cut across kinship lines, combine with other factors to make the Island people unwilling to leave and anxious to return. Economic opportunities are not available on the Islands except at the peak agricultural seasons. Some Islanders venture into the larger society to make money in the North for the sole purpose of coming home to their families on the Sea Islands on long weekends. Because of the linguistic barriers and the racial situation, some of the Islanders have a difficult time finding work in the outside world, where, among other disadvantages, they run into the temptations of illicit drugs. For women, in the past, prostitution was often one of the few available occupations. With almost every family in the Islands having someone "up North," a great deal of movement takes place between the Islands and the more northerly cities. Still others of the Islanders obtain educational or vocational opportunities off the Islands and, remembering the lack of economic opportunities and the segregation system of the past, do not want to return home.

In former times, the seasons of the agricultural year governed the lives of the Islanders. Their existence was patterned in accordance with the seasonal requirements of the climate and the demands of the planters to whom they owed work. It was a life limited by these constraints for people whose education or contacts might have led them to have other ambitions. For some, agricultural work was the only opportunity, and this fact controlled their lives. While they did fewer of the regimented tasks handed out by the overseers, the former slaves adapted themselves and their land to the only work they knew. Though the social situation had changed because of the Civil War, the Islanders continued to be bound by the land on which they had been enslaved. This transition to peasant status meant not change but continuity in many of their lives and folkways, since the agricultural situation and isolation remained two of the controlling factors. Some of the endemic problems discussed by Claude Kiser (1931) still exist today. For example, the drainage problems on St. Helena Island, South Carolina, described in Kiser's *Sea Island to City*, persisted forty years later on Johns Island, South Carolina. It was the continuity, however, of the agricultural situation which made it possible for Sea Island culture to remain stabilized through the years until increased transportation and communication began to disturb the traditional patterns.

The similarities between the predominantly agricultural economies of West Africa and the southeastern United States made possible the transference of some folkways and cultural attitudes on the part of the enslaved West Africans who composed the bulk of the slave population; the continuance of polygynous marriage customs in spite of the lack of a legal structure to support it is but one example (King 1875). The interrelated life of the African American family in the rural agricultural economy included fishnet making and using, oyster-picking and crab fishing, agricultural plowing, planting, pounding of rice, and raising of stock such as chickens and pigs. Marketing, savings clubs, insurance societies and lodges—all African carryovers—are significant integrative activities which require intensive family interaction, and which relate the families to the community as a whole. Economic activity is lowest on Herskovits's scale of African retentions in the Americas. The African Americans functioned within the plantation economy as slaves and later under the evolved peonage in the South as peasants and sharecroppers. In time they also participated in the open market, selling their produce and livestock much as they might have done in African or Caribbean market economies.

In reviewing the factors which qualify the Sea Islands as a laboratory for the study of the African American family, we commented on language, folk arts, education, population concentration, and religion among other cultural continuities. We utilized these indices of cultural retention to demonstrate the durability and survival of the African American family in the face of oppression and exploitation. The Sea Islands culture, though itself undergoing change, thus represents a crystallized stage of development of the total African American community.

FOOTNOTE

1. Some European Americans who have intensive contact with the African American community can and do speak Gullah in communicating with the African American Sea Islanders.

REFERENCES

BAIRD, K.E., 1980, "Guy B. Johnson Revisited." Journal of Black Studies, 10/4 June.

BILLINGSLEY, A., 1968, Black Families in White America. Englewood Cliffs: Prentice Hall.

BOTUME, E., 1983, First Days Among the Contrabands. Boston: Lee & Shepard.

CARAWAN, G., 1966, Ain't You Got A Right to the Tree of Life. New York: Simon & Schuster.

CHANDLER, A.D., 1946, "The Expansion of Barbados." Journal of the Barbados Museum and Historical Society, nos. 3 & 4.

CURTIN, P., 1955, Two Jamaicas. Cambridge: Harvard University Press.

DIOP, C.A., 1978, Cultural Unity of Black Africa. Chicago: Third World Press.

GILBERT, W.H., 1953, Compilation of material relating to the Indians of the United States and the tribes of Alaska including certain laws and treaties affecting such Indians. Appendix II U.S. Congress report and respect to the House Resolution authorizing the committee on Interior and Insular Affairs to conduct an investigation of the Bureau of Indian Affairs, Washington, D.C.

GUTMAN, H., 1976, The Black Family in Slavery and Freedom. New York: Random House.

HALEY, A., 1976, Roots. New York: Doubleday.

HERSKOVITS, M.J., 1941, Myth of the Negro Past. New York: Harper.

JOHNSON, G.B., 1980, "Gullah Dialect Revisited." Journal of Black Studies 10/4 June.

JOHNSON, G.G., 1930, A Social History of the Sea Islands. Chapel Hill: University of North Carolina Press.

JONES, K., 1960, Six Flags Over Port Royal. Indianapolis.

JONES-JACKSON, P., 1983, "Contemporary Gullah Speech." Journal of Black Studies 13/3 March.

KING, E., 1875, The Great South. Hartford: The American Publishing Co.

KISER, C., 1932, Sea Island to City. New York.

OTTENBERG, S., 1968, Double Descent in an African Society: the Afikpo village group. Seattle: University of Washington.

ROSE, W.L., 1960, Rehearsal for Reconstruction. New York.

TURNER, L.D., 1949, Africanisms in the Gullah Dialect. Chicago: University of Chicago.

WOOD, P., 1974, Black Majority. New York: Knopf.

CHAPTER TWO

Changing Agricultural Patterns on the South Carolina Sea Islands*

Paul Sanford Salter

Much has been written on the Sea Islands of South Carolina and Georgia, particularly concerning pre-Civil War plantation life and Sea Island cotton. However, there is little in the geographic literature on changes in this region since the Civil War period and the accompanying breakdown of the plantation way of life.

Much of the observable change during the past century represents an attempt to fill the economic void created by the collapse of the plantation system. It is the intent of this article to determine to what extent the agricultural geography of the Sea Islands, with particular emphasis on the South Carolina segment, has changed since the downfall of this unique land use system.

PHYSICAL SETTING

The coastline of South Carolina is approximately 281 miles in length and is distinguished by a string of low-lying islands separated from the mainland by numerous inlets, marshlands, and tidal creeks. These islands, regionally known as the Sea Islands, are but one segment of a longer chain that parallels the coast from Cape Romain southward to near Jacksonville, Florida. The number of islands that lie off the coast of South Carolina is

*This article was first published in the *Journal of Geography* 67:4 (1968):223-228.

approximately 100, but only fifteen of them are of economic and historical importance.

The Sea Islands are unusual in their origin, physiography, and geographical arrangement and have climatic and vegetation characteristics that differ from areas just a few miles inland at the same latitude. Single strands of islands are found in the northern and southern boundary extremes of this study, while in the central portions of the region two and three islands group parallel the coast (Seigler 1959). The South Carolina Sea Islands are under the influence of a warm marine environment. The subtropical climate is atypical for this latitude and is reflected in the various tropical and subtropical types of vegetation found on the islands.

HISTORY

The early history of the region can be divided into two distinct periods: (1) the early exploration and settlement attempts by the French and Spanish, and (2) the successful settlement of the islands and adjacent coast by the English. The latter period saw the beginning of a plantation economy based upon indigo, rice, and slavery. This plantation system reached its fullest development between the American Revolutionary War and the Civil War. The importance of indigo, the first plantation crop, terminated with the end of the Revolutionary War. Rice, which was introduced in the 1700s, continued as a major plantation crop along the mainland coast and adjacent areas of the Islands. The introduction of long-staple cotton brought an era of rapid agricultural expansion and new settlement to the islands and dominated the land use pattern until the Civil War brought about a collapse of the plantation system (Blackman 1880).

The ending of the plantation system created notable changes in land use patterns on the Islands as the larger plantations were either abandoned or reduced in size. Long-staple cotton continued as the economic mainstay of the Sea Islands until it was wiped out permanently by the boll weevil. Rice decreased in the decades after the Civil War and was finally terminated by a series of severe hurricanes in the 1890s (Harris 1894).

CHANGING AGRICULTURAL PATTERNS SINCE 1900

In recent times the agricultural life of the Sea Islands has leaned as heavily upon truck gardening as it did previously on indigo, rice, and cotton. It furnishes the livelihood of at least 150 large-scale growers and hundreds of small-scale farmers. The end of rice and cotton production brought some immediate land-use changes. The former rice plantations, which proved unsatisfactory for growing cotton and other field crops, were abandoned in large numbers and many have since been bought by wealthy sportsmen who have turned them into private estates and hunting preserves. The Sea Island cotton planters were more fortunate than the rice planters in that a majority of them held on to their land. After the boll weevil struck, some planters turned to the short-staple variety. However, a great number of them, and even some of the small farmers, went into truck farming. By the end of the first quarter of the 1900s, the Sea Island agricultural picture had been completely altered and the term "planter" was a word of the past; gone also were the tenant and sharecropping systems. Cotton acreage grew smaller and smaller with each passing year. The small farmers and the former tenants and sharecroppers, at a loss where to turn when the boll weevil ended the cotton industry, followed the example of the large truck farmers in the type of vegetables grown and the methods of planting, cultivating and marketing.[1]

TRUCK FARMING

The truck farms of the Sea Islands are located between the truck farming regions of Florida and the Eastern Shore. They are mostly concentrated between Charleston and Beaufort on the large erosion-remnant islands of Johns, Wadmalaw, Edisto, St. Helena, Ladies, and Hilton Head. Between the end of the Florida truck season and the beginning of the Eastern Shore harvest there is a lapse of approximately three weeks, and during this interval Sea Island truck farmers ship eighty percent of their vegetables.

The climate of the region is ideal for truck crops with a growing season averaging between 250 and 300 days, depending on the proximity to marine influences; this is very similar to the growing season of Central Florida, another prominent truck farming area. The scarcity of early or late killing frosts is due to the insular location of the region and the proximity to the Gulf Stream. The sandy loam soils found on the islands, particularly the larger, erosion-remnant islands, are extremely well-suited to vegetable production, although due to the flatness of the terrain and swampy conditions all the truck soils need to be drained. When drained, all respond well to fertilizers and lime.

The first large truck growers were absentee farmers who handled and transacted their business through supervisors and agents. Smaller truck farmers who lived on the islands farmed in the traditional style with their total planting in one or two vegetable crops—usually cabbage or potatoes. Meggett, a small community some twenty miles south of Charleston, became an important shipping center for vegetables, particularly cabbage, and developed as the headquarters for a small vegetable stock-exchange and trucking association (Murray 1949). The small truck farmers on the islands experienced great initial difficulty in marketing their products. It was not uncommon for a farmer to ship a carload of potatoes or cabbage north and receive only a bill for the freight charge for his effort.

In the late 1930s the truck farmers of the Sea Island region formed a cooperative vegetable market under the supervision of the Farm Credit Association in Washington, D.C., but the cooperative was strictly voluntary and operated as a nonprofit organization. The members earned a commission of five percent on sales, with profits placed into either a farmer's reserve fund or an operating fund. A similar organization, the Charleston County Wholesale Vegetable Market, opened in October, 1939. However, then as now, a majority of the truck farmers remained aloof from the cooperatives and marketed their products independently.

World War II created a labor shortage on the islands. This posed a serious problem for the growers, since farming in the area has always been dependent on large quantities of manual labor. The loss of the available labor supply forced a reduction in the acreage cultivated, which still exists to this day. Even after the end of hostilities the labor shortage continued, for most returning servicemen were unwilling to go back to farming and rural life; and those who did return wanted higher wages than the truck farm owners were willing to pay.

Thus, the late 1940s were a time of extreme pessimism. Acreage continued to decrease and production of vegetables fell far below pre-war levels. In 1948 the production of Irish potatoes was negligible in the Beaufort district, and in the Charleston area the potato acreage was down to 6,500 acres from a high of 12,000 acres planted in 1938. The acreage planted to cabbage, once one of the leading commodities of the area, was reduced two-thirds or more. Other vegetable crops declined in similar fashion.

During the depression years, it appeared that truck farming might disappear, as did rice and cotton. While this did not occur, the number of farm operators did decrease. In the 1940s there were several hundred truck farmers on the islands, but by 1964 there were only approximately 150 large truck operators. There still remain many hundreds of small part-time farmers, but most of the vegetables from the Sea Islands are shipped by a few big operators.[6] Even with the decrease in the number of truck farmers, the volume of vegetable shipments since the 1950s has remained steady or in some cases increased due to more efficient operations, which relate to farm consolidation and mechanization. As an example of farm consolidation and reduction in the number of growers: in the Charleston area in 1961, out of 361 growers harvesting vegetables, 28 growers produced 59 percent of the snap beans, 24 growers produced 80 percent of the tomatoes, 29 growers produced 86 percent of the cucumbers, and 31 growers produced

76 percent of the cabbage.[3] In the Beaufort district, out of 232 producers, 25 large growers accounted for approximately 96 percent of the 1960 sales.[8]

The leading crops in acreage in Charleston County in 1961 were snap beans, potatoes, tomatoes, cucumbers, and cabbage. These five crops totaled 13,641 acres and accounted for approximately 90 percent of all vegetable acreage in the county. The leading crop in value is tomatoes, followed by cucumbers. The five crops mentioned accounted for 94 percent of the value of vegetables grown in the county in 1961.[9]

In 1960, in the Sea Island truck area of Beaufort County, the leading money crop produced was tomatoes (39.7%); the second in importance was cucumbers (18.8%). Other important crops were broccoli (7.7%), snap beans (7.2%), greens (4.8%), and squash (4.3%).[10]

MARKETS

A major problem for the small truck growers is marketing the crops. For the large truck producers marketing is not a major problem, since they produce crops in large enough quantities to insure market control. However, the smaller producers do not exercise control over the market factor, because they are handicapped by the limited quantity and quality of the products which they offer for sale. The limited quantity of produce is not enough to attract buyers and the great number of small lots involves too many different grades of vegetables.

A majority of the vegetables produced in the region are sold in the fresh vegetable market (two exceptions: half of the potatoes sold are for potato chips and one-fifth of the snap bean crop goes to processors). The fresh vegetables produced in the region are marketed in sixteen major market centers, of which the more important are New York, Baltimore, Philadelphia, Chicago, Boston, Montreal, Nashville, and St. Louis.

PROBLEMS AND FUTURE OF THE INDUSTRY

The Sea Island truck farming industry is confronted with problems that may seriously reduce its importance if they are not solved. A major problem is that most fields are so small that the use of mechanical equipment is limited. Furthermore, the open ditch drainage system, which is still quite common, limits the use of mechanical equipment. A second problem is the lack of specially-designed mechanical harvesting machinery that is able to operate on the artificially high vegetable beds. Due to the poor drainage, plants are grown on artificially-raised beds approximately twelve to eighteen inches high. A third problem is the lack of new varieties of crops and modern processing facilities to capture new markets. New crops must be introduced to give the region a sequential series of plantings, ideally from March to late October. Today, the optimum value of the land is not being realized since the prime vegetable growing season is so short. Processing of the vegetables—either canning, radiation, or most likely, quick-freezing— is the next inevitable step if the region is to remain in competition with other vegetable producing regions and expand its economy. The Sea Island area must increase its volume of production to attract processors to the area. Perhaps the truck growing season can be expanded into the upper coastal plain as the cotton picture there changes. It has been suggested that cold resistant crops such as collards, broccoli, turnips, carrots, and okra could be planted inland. It has also been suggested that it would be in the interests of the orchard producers of the Sand Hills region of South Carolina to consider a co-partnership in processing with the Sea Island vegetable growers. A fourth problem, and one that has constantly plagued the growers is the lack of capital. Large sums of money are necessary for the development of processing plants. This could be raised in one of two ways; the farmers themselves can form their own cooperatives, or, with expanded acreage and volume, outside producers may be attracted into the region. At one time, Sea Island growers considered 600-700 acres of tomatoes sufficient to control the market. Today, buyers demand large quantities of high quality produce. The same demand applies to other vegetables. The truck growers must expand their production and quality if they are to insure market control.[11]

SUMMARY

Thus, in summary, although the end of Sea Island cotton and rice promoted the rise of the vegetable truck industry, and the Sea Island truck area does fill in the fresh vegetable gap between harvest from Florida and the Middle Atlantic Eastern Shore, and truck farming on the islands is a multi-million dollar enterprise, the industry faces the need to demonstrate flexibility. It must modernize, develop new processing centers, and expand its market potential if it is to remain in serious competition with other truck producing regions of the country.

FOOTNOTES

1. SEIGLER, J.M., 1959, Origin of the Sea Islands of the Southeastern United States. New York: The Geographical Review, Vol. XLIX, The American Geographical Society.

   SINHA, E.Z., 1959, Geomorphology of the Lower Coastal Plain from the

Savannah River Area, Georgia, to the Roanoke River Area, North Carolina. University of North Carolina: unpublished. For two interesting studies on the origins of the Sea Islands refer to the above. Doctoral dissertation.

2. A record of the accounts of the agricultural situation on the South Carolina Sea Islands is available in The Charlestown News and Courier for this period. An excellent example is J.K. Blackman, "The Sea Islands of South Carolina 1865-1880," The Charleston News and Courier, April 22, 1880.

3. HARRIS, J.C., Feb. 1984, The Sea Island Hurricanes, The Devastation. Scribner's Magazine, XV: pp. 242-243.

4. BARNWELL, B., retired Agricultural County Agent, Beaufort County, South Carolina, personal communications.

5. MURRAY, C.S., 1949, This Our Land. Columbia, South Carolina: R.L. Bryan Co. For an informative history of the Agricultural Society of South Carolina refer to above.

6. Agricultural County Agents of Charleston and Beaufort Counties, C.J. Livingston and William Johnson, personal communications.

7. Vegetable Crop Survey, Charleston County, S.C., South Carolina Crop Reporting Survey in Cooperation with the Department of Agricultural Economics South Carolina Agricultural Experimental Station, Clemson, S.C., Crop and Livestock Series, No. 30, May 1962: p. 2.

8. Vegetable Crop Survey, Beaufort County, S.C., South Carolina Crop Reporting Survey in Cooperation with the Department of Agricultural Economics South Carolina Agricultural Experimental Station, Clemson, S.C., Crop and Livestock Series, No. 26, August, 1961: p. 1.

9. Vegetable Crop Survey, Charleston, South Carolina: p. 2.

10. Vegetable Crop Survey, Beaufort, South Carolina: p. 7.

11. JOHNSON, William, Agricultural County Agent, Beaufort County, S.C., personal communication.

CHAPTER THREE

Gullah Folk Beliefs
Concerning Childbirth*

William Bascom

A long the Atlantic coast from New York City to Palm Beach lie a series of long sand bars, broken by the rivers which run into the ocean. They form a large number of low islands separated from the mainland by salt flats which are regularly covered by the tide, and by narrow channels of clear water. These channels have been made into the Inland Waterway, along which yachts and other small boats can pass back and forth between New York and Florida, seldom having to venture out into open water. Some of the largest of these islands, often ten to twenty miles long, lie right on the ocean and have fine, sandy beaches (Johnson 1931).

The Negroes of these islands and the neighboring mainland are known as Gullah in South Carolina and as Geechee in Georgia, but the term Gullah is frequently used to include both groups. Two origins of the name Gullah have been suggested, Angola and Gola, the latter being the name of an African group in Liberia. T.J. Bowen (1857), an American Baptist missionary who visted Liberia in 1850, said of the Gola: "These are the 'Gula negroes' of the southern states." Despite this categorical answer, the question still remains open.

---

*This paper was read at the annual meeting of the American Folklore Society at Andover, Massachusetts, on December 29, 1941. It is based on research conducted during the summer of 1939, in the course of which 114 informants were interviewed. The field work was made possible by a grant-in-aid from the Social Science Research Council of Northwestern University.

27

My field work extended from Beaufort in South Carolina to Brunswick in Georgia, between which lie the following large islands: St. Helena, Hilton Head, Daufuskie, Tybee, Wilmington, Skidaway, Ossabaw, St. Catherines, Sapeloe, and St. Simons. This was the region of some of the largest and most profitable plantations in the period of slavery. Until the bounty was removed from indigo and cheaper rice from other regions flooded the market, these two crops brought in good money. Then for a while the long staple Sea Island cotton perpetuated the plantation system, until the boll weevil and the Civil War together ended the era of prosperity. Port Royal was captured at the beginning of the war in an important naval engagement just off the northern end of Hilton Head, and soon afterward nearly all the slave owners destroyed their crops and fled inland with their slaves. They never returned; but Negroes gradually found their way back to the places where they had been born and raised. Following a brief period of carpetbagger prosperity and high wages, they bought up the plantations of their former masters at low prices, and settled down to subsistence farming and fishing.

Before the war many plantations had had more than a hundred slaves. To avoid isolation and malaria, the owners lived most of the time in Beaufort, Savannah, or Darien, leaving their plantations in the charge of a white overseer and one or two Negro drivers. The numerical preponderance of Negroes over whites, and the isolation of the islands and the immediate mainland, which is also cut up by salt flats and rivers so that the main roads must run some distance inland, are still characteristic of much of the coast of South Carolina and Georgia, and have combined to provide a field of study which has long been recognized as fruitful.

North of Sapeloe on Harris Neck, which is all but an island, there were between fifty and sixty Negro families in 1939 to about five white families, only two of which remained throughout the year. On Hilton Head there were 1,377 Negroes in 1930 to 97 whites, and by 1939 the latter figure had dropped to 40. Sapeloe Island, which was owned by R.J. Reynolds, had 339 Negroes and only the few whites that were necessary to manage the very elaborate estate at which Reynolds spent about two weeks each winter. St. Helena had only 168 whites to 4,458 Negroes in 1930; but there had been considerable contact with whites due to the fact that a bridge connected the island with the mainland since 1927, and to the fact that St. Helena is the site of Penn School, the first Negro school to be opened in the South. St. Simons Island was no longer isolated. Connected by a bridge to the mainland, it had already become an important seaside resort; in 1930 the census gave 662 whites to only 606 Negroes. Tybee Island preserved the least Gullah culture; located at the mouth of the Savannah River, it was important only as a bathing beach and week-end resort for the whites of Savannah.

Many changes in life on the Sea Islands have undoubtedly occurred since my field work in 1939, and very considerable changes since the beginning of Freedom were already evident at that time. Most of the older people still owned their farms and houses, but more and more of the younger people were deserting the hoe and the farm to go North or to the city, where they could earn money. Moreover, the younger people had little use for the "old fogeyisms" of their parents, so that folk beliefs and customs had to be studied among the older inhabitants. Discussions of the old ways of life frequently brought out the plaintive remark that "Them's kerosene times; it's gasoline time now."

Like their African ancestors, the Negroes of the Sea Islands regard abnormalities of birth as prognostic of the future. Probably the most widespread of the beliefs in this category is that a child born in a caul will be gifted with the ability to see "ghosses" and "ha'nts." Not only was this belief recorded on St. Helena, Hilton Head, Harris Neck, Sapeloe, Butler, St. Simons, and at Darien (1, 2, 3, 6, 8, 9, 10, 11, 12, 13, 15, 17), but three informants (11, 12, 17) claimed to be living proof of its validity.[1] The existence of techniques for destroying this power—for "blinding" such a person so that he cannot see ghosts—shows that it is not an unmixed blessing. An informant (12) told how ghosts frightened and tormented her until she ate some of the caul in which she had been born, and thereby "drove them down to hell." However, the usual attitude seems to be that ghosts are harmless, and that the ability to foretell the future that comes from being able to see them and talk to them is a distinct advantage. One informant (5) felt that to have "blinded" her own daughter, who was born in a caul, would have been cheating her; she added that as a midwife she always left the decision up to the child's mother, because a person should never be "blinded" until it is certain that ghosts are troubling him.

The belief that birth in a caul is a sign of luck or wisdom (1, 2, 3, 5, 15), seems to derive from this ability to "see everything" (2, 3, 5). On the other hand, this interpretation is not consistent with the view of one informant (1) that a child born in a caul is wise even after it has been "blinded." It is also said that a person who is born in a caul is able to tell if "whiskey has been dosed" (15), and thus avoid evil charms put into food or drink. And if he is about to become ill, his caul will sweat (5, 15); or if he is about to die, it will begin to mould (5).

When such a child is born, the caul is dried, usually on a piece of paper or tissue paper (1, 5, 9), and kept in a trunk or some other safe place (12) so that, if necessary, some of it can be used to drive away the ghosts. A small piece of the caul is usually broken off, along with some of the paper to which it has struck, and put into boiling water; this "tea" is then given to the individual to drink (1, 5, 7, 9, 10, 12) without his knowledge (5). It is also suggested that a piece of the caul could be baked in bread and eaten (1); and that if the caul had been lost, tea made from caul in which someone else had been born could be used. The informant (12) who made this last statement said that some of her own caul had been consumed by herself, and some by others.

There is more variation in the significance ascribed to the various positions in which the child emerges. A head first delivery is generally believed to be the normal position and no sign at all; but some held that it meant luck (1) or wisdom (12); and one informant (11) claimed that she had never heard of a child being delivered head first. It is said that a "foot foremost child" is destined to be lucky (1, 3, 15) or wise (5, 11; just the opposite view was held by 12) and, like one born in caul, can see spirits and tell whether or not food has been "dosed" (5, 15). One informant (11) cited her own son as proof of the fact that a "foot foremost child" loves to travel and is able to forecast his own death; she added that such children are usually sensible, but "if they aren't the wisest, then they are the ignorantest." A "hand foremost child" is said to be unlucky (1), but one informant (11) who had never seen such a delivery argued that he must be a good swimmer; another (3) held that this was the normal position.

One can also tell about a child by examining the shape of its head. Thus it was explained that a square head means that the child is smart (8). A "long head (i.e., one that is tall or high) is said to mean that the child may be either desirable or undesirable. A short, flat head means just a good hard worker (8). A "two-headed" child is another sign, but there is some disagreement about the meaning of this term. The usual interpretation is that it means a large head, bulging markedly at the rear, and is the sign that the child has "plenty sense" (5, 12, 15). But one informant (8) held that it means that there are two bumps on the person's head, so that he "doesn't know where to put his hat"; he is "sharp," "slick," and "double-tongued," and while he is smart, he uses his cleverness only for his own advantage and doesn't "suit the other fellows."

Though some informants (1, 3, 4, 15) regarded twins as only natural, others attributed special significance to multiple births. One informant (1) said that triplets are a good sign; and another (15) who had heard of, but never seen them, felt that triplets could be a sign even though she did not know its meaning. Twins are liked and not feared, and one of the pair is certain to be good and wise; this will be the boy if there is a boy (12). An informant (4) who personally felt that twins are not a sign, said that she heard others say that one of the twins "has to die." Another (15) said that if one of them dies, the other is apt to follow it back; but others (1, 3) had never heard of this belief. Several informants (3, 4, 12, 15) were able to cite cases of twins both of whom reached maturity. Children born after twins are not considered as signs (15).

For a child to be born with hair on its head is regarded as a sign of luck (1, 12) or as no sign at all (15). An erupted tooth at birth is interpreted as a sign of a quiet and lucky person (5, 7, 12) or more often as a sign the meaning of which was not known (4, 5, 10, 11, 15). An individual whose career was cited as evidence of the validity of these two beliefs was born with both a tooth and a lock of gray hair, so that his luck was doubly assured (12). None of the informants questioned had ever seen an albino, but on the strength of a description one of them (5) volunteered that this must be a "mark" or punishment for some sin of the parents rather than a sign. A child who favors his mother is lucky (12). On the characteristics of a "seventh child" there was emphatic agreement; these are "*lucky* babies" (1, 5), and they are as wise as a child born with a caul (3, 5). In spite of the importance of the moon and the tide in planting and butchering, these were said to have no significance for childbirth (15).

Midwives say that they are able to predict the sex of an unborn child. Two (5, 15) said that if a boy "hankers with the pregnant woman," the child will be a boy. Another midwife (1) held that just the reverse was true; but she agreed that the sex of a child could be foretold by the shape of the mother's abdomen: a girl lies flat in the belly, while a boy stands up, making it bulge sharply (1, 5).

Especially on the islands and in the more isolated regions of the coast, the midwife or "granny" was very important. For the people on Hilton Head Island the closest doctors, even in 1939, were in Savannah and Beaufort. These could be reached only on one of the thrice-weekly round trips of a slow and rickety ship, the *Clivedon* of the Beaufort-Savannah Line, or by rowing to the mainland and then driving to town. Nancy Christopher, who was recognized as the most important midwife on the island, complained that she was kept so busy that she never got to the mainland. There were three other midwives (Hanna Barnwell, Adrianna Ford, and Helen Sampson) on Hilton Head, none of whom lived within fifteen miles of her house. According to her own reckoning, Nancy Christopher had delivered 388 children since 1890, when she "catched" her first child alone. Many of these were still on the island, but others had scattered all up and down the coast. Nancy first learned her profession from an old "slavery-time" midwife, and then received instruction from a white doctor during World War I when it was required that all midwives be licensed. Only when a case was difficult did she suggest that a doctor be called in.

Fanny Burke, who had been a midwife on Hilton Head before licensing was required, said that Aunt Nancy (Christopher) had "catched the whole world." Emma Mack, whose mother was a midwife before her, was raised on Butler Island, the former home of Fanny Kemble (1832), but she was practicing in Darien. Christina Daise of St. Helena, whose beliefs and practices showed the greatest white influence, was also carrying on the profession of her mother. From these four midwives, most of the following information was obtained.

Although midwifery was under the control of the white medical profession, a number of folk beliefs were still maintained. It was believed that if a woman acts as midwife while still able to bear children, she will "catch the pains" of childbirth from the woman she is attending. Three of the midwives interviewed (4, 5, 15) volunteered the information that it was for this reason that they had not taken up the profession until after menopause. It was likewise held that if the midwife is not paid promptly for her services, she will become blind (5, 15). Emma Mack commented that this was what was the matter with her eyes. However, Nancy Christopher explained that a token payment is sufficient to prevent blindness, so that she did not hesitate to assist families who were known to have little money or to be lax in payment of debts. Her regular rates were $10 for a girl and $15 for a boy. The higher fee for boys was justified by the statement that there is more and harder work in delivering them, not because boys are more desirable. Emma Mack charged a straight $10 per child, in addition to which the family paid $20 to the doctor with whom she usually worked.

A special relationship exists between the midwife and the children she delivers; it is said that a midwife is "just like a mother" to them (1). During a discussion of the Gullah custom of putting objects which had been used by the deceased on his grave, Christina Daise's daughter jokingly suggested that when her mother died, two boys should be put on her grave. Christina objected that she wouldn't let them take the one *she* had "catched," and who happened to be visiting her at the time. Nancy Christopher said that she liked the children that she had delivered, and frequently gave them presents; in return they treated her with a kindness and respect that did not seem to be due simply to her old age. She added that when she went to church and they all gathered around her, many of them already with their own grandchildren, she was "almost ashamed."

One of the important remedies used by midwives is tansy. The properties ascribed to the two varieties of this plant which are employed, however, are directly contradictory. According to Emma Mack, single tansy kills a baby, and double tansy helps the mother hold it and eases the mother's pains after delivery. On the other hand, Nancy Christopher stated that a tea made of single tansy is used to help an expectant mother to hold her child until the proper moment for delivery; but she pointed out that it must be administered in time, as it can have no effect if the baby has already "left the mother's back." According to Nancy, single tansy is also used to ease the pain during delivery; and double tansy is used, not only as a remedy for colds, but also to "drop the baby" when the proper moment for delivery has arrived. According to Emma, tea made from the nest of the mud dauber, mixed with gunpowder, will also ease the pain and "drop" the child.

Another, and perhaps even commoner method of "cutting after pains" is to place a sharp piece of iron under the mother's bed (5, 9, 15) without her knowledge (9). This may be a knife, razor, hatchet, ax, or plowshare—anything sharp—and the sharper it is, the better it "cuts the pain." One informant (9), who said that any piece of iron is satisfactory and that a "smoothenin' iron" is often used, described how, when it was used for her even though she did not know it, she felt great relief. She wondered what had happened to make things so much easier for her. On the other hand, Christina Daise said that she used only hot water and the medicine prescribed by the white doctor.

A new-born child is not spanked. The "slop" is cleaned out of its mouth, and if it does not cry cold water is sprinkled on it or spewed on it from the midwife's mouth (5, 15). Or the midwife may scrape the baby's face (15), or blow in its mouth. Emma Mack claimed that she saved "many a one" after the doctor had given up, but Christina Daise said that in all her fourteen or fifteen years of work as a midwife, she had never seen a baby that wasn't "born howling." Sprinkling and blowing are done only if required; they are not rituals which are performed at the birth of every child.

A midwife devotes special attention to the umbilical cord, or the "navel string" as it is commonly called. She must take care of it "like a body" (5). When it has been cut with scissors, it and the afterbirth are salted and wrapped with newspaper (5, 15), and then either burned (5, 15) or buried (1, 5, 12, 15). The afterbirth must not be allowed to touch the floor, for fear that the baby will wet the bed (15). It is said that the old people always used to burn the cord, because if it was buried in the yard, boys or dogs might dig it up and thereby stop the mother from "breeding" (15). However, it was also said that the cord should be buried in the yard in a place which was not revealed to the owner (12), and that it should be buried in the chicken coop (1). The informant who suggested the chicken coop was not worried about the possibility that it might be dug up by the chickens; she said simply that they do not do so, and that she did not know what would happen if they did. The emphatic reactions to a suggestion that the umbilical cord might be simply thrown away are significant. Nancy Christopher protested, "If I did that I wouldn't be a midwife"; and Emma Mack said that if you throw away "the navel string, you throw away the baby."

A midwife has the further responsibility of seeing that the cord is buried or burned properly, because if this is done in the wrong position the mother will be unable to bear children in the future. The cord must be placed in an upright position (15), with the "mouth" up, and the bottom down "like a jug," in the same way that it emerges (5). As the latter informant (5) explained, this is the way that "God taught her," adding that she did not *want* to know how to stop babies from coming, since that is "God's business." The former informant (15), also a midwife, also felt that the use of abortives such as mistletoe and single tansy is "tampering with God's business." But she added that some women had begun to steal such medicines from midwives when they came to call.

A newborn child is first bathed, and then a "belly band" is tied around its abdomen "to pull his body together" and to strengthen its back and hips so that it can walk earlier (5, 15).

According to a man who lived under slavery (14), on his master's plantation on one of the small islands near Darien, two "hospitals" were maintained. One of these was for the older children, and the other, in the charge of a Colored midwife, was for pregnant women and nursing children. A woman was not allowed to work in the fields after she became too heavy with child, and she was permitted to stay in the hospital for two months after delivery. When the mothers went back to work, the children were taken down to the fields "like cattle" to be nursed for an hour or so. After weaning, the children were transferred to the other "hospital," where they remained until they "had sense enough" to do what they were told. There is reason to believe that there was considerable variation in such practices from one plantation to another, even as there was in methods of agriculture and in the privileges allowed to slaves.

In 1939 and in the period immediately following freedom, there were also variations in the period of confinement of the mother. It was said that one woman went back to work in the field or "yard" the day after delivery; and it was explained that if the mother does this at the birth of her first child, she can do it for all others (1). However the same informant said that one week was more usual, during which the mother spent two or three days in bed. It would seem that three or four days or one week was the more usual period of confinement (16), but that it had decreased since earlier times. One informant (15) stated that while it was three to four days, it had been ten days in the past. Another (9) said that it was three to four days against about three months in earlier times. Only Nancy Christopher of Hilton Head indicated an increase in the period of rest, while the period of confinement remained the same. She stated that women often caught cold, and often died, if they went back to work immediately after their three week confinement; therefore they waited an additional week after coming out of the house before resuming field work.

The confinement of the mother applied also to the child. No evidence was found of any ceremony for the child on its first coming out of the house, except for its attendance at church. On Hilton Head this took place about a month after the end of confinement (5), but on Harris Neck immediately afterward, and the approach of the end of a child's confinement was commented upon by the remark that "So-and-so should come to church tomorrow" (9).

For a time, at least, the West African custom of carrying the child on the mother's back persisted. One informant (2) told how her own grandmother, who came from Africa, carried her own mother in this manner. Women sometimes carried their children on their back when hoeing (5, 15), or when "shouting" (15). And women have been seen nursing their children from this position, by swinging them around under the mother's arm (15).

The period of nursing the child, which had been markedly shortened in those families where the bottle was used, had formerly lasted for ten months or a year within the memory of informants (5, 15, 16), until they cut their eye teeth (16). However, in some cases it had lasted two years (5) or even longer. One informant (14) held that in olden times children were nursed even after they were old enough to be sent for water. Weaning was accomplished by rubbing the breast with pepper or turpentine (15). Continence was not required during the period of nursing; on the contrary, midwives explained that they sent the parents "back to family business" after one month, because this "thickens the milk" and it is good for the child (5, 15).

Although several references have been made to African parallels (Savannah Unit, 1940), I am not concerned here with an analysis of the origins of Gullah culture. Many of the questions I asked, following my first field research in Nigeria in 1937-38, were phrased in terms of these parallels, but this is no simple problem. I certainly do not wish to imply that all Gullah culture is derived from Africa, or that Europe has not contributed markedly to it. In fact, one of the difficulties in seeking the provenience of Gullah customs and beliefs is that analogues to them are found in both groups of Europe and Africa (Bascom 1941).

FOOTNOTE

1. The numbers in parentheses refer to the following informants, listed in approximate geographical order from North to South:
   1. Christina Daise, St. Helena Island, South Carolina
   2. "Old Lady" Miller, St. Helena Island, South Carolina
   3. Flora Rivers, St. Helena Island, South Carolina

4. Fanny Burke, Hilton Head Island, South Carolina
5. Nancy Christopher, Hilton Head Island, South Carolina
6. Richard Jones, Hilton Head Island, South Carolina
7. Robert Butler, Thunderbolt (near Savannah), Georgia
8. Anna Elisa Baisden, Harris Neck, Georgia
9. Rosa Sallins, Harris Neck, Georgia
10. Josephine Stevens, Harris Neck, Georgia
11. Kate Brown, Sapelo Island, Georgia
12. Hannah Givens, Darien, Georgia
13. Lawrence Baker, Ridgeway (near Darien), Georgia
14. Henry Hutson, Carnegan (near Darien), Georgia
15. Emma Mack, Butler Island (but living in Darien), Georgia
16. Levinia Abbot, St. Simons Island, Georgia
17. Kate Ramsey, St. Simons Island, Georgia

REFERENCES

BASCOM, W., 1941, Acculturation Among the Gullah Negroes. American Anthropologist, Vol. 43, no. 1: pp. 43-50.

BOWEN, T.J., 1851, Central Africa, Adventures and Missionary Labors in Several Countries in the Interior of Africa; from 1849 to 1856. Charleston: Southern Baptist Publication Society.

DRUMS and SHADOWS, 1940, Athens, Ga.: University of Georgia Press.

JOHNSON, G.G., 1931, Social and Economic History of the Sea Islands. Chapel Hill: University of North Carolina.

KEMBLE, F., 1864, Journal of a Residence on a George Plantation. New York: Harper.

LEIGH, F.B., 1883, Ten Years on a Georgia Plantation (1866-1876). London: R. Bentley & Son.

PETERKIN, J., 1924, Green Thursday. New York: Knopf.

_____, 1927, Black April. New York: Grosset and Dunlap.

PRINGLE, E.A., 1913, Patience Pennington: A Woman Rice Planter. New York: Macmillan.

PUCKETT, N.N., 1926, Folk Beliefs of the Southern Negro. Chapel Hill: University of North Carolina.

SAVANNAH UNIT OF THE GEORGIA WRITERS' PROJECT, 1940, Drums and Shadows. Survival Studies among the Georgia Coastal Negroes. Athens: University of Georgia Press. Some comparative notes from Africa and the Caribbean are given in the appendix to the above by the Georgia Writers' Project, Work Projects Administration.

CHAPTER FOUR

Names and Naming in The Sea Islands*
Keith E. Baird and Mary A. Twining

In the Sea Islands it is not unusual for a person to have two given names. One is an official, generally English (or European) name; the other is a nickname, or "basket" name. The official name (e.g., Joseph, George, Mary, Jane) is likely to appear on the individual's birth or baptismal certificate, school records, social security card, and other documents relating to dealings with the outside European American community. The nickname or "basket" name is known and used only in the family circle and within the individual's home community. There is a distinction between a basket (or pet) name and nickname. The basket name is usually given soon after birth, when the infant is still carried in arms or placed in a cradle (or basket), but a nickname may be acquired during adolescence or later in life because of some physical or temperamental characteristic, or some incident in which the person has been involved. In any case, for Sea Islanders the nickname, basket name, or pet name by which an individual is known within the community is the owner's operative personal name.

Basket naming and nicknaming is one of the issues in the "Sea Island creole controversy," chiefly between Johnson (1930, 1967) and Turner

*This article was first presented as a paper at the Annual Symposium on Language and Culture in South Carolina at the University of South Carolina, April 1984. The authors gratefully acknowledge the invaluable assistance rendered them in the conduct of the research by Mr. William Saunders and his brother Mr. Alphonso Saunders, both lifelong residents of the Sea Islands.

(1949), since it relates to the questions both of the African influences in Sea Island language and culture, and the contemporary persistence of African folkways in the region. Turner unequivocally states that the Sea Island nickname is nearly always a word of African origin, and declares:

> In many instances both the given-name and surname are African words. Some of my ex-slave informants explain this by saying that during slavery they used for their surnames (which they called "trimmin") the surname of their owner. After slavery, many of them refused to use any longer the name of their former enslavers. Likewise, many former slaveholders refused to allow the freedmen to use their names. Thereupon, the former slaves chose their nickname for their surname and gave themselves another nickname. This also is frequently an African word (Turner 1949, 40).

Against Johnson's minimizing of African linguistic continuities in the Sea Islands, Turner argued that the distinctive speech of Sea Islanders (known as Gullah or Geechee), including personal names, was strongly influenced by the people's African origins.

Sometimes a nickname may seem to be simply an English name; so that a person whose official name is, for instance, Richard, may come to be known as Joe. The reason for this might be that the African-originated name "Kojo" (the Ga and Ewe name for a male born on Monday) has either been affectionately apocopated by the bearer's fellow Islanders, or mistaken by European Americans for the familiar short form of the English name Joseph, as Wood (1974) has demonstrated. Dillard (1972) shows how an African-originated "Fiba" (from the Ewe name for a girl born on Friday) was incorrectly heard and perpetuated by European Americans as Phoebe (a name in ancient Greek for the moon).

Traditional attitudes towards names and naming persist in the Sea Islands. A man on Johns Island who had been burned so that his skin showed a most atypical pink-and-white mottled complexion was called "Buckra" by his friends. By this appellation they were commenting jokingly on his resemblance to a European man; in Efik "mbakara" means "European person." A remarkable feature of the physiognomy of Joe Bligen, nicknamed "Cunjie," is his broad cheekbones. The nickname closely approximates the pronunciation of the Hausa word "kunci" which means "cheek" or "the side of the face." Joe Bligen's sister, Ms. Hunter, worked for a family down the road from her home and the children there call called her "Dada," which means "mother" in Ewe. She is also known as "Miss Delia" and Janie Hunter.

Turner (1949) lists over 1,000 Sea Island (Gullah) personal names which he traces back to their origins in some thirty African languages. The research on which these data are based was conducted by Turner between 1932 and 1940, and the extent to which African-derived naming practices persist today, around a half century later, is a matter of continuing scholarly interest. Even in the 1930s, it was not easy for a researcher from outside the culture to obtain information from the Sea Islanders concerning their naming practices. Dillard (1972) praises Turner's achievement in the face of the difficulties involved, and explains his success in these terms:

> It thus took an outstanding act of sympathetic and discrete inquiry by a Black researcher, Turner, to come up with the fact that thousands of naming patterns traceable to West African practices were still in effect among the Gullah speakers.

It should hardly be surprising that African names and African attitudes toward naming were retained and continued in the Sea Islands. One reason was certainly the importance attached in African societies to the naming of a child, since "in the African tradition, today as yesterday, a name is not a mere identification tag; it is a record of family and community history, a distinct personal reference, an indication of present status, and an enunciated promise of future accomplishment" (Baird 1972). The choice of a name for a child might be influenced by a number of considerations, such as the day or time of day the child was born, its place in numerical order as regards its siblings, whether it was the elder or younger of twins, or if chldren preceding it had not survived. Circumstances existing in the family or in the community, as well as more cosmic events such as flood or famine or war occurring at the time of birth, might determine the child's name. The Yoruba people of Nigeria neatly encapsulate the notions connected with this African attitude in the saying: "We consider the state of our affairs before we name a child."

Africans are extremely fond of children, so that generally when a child is born in the family the new arrival is seen as a cause of rejoicing, as may be seen in the following examples of names from West Africa, whence most of the ancestors of the Sea Islanders came to America.

The Yoruba male and female name "Ayo" means "joy," and forms part of another name, "Ayodele," the meaning of which, "joy comes to the house," is an even more explicit expression of a family's gratification at the long-hoped-for arrival of a child. The Igbo people of eastern Nigeria express a similar sentiment when they bestow on a newborn male child the piously thankful name "Chukwuemeka." The day on which a child was born is celebrated through the bestowal of a dayname: thus the name "Yaa" among the Ewe people of Ghana indicates that the baby girl who bears it was born on Thursday; a baby boy born on that day would be named "Yao." The attention given to birth order as well as multiple births is to be observed in the name "Twia" given by the Fante ethnic group in Ghana to a boy born following twins.

The basket names and nicknames of Sea Islanders listed by Turner (1949) are shown to have come from countries of West Africa as far north as Senegal, and as far south as Angola. The African names in Turner's listing thus indicate that among the ancestors of the Sea Islanders were speakers of a variety of languages which he identifies as Bambara, Bini, Bobangi, Djerma, Efik, Ewe, Fante, Fon, Fula, Ga, Gbari, Hausa, Ibo, Ibibio, Kikongo, Kimbundu, Kpelle, Mende, Malinke, Nupe, Susu, Songhai, Twi, Tshiluba, Umbundu, Vai, Wolof, and Yoruba. The linguistic and cultural patrimony of Sea Islanders, therefore, is seen to involve an expanse of territory which includes Senegal, Gambia, Mali, Guinea, Sierra Leone, Liberia, Ivory Coast, Ghana, Togo, Benin, Niger, Nigeria, Cameroon, Equatorial Guinea, Gabon, Congo, Zaire, and Angola.

In the foregoing discussion, attention has been focused on names rather than on naming. Emphasis has been laid more on the sounds, shapes, meanings and provenances of the names, and less on the acts and attitudes associated with the conferring, accepting, or assuming of nicknames in the Sea Islands, and the socio-historical context in which this behavior takes place. Turner, himself a linguist, was mainly preoccupied with linguistic considerations. He was not, however, neglectful of those customary practices of Sea Islanders regarding naming which reflect their familial attitudes and societal values. Thus he was careful to indicate those personal names which his African informants could identify as well-known African names as he included them in his list. Noting, however, that various methods were used in West Africa in naming children, Turner remarked that African-originated Sea Island names in his list which he did not mark as known by his African informants to be employed on the continent, might nonetheless have been used as personal names by the African ancestors of the Sea Islanders. He went on to make this significant comment:

> Even though my Gullah informants do not remember the meanings of these unmarked personal names (nor the precise meanings of most of those that are marked), they continue to use them in naming their children because their older relatives and friends so used them. That they would choose many words whose meanings they do not know is not surprising. As already indicated, even though the Africans attach very great importance to the meanings of the words they use as personal names, they do not follow this practice exclusively. The meanings of many of their names are not known. Like many other peoples, the

Africans sometimes choose a name because it is that of some ancestor (Turner 1949, 41).

Some writers on Sea Island culture besides Turner have commented on attitudes and customs regarding naming. Parsons (1923), for example, has reported that Sea Islanders named a child on the ninth day after birth. Twining (1977) records that "the custom of a person's having several names is particularly well developed on the Islands." Twining's statement is based on her fieldwork carried out in the area from 1966 to 1975, and is thus quite recent as compared with the observation to the same effect made by the schoolteacher Elizabeth Botume in her *First Days Amongst the Contrabands* (1893).

Pressures toward acculturation have no doubt caused some African personal names to disappear (at least from official use), being supplanted by the more usual Anglo-American names. Other African names have acquired negative associations and have fallen into disuse, or been changed into an innocuous, more acceptable, form. Dillard (1972) comments on how "Sambo," a Hausa name for the second son in the family (but meaning "disgrace" in Mende and Vai) came to have an exclusively pejorative connotation.

Turner's (1949) study of Africanisms in the speech of Sea Islanders has received merited recognition for the contribution his findings on African personal names has made to the African substrate theory of the origins of the Atlantic creole languages. His approach and consequently his conclusions, however, have not been without challenge or at least mild demurral. In a recent paper, Mufwene (1985) has identified and responded to some of Turner's critics, such as Swadesh (1951) and Hair (1965) who, while not strongly disputing the African substrate theory, nevertheless question whether the African names in Gullah are sufficiently probative of that view. Mufwene observes that the African names in Gullah exhibit some African phonological features, and remarks that until other, essentially grammatical, evidence is offered, "it is doubtful that the African proper names prove anything in support of the linguistic Afrogenetic hypothesis . . ." Mufwene does not dispute, however, that the names identified by Turner as African are such in fact, but concludes regarding their persistence in use that "the best we can now tell is that they certainly represent cultural, non-linguistic, africanisms [*sic*], since in this regard the custom seems to have continued."

It can be asserted from the foregoing discussion that irrespective of whether Turner's list of Sea Island names does not offer satisfactory proof that Gullah (and by extension Afrish, the so-called "Black English") is fundamentally African in its grammatical structure, the African origin of the names is not now substantially in dispute. If these names, and the practices and attitudes associated with them, are still to be found in the Sea Island region, it is reasonable to conclude that they are functional within the society, and that their persistence may therefore properly be regarded as expressive of African cultural continuity.

The present writers were interested in discovering the extent to which distinctive basket names and nicknames are to be encountered in the Sea Islands today, nearly forty years after the publication of Turner's *Africanisms in the Gullah Dialect*. The informants for our study are at this writing between forty and fifty years old. The names in our list, most of which they have supplied, are of individuals personally known to them, mainly from their native Johns Island, South Carolina, but also from other parts of the Sea Island region, including the city of Charleston. The youngest of the bearers of the names are around twenty years old, but these are conspicuously few. The majority of the names are of persons thirty-five years of age and above.

The following list is of names which our informants called "nicknames" because they are not the official names of the bearers. A large number of the names (e.g., Chance, Monkey, Nuttin', Plum) are recognizable English or near-English words: what makes them distinctive in the Sea Island context is that (1) they relate specifically to physical, mental, or moral characteristics of their bearers as perceived by their fellow Sea Islanders, or (2) they refer to some incident or situation in which the nicknamed individual was involved. There are other nicknames, however, that are neither Euro-American names, nor English words; neither are they Sea Island creolisms such as Chanceum, Lickey-too, and Do-um Bubba; but like Buckra and Minna they can be documented as African-originated words. Also listed, finally, are some names for which to date there is no explanation except in terms of conjectural African origins. For these entries we have had recourse to Turner (1949) when the name in question appeared to bear some relationship to an item listed in that work. References to the Turner study in this connection are indicated in the comment on the particular entry by the initial T followed by the relevant page number: thus, T 141 = Turner (1949, 141). Conventional English spelling has been used for the names, since the majority of them are either English words are are based on English words.

In the commentary on the following Sea Island names appear a number of names and other words from African languages as recorded by Turner (1949). In order to show how some Sea Island names reflect phonetically their origins in African languages, the alphabet Turner used to represent the sounds of the African words is "a slight modification of that recommended by the International Phonetic Assocation." Many of the African languages referred to in the comments are tone languages, that is, languages in which musical pitch (or tone) in the pronunciation of the syllables of words conveys meaning and shows grammatical relationships. The numerals 1, 2, or 3 are placed after the vowels or syllabic consonants carrying tones. The numeral 1 indicates a low level tone, 2 indicates a mid level tone, and 3 indicates a high level tone. (For a more extended discussion, see Turner 1949, 15-30).

Beep-beep (m.): The individual so nicknamed was saved from possibly fatal injury by the timely sounding of an automobile horn which warned him to leap to safety.

Betsy Ben (m.): A matronymic, indicating that Ben is the son of Betsy.

Big (m.): Descriptive of the individual named.

Blue (m.): The individual is so named because his complexion is so dark as to appear blue.

Old Bo (m.): The word "old" distinguishes the bearer from his son, Young Bo. Ewe "bo" means "far away," "high up" (T 66). Fon "gbo" means "charm" (T 67).

Boda (f.): Daughter of Old Bo, preceding. Fon "gboda" means "to play" (T 67).

Bodick (m.): Cousin to Old Bo, above. Ewe "bo" = "far away," "high up" (T 66); Fon "gbo" = "charm" (T 67); Fon "digi" = "long," "be long" (T 74).

Bo Jibba (m.): For "Bo" see "Old Bo" above. Fula "dziba" = "pocket" (T 100).

Boody (m.): The individual so named has remarkably long arms, and is fond of gambling. Kongo "budi" = "cat" (T 68).

Boogah (m.,f.): Vai "bu'2gi2kai1" = "something frightful" (T 68). The individuals bearing this name share no specific characteristic, for example, attractiveness or unattractiveness. Africans often traditionally name a child on the basis of a positive physical, mental, or moral characteristic; they may also give an uncomplimentary name to a child to deceive the ancestors who might otherwise, it is thought, wish to take back to themselves a very desirable infant. (See Baird 1972, 76)

Boot (m.): The individual so named is of a very dark complexion.

Bubba (m.): As a family term this name corresponds to the English "brother" of which it is a childish pronunciation (Botume 1893). It is possible, however, that there is also a convergence with Vai 'boɪ boɪ', the name given a boy when his real name is not known (T 65), which extends its use into the community at large.

Buck (m.): The individual bearing this nickname is robust, very masculine.

Buckaroo (m.): The bearer of this name worked on a farm where he developed a reputation for his skill in handling animals. The name is an Anglo-American rendering of the Spanish "vaquero" = "cowboy."

Buckra (m.): From Efik "mbakara" = "he who surrounds or governs," hence in the slavery and early post-slavery period, "European (especially English) person." This term has been applied as a nickname to a man who suffered burns on his face which removed his dark pigmented epidermis, leaving the pink under-skin visible.

Butcher (m.): The bearer of this nickname is a big, tall (6' 6") man noted for his aggressiveness (i.e., his "readiness to slaughter" anyone who offends him).

Cat (m.): The individual bearing this name is reputed, it is not established whether justly or unjustly, to be a clever and agile burglar.

Chance (m.): This name is borne by an individual known for his willingness to take a risk.

Chance-um (m.): That is, "risk it," whether in the area of business or romantic relations. There are several persons who have that nickname.

Cheetah (m.): The face of the bearer of this name is spotted, on account of burns.

Coodle (m.): The individual so named has a particular attraction to funerals, and attends the ceremonies whether he is acquainted with the deceased or not. These facts point firmly to the origin of this name in the Ewe 'ku3duɪ' = "announcement of a death" (T 117).

Country (m.): Nickname given to the bearer because of his very pronounced rusticity in speech, dress and general comportment.

Croak (m.): The individual has a physical condition which gives his skin an unusual roughness, seen by his associates as comparable to that of a "croc," or crocodile.

Cunjie (m.): The bearer of this name has very broad cheekbones. Hausa "kun3t i:3" = "the side of the face, the cheek."

Cuteness (f.): This nickname is accurately descriptive of the young lady who bears it, according to our informants.

Dada (f.): This is the term of address used by children and young adults to an older woman, especially when she has responsibility for their care. Ewe "da1 da3" = mother (T 70).

Dahlin (f.): The Sea Island form of the English "darling." This term of endearment is the name by which the bearer is known not only within the intimate circle of family and close associates but also within the wider community.

Dan (f.): This is the nickname of a very beautiful young woman who is a professional model. "Dan" is a possible abbreviation of either one of two names listed by Turner, considering a certain degree of correspondence between the description of the bearer of the name and the connotations of the suggested etyma. The full entry for each of the two Sea Island names as given by Turner is here cited (slightly edited for the purpose of simplicity):

    dana (f.): Yoruba "da3na2" (personal name) = "to pay a dowry"; "da3na3" = "to make a fire"; "da3na1" = "to commit robbery on the highway"; Bambara "dana" = "faith, confidence"; "ndana" = "a bell" (T 71).

    dane (m.): Mende "ndane" (personal name), literally = "mouth sweet" (T 72).

Delia (f.): It is easy to assume that we have here the English form of the epithet of the Greek goddess Artemis (Diana to the Romans) as worshipped at Delos (see Partridge 1959, 38). "Miss Delia," however, is known on Johns Island as the nickname of a matron and folk artist whose official first name is Janie. The explanation of this name, admittedly conjectural, seems to relate, not to the distant isles of Greece, but to the much nearer Sea Islands. Turner records the name 'dileli' (f.) stressed on the first syllable, and supplies the following further information: Mende "ndileli" (personal name) = "peace, contentment" (T 74). The name is fully in accord with the calm and gentle nature of its bearer.

Dink (m.), Dinky (m.): Mandinka "dinke" (personal name) = "male child" (T 75).

Dog (m.): The individual bearing this name is not considered to be handsome. It should be noted, however, that the Yoruba people of Nigeria give the name "Ajayi" = "this dog" to a child born with his face down (Abraham 1958). Turner includes this name in his list (T 47), as well as the name "imbuwa" which he shows to originate in the Kimbundu "imbua" (personal name) = "dog" (T 96). Thus there exist African precedents for naming a person "Dog," and such an appelation would not necessarily be pejorative any more than is the English surname, Hogg.

Do-um (m.): That is, "do it": an injunction to assiduous aplication to an endeavor, or an incitement to audacity in sexual adventure. The bearer of this sobriquet is reputed to have earned it by reason of his conduct which embraced both acceptances of the name. He was in his twenties at the time.

Do-um Bubba (m.): (Younger) brother of "Do-um," preceding.

Dreg (m.): The individual so named was regarded as lazy and, therefore, worthless.

Dukey (m.): The bearer of this name was a great admirer of the actor, John Wayne, who was called "the Duke." He affected many of Wayne's mannerisms; his fantasy identification with the actor was aided by the fact that he was so light-complexioned that he could have "passed" for a European American.

Essie (f.): Bini "eɪseɜ-ɪ" = "goodness, favor" (T 84).

Fair (m.): This nickname was bestowed on a young man of particularly respectable character and engaging disposition, "a really nice person."

Fat (m.): Nickname of a man who returned home to the Sea Islands after having become rather affluent in New York City.

Foxy (m.): Name of a clever gambler.

Gal (f.): That is, "Girl." It is not unusual for African peoples to give a child a name that is simply the gender designation "both" or "girl." "Boysie" is a common nickname for a boy in the English-speaking Caribbean. (Cp. "Dinky," above.)

Gotta love me with a feeling (m.); This name was taken from the favorite song of the bearer, for whom it seemed to serve as an admonition to any potential female admirers.

Gussie (m.): The bearer's official name is nothing like Augustus or Gustavus of which it might be presumed to be an abbreviation. Turner, however, lists the Bambara derived female personal name "gasi" = "misforutune" (T 90). Since some names both in Africa and in the Sea islands are not absolutely restricted either to males or females, the Bambara name might conceivably have been the original.

Handful (f.): The old lady who bears this nickname is now around ninety years of age. It was not possible to establish whether it was due to diminutive size, forceful disposition, or a combination of the two characteristics that she received this name in her youth.

Head (m.): This name was conferred on its bearer because one of his most conspicuous features was his rather sizeable head.

Hog (m.): The bearer of this name received it because he was aggreessively acquisitive; he "hogged everything."

Jackie (m.,f.): Not an official name of any of the bearers. Turner lists the male personal name "Jake" and relates it to Vai "dza₃ke₁" = "to prophesy" (T 98). A Sea Island woman bearing the name "Jackie" is reputed to have the gift of precognition.

Kyah (m.): This is not the abbreviation of another name (such as Hezekiah, for instance). Turner lists the Sea Island name "kiya" from the Vai "kai₃a₃" ("kai₃a₃") = "a fish trap made by placing sticks across a creek so that only a small opening is left into which a long cone-shaped basket, made of bamboo sticks from three to six feet long, is inserted in such a way that the fish are forced into it by the strong current of the water" (T 113).

Lab (m.): A number of persons whose official name is Arthur have this name. Our Sea Island informants could offer no explanation of the connection between the two names. A possible explanation which we venture is that the first Arthur to bear the name had the initials L.A.B. which became the nickname "Lab." Other individuals having the official name Arthur subsequently either had conferred on them or assumed the nickname.

Lady (f.): This name indicates the attractive appearance, dignified bearing and exemplary personal reputation of its bearer.

Lilah (f.): Turner lists "Laila," giving its origin as "la ila!" = "Oh God!," an exclamation used by the Mandinka and other people of the Gambia, whether Muslim or not, to express great astonishment (T 120).

Licky-too (m.): The bearer of this name defeated an antagonist not only in a verbal confrontation but in physical combat as well.

Lizard (m.): The individual so nicknamed is an excellent dancer, noted for the nimbleness of his feet.

Louse (m.): This name was conferred on its bearer because he was perceived as conspicuously lacking in amiable personal qualities.

Lovey (f.); There are at least three persons so called on Johns Island. The origin of the name most readily appears to be the English word "love," and would be thus expressive of affection felt for the bearer by those who bestowed the name on her. Another possibility is that "Lovey" is an Anglo-American oriented acculturative adaptation of the Sea Island name "lafiya" listed by Turner as derived from Fon "lafiya" = "to be in good health"; also, Hausa "la₃fi₃ya₁" = "health, outward prosperity" (T 120).

Lula (f.): This fairly common name is not the official name of any one of its bearers. Kimbundu "mululu" = "great -grandchild" (T 134).

Mattus Momma (f.): Mattus is a place on Johns Island. The bearer of this name is the respected matriarchal individual of the locality.

Minna (f.): Turner lists the name "mina" (m. and f.) and relates it to the Vai personal name "miₙna₃," and the Fon "mina," denoting an African from Elmina or Accra in the former Gold Coast (present day Ghana) and refugee to Popo in the present day Republic of Benin (T 131).

Minna Bill (m.): That is, "Minna's Bill," nickname of Minna's grandson, Bill.

Monkey (f.): The nickname of a very attractive young woman whose charming antics as a child amused and delighted her elders.

Neen (f.): Turner lists the Sea Island name "nina" from the Bambara "nina" = "a gift" (T 137).

Neeny (f.): Diminutive of "Neen," above.

Nubber (m.): The bearer of this name "butted people." Butting as a form of physical assault consists of one person's use of the head to deliver a blow to the head of another person, often with stunning effect. The Oxford English Dictionary (Compact Edition, 1971) lists as boxing slang the word "nob," meaing "to strike one on the head" (attested for 1812). "Nobber" = "a blow on the head" is attested for 1818, and the same word is attested for 1821 as meaning "as pugilist skilled in nobbing." It seems, therefore that there is some justification for assuming that the unusual word "nubber" is a variant of "nobber."

Numprel (f.); The French "nombril" = "navel" has been proposed as the original form of this nickname (Cassidy 1985). In many African populations, both continental and diasporic, it is not uncommon to see infants and small children with notably protuberant navels. In our research, however, we have identified only one individual with the name "Numprel." One of the authors of this paper (Baird) sees the name as possibly related to "pela" (f.) cited by Turner as originated in Kimbundu "mpela" = "the season when the grass is burned (from July to October)"; "the ground which has been cleared by five"; also Mende "kpela" = "to mature, to reach puberty," used of females (T 148.).

Nuttin (m.): That is, "Nothing." This appears to be a basketname, given at birth, as distinct from a nickname which might be acquired or assumed during later periods of life. The bestowing of the somewhat derogatory name is in accord with the practice among some African peoples of giving an uncomplimentary name to an infant, especially if it is very healthy or good-looking, so that the ancestors might not become jealous and take the child back. (See Baird 1972, 76)

Peewee (m.,f.): Turner lists "piwi" as a female name, but males also have this name. Its origin is Kimbundu "mpivi" = "an orphan" (T 149).

Pig (m.): The individual so nicknamed has a reputation for over-indulgence.

Plum (m.,f.): Persons with this nickname have a light, smooth complexion.

Plummy (m.,f.): Diminutive of "Plum" above.

Pompey (m.,f.): The similarity of this name to that of the ill-fated rival of Julius Caesar is accidental and potentially misleading. Turner lists a Sea

Island name "pambi" from Mende "kpambi" = "line, course"; "a red handkerchief" (T 147). The misperception of African names and their alteration into forms more familiar to speakers of English has been remarked by such scholars as Dillard (1972, 129) and Woods (1974, 183).

Pook (m.): The pronunciation of this name requires the rounding and protrusion of the lips, thus reproducing the physiognomical feature of the bearer, for which he receive the sobriquet.

Poor-Man (m.): This nickname was given to the bearer because he was regarded as jealous, "tough" and "stingy."

Pop (m.): Not a reference to its bearer's name as a father, but to his paunch or 'pop-belly," that is, "pot-belly."

Prosper (m.): The bearer of this nickname is a distinguished Sea Islander. The very auspicious meaning of the name calls to mind the "oriki" or "praise-name" which is a feature of Yoruba naming practices.

Puddin (m.): That is, "Pudding." The nickname reflects the fact that the bearer likes to eat, and also that he is "a loveable character."

Queen (f.): Name of a young lady much admired for her beauty and meticulous good grooming. The name "Queen" or "Queenie" is found quite widely not only among African Americans but also among English-speaking Caribbean people. Both of these groups appear to have a greater consciousness of the complimentary character of the name than exists generally in the United States and in the Caribbean regarding its Latinate equivalent "Regina."

Rabbit (m.): The bearer of this name is perceived as being "tricky" like the Br'er Rabbit of African American (and originally African) folklore.

Reb (m.): That is Rev(erend). The bearer of this nickname, even in Sunday School carried a pack of cards with a constancy and pride similar to that with which a clergyman carried the Holy Book.

Sambo (m.): Turner lists this name, relating it to Hausa "sam₃boɪ" = "name given to the second son in a family"; "name given to anyone called *Muhammadu*"; "name of a spirit"; Mende "sambo" = "to disgrace"; "to be shameful"; Vai "sam₃boɪ" (personal name) = "to disgrace" (T 155).

Shadda (m.): That is, "Shadow." Individual so nicknamed is very dark-complexioned.

Shine-eye (m.): Nickname of an individual whose eyes had an extraordinary glitter.

Shug (m.,f.): Diminutive of "Sugar," a widely current sobriequet indicating the affection in which the bearer is held.

Sip (m.): The personal feature which characterizes the individual so nicknamed is alluded to by its opposite in this case. The bearer of the name is in fact a very tall person, such as is humorously described as "a long drink of water."

Sister (f.): Persons called by this kinship designation used as a nickname are not necessarily related familially to those who know and address them by the appellation, even though the name may have first been given within the family. The institutional (e.g., church) use of the title "sister" is different, and is not relevant here.

Skinny (m.): The bearer of this name is in fact presently rather corpulent: "he has a gut on him." He was, however, quite slender at the time the nickname was first conferred. In this case the name has outlasted the circumstances which gave it origin and justification.

Slim (m.): A number of persons so nicknamed are, as a matter of fact, slim. Some persons called "Slim," however, are, as in the case preceding, now fat.

South (m.): The bearer of this name is left-handed.

Spike (m.): The person so nicknamed is very tall, very thin, and has a long head.

Step (m.): The bearer of this nickname is a very short person.

Stretch (m.): Persons called by this name are very tall and slim. The head is not necessarily long as with "Spike."

Sugarnun (f.): The first element of this name "Sugar" is readily recognizable. The element "nun" (or "none") requires some explanation. There is no cultural basis for presuming any conventual connection, and the ungenerous prohibition suggested by the concept "none" negates the pleasant indulgence associated with "sugar." A review of the "sugar"-related terms which have or have had currency within the African American community reveals the word "sugar-tit." The article thus designated is a piece of cloth folded or rolled into a cone so that a kind of nipple is formed at the end. This end-part, dipped into sweetened water and inserted between the lips of a fretful infant, is sucked upon by the child who is thus calmed into a more complacent mood by the artificial but nonetheless gratifying "sugartit" or "sugarteat." Turner lists the name "nono" from Hausa "no₃no₁" = "the mammary gland of the female, and the corresponding structure in the male;" "the fins below the head of fish"; "a cluster of fruit" (T 137). The name "Sugarnun", accordingly, is apparently synonymous with "sugartit"/"sugarteat" and is connotative of oral pleasure and sensory satisfaction.

Swag (m.): The individual so nicknamed wore pants that were too big and as a result "sagged" or "swagged."

Sweet (f.): A complimentary description of the person so named.

Toady (m.): The bearer of this name was considered to resemble a frog.

Tuhmee (f.); Turner lists the name "toma" (f.) and relates it to Kongo "toma" = "to be good, to be pleasant"; "to taste sweet"; Kimbundu "toma" = "to stick"; Vai "to:₃ma₃," (personal name, m. and f.) (T 171).

Trader (m.): The individual bearing this nickname "like to swap stuff."

Ucker (m.); Turner records the name "okra" (m.), and relates it to Twi "okra" (personal name, m.) = soul (T 141). Bearer is an elderly man.

Wah-wah (f.) The bearer of this name, an older woman, is very religious. Turner records the name "wawa" (m.) and relates it to Hausa "wa:₃wa₃" = "a fool"; "a cloth of native make worn round the body and thrown over the shoulder"; "wa:₃wa₁" = "scrambling to obtain possession of a portion of an animal which has been killed"; Kimbundu "vava" = "to wish for"; "necessity"; Ewe "Ba₁vã₁-₃" = "a wasp." (T 178)

Yacky (m.): This name could be a variant pronunciation of "Jackie," above. A possible alternative source might be the name "yako" (m.) which Turner records and relates to Yoruba "ya₂ko₂" (personal name, m.) = 'to be male'; 'to be odd'. (T 184). The individual so named is an elderly man.

The foregoing list, by no means exhaustive, is intended to indicate the shapes, the sounds, the semantic associations, and the origins (actual and conjectural) of extant Sea Island personal names. The names included have been selected on the basis of the following criteria:

(a) they are the basket names or nicknames of the bearers, as distinct from their official given names;

(b) they are known and used by Sea Islanders within the family and the community to which the bearers belong. The family is to be understood in this context not as conforming to the European and European American nuclear model but as the African (so called extended) family which through its ramifying interconnections becomes, at its maximal extension, the community.

(c) their family and community connections, and the circumstances under which they were conferred or assumed, could be accounted for by our informants;

(d) their origins could be traced to African or other etyma so as to explain their occurrence and use.

The bearers of the basket names or nicknames listed are about twenty years old and above. No names of young or adolescent individuals have been included in our list. It appears that due to acculturative influences fewer parents are giving basket names to their children. Moreover, the greater mobility of Sea Islanders today, together with their rising socio-economic expectations and achievements, move the younger element into a wider sphere of life activity in which the more formal, official, European American name is more appropriate. Thus, even if a child is given a basket name or nickname, the period of time during which the recipient lives in an undiluted folk society is not long enough to ensure the lifetime attachment of the name.

The evidence indicates that some basket names and nicknames are still to be found in use in the Sea Islands today, even though the number of them is gradually being reduced. It is clear, to the extent that they continue in use at the present time, that these names form a part of the intimate family and community interrelationships between people in the culture. The attitudes and values expressed in these names would seem to constitute an inner core of cultural integrity and thus have been remarkably resistant to outside influences. The extant names continue to express familial affection and friendly regard, to compliment praiseworthy characteristics and to remark less laudable features, to commemorate personal incidents and communal events. In view of these considerations it is fair to conclude that some elements of traditional Sea Island naming practices persist to the present day, even though in attenuated form and in declining vigor.

References

ABRAHAM, R.C. (1958) A dictionary of modern Yoruba. London: Univ. of London Press Ltd.

BAIRD, K.E. (ed.) and CHUKS-ORJI, O. (1972) Names from Africa: Their Origin, Meaning and Pronunciation. Chicago: Johnson Publishing Co., Inc.

BOTUME, E.H. (1893) First Days Amongst the Contrabands. Boston: Lee and Sheperd.

CASSIDY, F.G. (1985) Personal communication.

DILLARD, J.L. (1972) Black English. New York: Random House.

HAIR, P.E.H. (1965) "Sierra Leone items in the Gullah Dialect of American English." Sierra Leone Language Review 4:79-84.

JOHNSON, G. (1930) Folk Culture on St. Helena Island, South Carolina. Chapel Hill: Univ. of North Carolina Press.

___ (1967) "The Gullah Dialect Revisited: A Note on Linguistic Acculturation." Paper read before the American Anthropological Association, December. Published in Journal of Black Studies 10, 4.

MUFWENE, S.S (1985) "The Linguistic significance of African proper names in Gullah." Presented at the Ninth Annual Language in South Carolina Symposium, April. To appear in New West Indian Guide 59, 3 and 4, Fall 1985.

OXFORD ENGLISH DICTIONARY (1971) Compact Edition. Oxford University Press.

PARSONS, E.C. (1923) Folk-Lore of the Sea Islands, South Carolina. Cambridge and New York: Memoirs of the American Folklore Society 16.

PARTRIDGE, E. (1959) Name this child; a handy guide for puzzled parents. London: Hamish Hamilton.

SWADESH, M. (1951) "Review of Turner's *Africanisms in the Gullah Dialect*," Word 7: 82-84.

TURNER, L.D. (1949) Africanisms in the Gullah Dialect. Chicago: Univ. of Chicago Press.

TWINING, M.A. (1977) "An examination of African retentions in the folk culture of the South Carolina and Georgia Sea Islands." Ph.D. dissertation, Indiana University.

WOOD, P.H. (1974) Black Majority: Negroes in Colonial South Carolina from 1670 through the Stono Rebellion. New York: Alfred A. Knopf.

CHAPTER FIVE

Family Life on Wadmalaw Island

Bamidele Agbasegbe Demerson

[A]ttempt ... to connect present conditions with the African past. This is not because Negro-Americans are Africans, or can trace an unbroken social history from Africa, but because there is a distinct nexus between Africa and America, which though broken and perverted, is nevertheless not to be neglected by the careful student.

W.E.B. DuBois (1908: 9)

The ... issue that requires clarification in studies of African and Afro-American family structure concerns the principles upon which these families are organized. The implications of the operation of the principle of consanguinity in relation to that of conjugality must be fully explored before the dynamics of Afro-American families can be appreciated and their similarities to African families and differences from Euro-American families fully understood.

Niara Sudarkasa (1980: 54)

In the rural communities of the South Carolina Sea Islands,[1] African Americans—known by their African derived ethnic designations, *Gullah* and *Geechee* (Turner, 1949: 194)—have traditionally maintained three multi-generational domestic groups whose members co-reside in compounds, i.e., clusters of contiguous or adjacent households. Each domestic group, moreover, is structured around a *building block, nucleus,* or *core* composed

57

of the adult male household heads who are also related to each other through paternal consanguineal ("blood") linkages. The Sea Islanders therefore may be characterized as having localized extended families. A contrasting phenomenon may be observed among the highly urbanized European Americans for whom the ideal family consists of a married couple and the offspring of that union living in a household apart (although not necessarily isolated) from other kinsfolk. In other words, for urban European Americans the family is based on conjugal (marital) bonding rather than consanguineal bonding as in African American Sea Island communities. And while the normative domestic group of these rural African Americans contrasts with that of urban European Americans, extended family life in the Sea Islands bears a remarkable resemblance to extended family among African peoples in Africa, the Caribbean, Central America, South America, and various parts of North America.

Of course the people of the South Carolina and Georgia Sea Islands are regarded by many to be distinctive because they appear to be somewhat less "acculturated," hence more African-like, than other sectors of the African population in the United States. Those who have studied Sea Island society and culture have pointed to at least three significant factors underlying this perception. First, as late as 1858,[2] captives were being imported directly from Africa to this region. Thus African patterns of life were receiving constant reinforcement and cultural enrichment in the Sea Islands. Second, during the period of enslavement and until recently on some islands, Africans have traditionally constituted a significant majority of the islands' population. And third, well into the twentieth century, the African descendants in the Sea Islands have been geographically isolated from the mainland and some aspects of mainstream American life. These three factors, then, are said to have facilitated the preservation, strengthening, and growth of an African-derived culture in the Sea Islands.

A perusal of the entries in bibliographies on the Sea Islands (Demerson, n.d.; Szwed and Abrahams 1978: 768, 776, 810, and 813; and Twining 1975) reveals a significant preoccupation of scholars with documenting the persistence and transformation of the African-derived culture in this region. While a diverse array of topics have been covered, documentation of the Sea Islanders' resilient Africanity in the area of family life—in spite of the horrors of slavery, the pressures of Reconstruction, and the dramatic social and economic changes of the late twentieth century—has yet to be systematically detailed. Such a worthy research objective is a mammoth task certainly beyond the scope of this paper. However, in moving toward this objective this paper provides an ethnographic portrait of the localized extended family in the South Carolina Sea Islands region. While the detailing is not exhaustive, the most characteristic features of kinship and residence will be discernible. A physical description of the compound is sketched. And a social description of the compound is illustrated with case study data regarding "the Smiths" (a pseudonym) who are used as a point of reference in discussing norms and variations in the extended families observed on Wadmalaw Island, Charleston County, in 1971. So that the Africanity of Sea Island family life may be perceived more fully, the presentation of ethnographic data from South Carolina is preceded by an overview of extended family life in African traditional arrangements.

EXTENDED FAMILY LIFE IN AFRICA: A BRIEF OVERVIEW

When African people were captured, herded onto ships, and forced to undertake the horrendous middle passage across the Atlantic to become enslaved in the Sea Islands and other areas of the Western Hemisphere, their "cultural baggage" included among other things fundamental principles and values regarding kinship; extended family structure and organization; and a complex set of rights, responsibilities, and behavioral codes attached to age, sex, marital status, and other markers of social differentiation. The differences in the structure and organization of extended families discernible to the ethnographic literature on Africa, and the Americas too, reflect in part how each society—given its unique history, political structure, economic organization, ecological niche, etc.—combined and elaborated upon those fundamental structures, principles and values.

In virtually every society of precolonial (as well as present day "traditional") Africa, a person was affiliated at birth with a set of unilineally determined consanguines. Whether the members of a society traced "blood" kinship through males, hence being patrilineal as among the Yoruba (see e.g., Fadipe 1970: 65-146; and Sudarkasa 1973: 97-116), or through females, hence being matrilineal as among the Ashanti (see e.g., Fortes 1950), the fundamental emphasis on the lineage—a corporate descent group to which one had obligations and through which one acquired rights—was (and is) widespread in Africa. In fact it was through lineage membership that one gained access to the use of land; inherited land and other properties; succeeded to political and religious offices owned by or allocated to a descent group; and acquired specializing training and an occupation predominantly practiced by members of that group. (See Sudarkasa 1980 and 1981 for further details.) Of course the emphasis on unilineal descent group membership did not rule out cognizance of one's bilateral genealogical connections to the kin of both one's father and one's mother. Indeed in many societies with unilineal kinship systems, a fundamental rule of bilateral kin exogamy prevented one from marrying relatives, however distant, of either parent.[4]

A segment of the lineage would serve as the *building block, nucleus*, or *core* or a localized extended family. This emphasis on a consanguineal core as the fundamental basis of *the family* meant that the recently wedded did not establish a new residence. Rather, as determined by the norms of the society, a couple's residence was established with the localized extended family of the husband (virilocal) or that of the wife (uxorilocal). Some men were even polygynists, i.e., concurrently married to a plurality of wives. The extended family, then, comprising a consanguineal core and the "in-marrying" spouses, co-resided in a compound. Headed by the most senior male of the consanguineal core owning the compound, the localized extended family had a tradition of being an institution with manifold functions. That is to say, members interacted so as to provide mutual assistance in goods, monetary contributions, and a variety of services that ensured the social and economic well being of all—the young, the elderly, the able-bodied, and the disabled. (See Sudarkasa 1980 and 1981 for further details. See also Agbasegbe 1976a; Fadipe 1970: 65-146; Fortes 1950; Kerri 1979; Marshall 1968; Okediji 1975a and 1975b; Onwuejeogwu 1975: 57-112; Shimkin and Uchendu 1978; and Sudarkasa 1973: 97-116).

Enduring marital bonding was encouraged in African traditions. And although significant, a married pair and the offspring of that union neither constituted an entity unto itself nor was it the building block or nucleus of the extended family. A corollary of this observation is that divorce, albeit a shocking experience for those directly concerned, did not lead to a "broken family" especially since the African family was an "extended" institution built on bonds of consanguinity rather than conjugality (Sudarkasa 1980 and 1981). Even in the case of a death of a spouse, some societies sanctioned secondary marriages (sororate, levirate, and widow inheritance) between the surviving spouse and a member of the deceased's lineage (Marshall 1968). And any number of adults within the compound could serve as parental surrogates to minors who had suffered the loss of a parent, whether from death or divorce.

The foregoing sketch, although devoid of detailed behavioral codes operative within the extended family, nevertheless suggests a few of the shared fundamentals that culture bearing Africans, forcibly uprooted from their societies and forcibly transported to "a new world," would draw upon in an effort to reconstruct a family life within the context of the enslavers' regime. Of course the dominant cultures of the planters (British, French, Portuguese), the demographic realities of the plantations (especially sex ratio), and the economic dictates of the times were among the many factors that forced the captives to combine and/or elaborate upon their pool of shared fundamentals in a variety of ways. A task for scholars today is the documentation of the persistence of these fundamentals of Africanity that are still recognizable in twentieth century life.

CLUSTERS OF CONTIGUOUS HOUSES IN THE SEA ISLANDS: A PHYSICAL DESCRIPTION OF THE EXTENDED FAMILY COMPOUND

On Wadmalaw and other islands in the region, many of the neighborhoods continue to bear the names and continue to be demarcated along the perimeters of the antebellum plantations. Within the neighborhoods one encounters roads and foot pathways that lead to clusters of households. To the person who is "off island"[5] these clusters of households or compounds are perhaps the first clues or physical evidence that African-descended Sea Islanders, like persons in "traditional" African societies, are born and reared in families that transcend the conjugal households idealized in Euro-America.

The evolutionary development of clusters of related households along with their landholding histories have not been neatly and carefully preserved in (or for) each family. Nevertheless we know from general histories of South Carolina and the Sea Islands in particular, that in some families, land tenure and compound development were integrally linked to events of the nineteenth century. Of particular significance were the federal occupation of the Sea Islands, the liberation of the enslaved Africans, and the land redistribution scheme (albeit precarious) that occurred during the Civil War. The Freedmen's Bureau, the Direct Tax Act of 1861, and the South Carolina Land Commission provided avenues through which an ex-bondsman or a cooperative association of ex-bondsmen could become a landholder of the estate (or portion thereof) on which Africans and their descendants were once enslaved. This redistribution of estates, abandoned by planters fleeing the war, was a pilot test conducted in large measure by agents of the federal government. Predating the beginning of the Reconstruction Era, this test was to ascertain the extent to which the formerly enslaved population had the capacity to become landowners and thereby develop a stable community and family life. Thus, before the end of the Civil War and the commencement of Reconstruction, there were indeed landowning Africans in the Sea Islands (Abbott 1967; Agbasgbe 1977; Bleser 1969; Hoffman 1956; Pease and Pease 1963; Rose 1964; and Verney 1983).[6]

In reference to the St. Helena Islanders of Beaufort County, one sociologist has remarked: "When the lands were sold to the Negroes, cabins in [alignment along both sides of] 'de street' . . . as the plantation quarters [for the enslaved] were formerly known, were moved to the center of the ten acre patches scattered all over the plantation" (Woofter 1930: 213-14).[7] And with the continued sales of portions of huge plantations on St. Helena and other islands in South Carolina, scattered clusters of multihousehold family settlements increased in number during the late nineteenth and early twentieth centuries.

On Wadmalaw today, the extended family settlement or compound usually comprises three to eight households arranged so that the distance between adjacent units is not more than thirty or forty feet. The houses in some compounds are situated along both sides of a foot pathway or road, reminiscent in some ways of the enslaved's quarters during the antebellum era. And in some compounds, the households are arranged so that a door of each domicile opens to a shared courtyard area where children play and kinsfolk gather. If the houses in a compound do not have indoor plumbing, they may also share an outdoor manually operated water pump and an outdoor toilet. In a family where agriculture is the major economic pursuit, cleared farmland is located not far from the compound. However when large scale cultivation is no longer an extended family's economic focus, often one or more members of the compound will maintain a garden adjacent to one of the family's households.

This description of the physical layout of the extended family compound on Wadmalaw has also been corroborated by social scientists researching family life on the neighboring islands. Regarding Johns, James, Younge's, and Edisto islands (in addition to Wadmalaw) in Charleston County, an educator and anthropologist from the Sea Islands has said that: "The . . . household is situated in a large gap. Three, five or more units may have been built in this gap. This would be home for one family. . . . The general pattern [i.e., spatial arrangement] of these units is circular to semi-circular" (Smith 1973: 19). Indeed the "extended design" of the "family gap . . . is the most prevalent family structure in the Sea Islands" (Smith 1973: 39). And for the St. Helena family, another anthropologist has reported that: "Households tend to be grouped together in residential compounds" (Moerman 1974: 75).

The physical structures (building materials and floor plans) of the houses in one compound may vary tremendously. Mobile homes and cinder block constructions, for example, are increasing in popularity in the region; however the wooden frame house is still predominant on Wadmalaw. In earlier days when the former captives began to establish wooden houses on their newly acquired lands, their homes evidently bore some resemblance to cabins known during slavery. On St. Helena, "The majority of these first homes were one and two room cabins with stick and mud chimney" (Woofter 1930: 214). Today in the late twentieth century, there are some houses on Wadmalaw that recall these nineteenth century dwellings. Most of the wooden frame houses today are larger with more rooms than the earlier ones. One floor plan utilized in some of the rectangular houses contains four equal sized rooms: living room, kitchen, and two bedrooms (Figure 1). Often the living room functions as a sleeping quarter at night. Insofar as possible the doors and windows of the houses are aligned in a parallel manner so as to facilitate maximum cross ventilation of the unit.

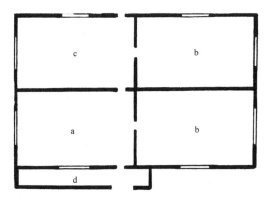

a   living room
b   bedroom
c   kitchen
d   porch

This floorplan may be seen in both wooden and cinder block homes. The approximate size of this house is 20' × 23'. Indoor plumbing is not available.

Figure 1. Floorplan of One Dwelling.

Other houses follow different floor plans. Moreover some houses, remodeled over the years to accomodate the growing size of the extended family, come to resemble duplexes (Figure 2). Such a dwelling is seen not only on Wadmalaw but has been reported for other islands as well (Smith 1973: 3).[8] Of course, wooden houses have been traditionally whitewashed. And a waning practice on many islands, that of painting outside door and window frames blue, is said to thwart malevolent spirits' attempts at entering the home.

KINSHIP, LAND, AND RESIDENCE IN THE SEA ISLANDS: A SOCIAL DESCRIPTION OF THE EXTENDED FAMILY COMPOUND

African American elders in various Sea Island communities, when queried about family life during slavery, affirm unreservedly that their foreparents valued kinship, family, and marriage. With a mixture of humor and sadness these elders recount the poignant incidents—transmitted intergenerationally by word of mouth—illustrative of their enslaved foreparents' never-ending struggles to keep intact marriages, to avoid parent-child separations, and to maintain mutual support and a sense of bonding among "blood," affinal (in-law), and "fictive" kinsfolk within (and

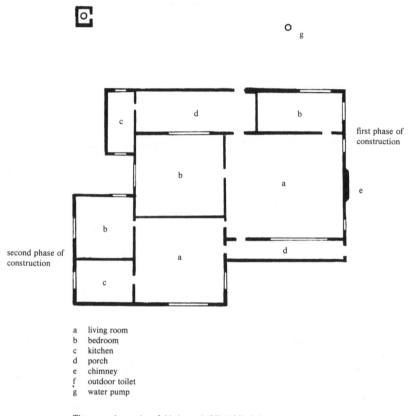

Figure 2. Floorplan of a "Duplex".

presumably across) the plantations.[9] Apparently on the large antebellum Sea Island plantations, some cabin households in "the street" were linked to each other in some form of an extended family relationship.

One might hypothesize that this extended family relationship represented an adaptation or transformation of African fundamental patterns and values. Regarding this, one may note that one Africanist who has both examined the narratives of enslaved Africans and surveyed the retrospective scholarship on slavery has remarked: "The writings . . . suggest that blacks on the plantations *behaved as slaves* towards whites and in relations to matters concerning the 'Masters' or their surrogates [yet] *behaved toward each other as Africans*, albeit Africans whose customs had to be adapted to the context of slavery" (Sudarkasa 1980: 54). Moreover, in the assessment of this Africanist anthropologist, the historical writings "reveal the presence of African patterns in Afro-American consanguineal kin groupings ('kin networks'), husband-wife relations, sibling bonds, socialization practices, patterns of exogamy, marriage rules and rituals, naming practices, relationships between alternate generations (grandparents and grandchildren), patterns of respect and deference, and the extension of kinship terminology to elders throughout the community" (Sudarkasa 1980: 52).[10] It should be noted, of course, that scholarly studies of the social life of those held in slavery draw significantly upon sources pertinent to South Carolina, Georgia, and the Sea Island region (e.g., Blassingame 1972; Genovese 1974; Gutman 1976; Owens 1976; see also Allen, English, and Hall 1986: 231-33).

Anthropological examination of the historical and ethnographic records pertaining to post-emancipation Africans have called attention to yet another facet of Africanity, the phenomenon of land ownership by kin groups. Some studies in the United States (e.g., Agbasegbe 1976b; Aschenbrenner 1975; Martin and Martin 1978; Shimkin, Shimkin, and Frate 1978) support the interpretation that *"after slavery*, when Black American extended family organization was not encumbered by . . . restraints . . . we find the reemergence of kinship groupings that exhibited many of their African antecedents" (Sudarkasa 1980: 56). Given that slavery would have rendered inoperative the function of lineages, it is particularly interesting to observe that "after slavery, some of the corporate functions of African lineages reemerged in some extended families which became property-owning collectives" (Sudarkasa 1981: 48).

Caribbeanist anthropologists have also emphasized that "one might well be surprised by the extent to which people may keep alive, even under conditions of extreme repression . . . fundamental ideas about kinship . . . widespread in West Africa" (Mintz and Price 1977: 39). Thus in some areas of post-emancipation Jamaica: "Once individuals had gained access to land ownership, large kinship groups . . . may have been built in at least some ways upon African models" (Mintz and Price 1977: 39). These land-based groups in Jamaica were non-unilineal and had a resemblance to those of the Para region of Suriname where former captives linked through ties of kinship, communally purchased the plantations on which they were formerly enslaved (Mintz and Price 1977: 36 and 39). During the period of slavery in Haiti, extended family compound-like settlements did exist among the captives (Laguerre 1978: 440). And following the early nineteenth century acquisition of land by the former captives, "they developed—perhaps reinstituted—a kind of familial settlement similar to existing patterns in [West African Fon communities of] Dahomey"

(Laguerre 1978: 441). The Haitians have a bilateral kinship system; however, the extended family compound is patrikin based (Bastein 1961; Laguerre 1978; Mintz and Price 1977; 39). In each of the aforementioned ethnographic cases, there is a correlated ritual association between ancestors and the land—they owned it while living—now serving as their place of interment. This ritual association between land and ancestors enacted by kin groups is certainly observable among the Saramaka so-called "maroons"[11] of Suriname whose well developed matrilineal kinship system reflects this descent principle operative in their ancestral African societies, poignantly reinforced by an inordinately high sex ratio during their early history as "runaways" (Mintz and Price 1977: 36 and 49; cf. Köbben 1973).

The phenomenon of land ownership by kin groups among post-emancipation African Americans of the Sea Islands parallels in some ways the same phenomenon in some post-emancipation African societies in other parts of the Western Hemisphere. Given the apparent presence of extended families on the pre-Civil War Sea Island plantations (as suggested in the discussions with present day elders recounting their oral histories), one might hypothesize that those ex-bondsmen who formed cooperative associations for the purpose of purchasing abandoned plantations were already linked to each other through ties of kinship (consanguineal, affinal, and "fictive") and friendship. And given the existence of consanguineal links between some of the neighboring extended family compounds today, it also seems reasonable to suggest that since the time liberated Sea Island Africans began acquiring land in the early 1860s, "blood" related kin would often purchase plots not too distant from one another, sometimes on the same plantation.[12]

As years passed, one might expect the complexity of the intraplantation relationships to increase. Not surprisingly, an observer of one island during the 1920s commented: "The plantation is a larger extension of several families which have intermarried. It is a face-to-face neighborhood where relationship is complicated but well recognized" (Woofter 1930: 213). Moreover: "This closeness of neighborhood, the recognized family relationship, and the simple community organization, give the plantation a solidarity and unity of action which is remarkable" (Woofter 1930: 213). Decades later, in the 1970s, another observer of that island would further comment: "On occasion, one had the feeling that everyone on the island was related to everyone else" (Moerman 1980: 31). This late twentieth century observer parenthetically added: "and counting relatives by marriage, probably everyone is" (Moerman 1980: 31; cf. Reid 1956: 41 regarding an island in Georgia).

The wide ranging acknowledgement of consanguineal, affinal, and "fictive" kinship by the people of Wadmalaw also gives one the impression that any person is related virtually to everyone else on this small island. As intriguing and perhaps startling as this perceived phenomenon may be to one who is "off island," it is less overwhelming to the Sea Islander. In any society or community, including the Sea Islands, one is enculturated so that he or she is able to distinguish non-kin from kin and distant kin from family. Thus an examination of some of the characteristic patterns of kinship and residence discernible on Wadmalaw leads one toward an understanding and appreciation of the compound as a dynamic social entity.

African Americans in the Sea Islands, like African Americans in various communities of the mainland United States, acknowledge ties of bilateral kinship. That is to say, one has a culturally recognized genealogical relatedness to the kinsfolk of one's father as well as to the kinsfolk of one's mother. However, in the Sea Islands, as typified by the Smiths' compound (documented in Figure 3 and Table 1), the localized extended family is structured around and identified by reference to a "core" group consisting primarily of consanguineously related adult males. More specifically, those males who make up the core of any given family trace kinship to each other through "blood" ties that are predominantly based on *paternal* linkages.

Among the Smiths, like many other families in the region, land has passed from one generation to the next by intestacy. In such cases, the land on which a compound is based, presumably passes to all descendants of the original title holder. In other words, property ownership is not exclusively vested in the male consanguineal core of the co-residing extended family, but in a group of male and female "blood" related heirs. And because the Sea Islanders do have a bilateral kinship system, both males and females would in theory have an equal right to inherit and transmit land. In a community where wills are rarely made—thereby not specifying or restricting the transmission of property—one could conceivably have claims to many tracts of lands from many different foreparents.

Customary "folk" attitudes and their behavioral correlates, as well as financial circumstances, may work to narrow one's theoretical possibilities or "choices" to land as noted in the following impressions. The third or fourth generation urbanites whose progenitor was a migrant to New York City, for example, may simply be content to be able to point with pride to the fact that their island kinsfolk own "family land." These persons may even periodically visit the island, especially to attend various rites of passage. But having no intention of ever living in the rural setting, they may not pay taxes on the "family land" and may have no intentions of every pressing their claim to its use and ownership. It is also possible that a deceased female's descendants may perceive no obligation to pay taxes on land that would by law accrue to them. And with the passage of time, her third or fourth

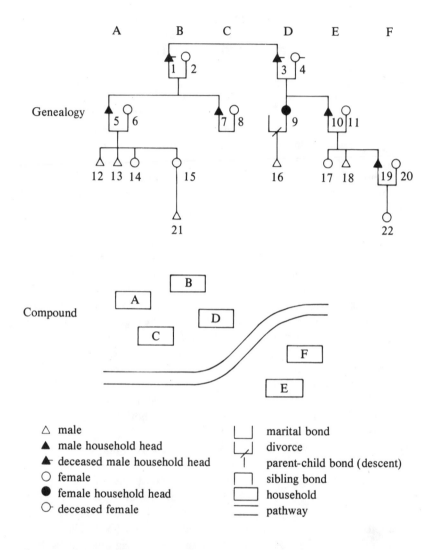

The genealogy is a partial one in that only co-resident members are depicted. (Of course those deceased members whose inclusion is necessary for a comprehension of the genealogical connections among the co-resident members are illustrated.) Thus those males and females who have migrated, and those females who have moved to their husbands' compounds, are not represented here. It should also be noted that siblings are not always presented in order of seniority based on age.

Figure 3. The Smiths: A Sea Island Extended Family Genealogy and Compound.

Table 1. Household Compositions in the Smith Compound.

Household	Head	Members (and relation to head of household)
A	5	6 (wife); 12, 13 (sons); 14 (daughter)
B	5	2 (mother); 15 (daughter); 21 (grandson)
C	7	8 (wife)
D	9	16 (son)
E	10	11 (wife); 17 (daughter); 18 (son)
F	19	20 (wife); 22 (daughter)

generation descendants may not even conceive of such land as belonging to them. Equally significant, in Sea Island communities where residents are certainly impoverished and underdeveloped (see e.g., Agbasegbe 1975; Demerson 1974; Moerman 1974 and 1980; and Moore and Washington 1970), it is also possible that sons or grandsons may feel a primary obligation or pressure to use their limited resources to keep up with the payment of taxes on land identified with the paternal kin groups of their fathers rather than those of their mothers.

The aforementioned impressions, gleaned from conversations with the Islands' residents and with the migrants (both temporary and permanent) from the islands to cities like New York, obviously need corroboration in further research efforts. Pending such research, one may hypothesize that these impressions signal the Sea Islanders' recognition that a large scale group of bilaterally related heirs as a property owning "corporation" may be problematic. Nevertheless, whatever the reasons underlying the phenomenon, in many extended families, one's rights to the use and ownership of land (as well as the obligation to pay taxes) certainly appears to accrue from one's membership in a paternal kin group. In other words, without a *bona fide* unilineal descent system, "unilineal-like" paternal consanguineal bonds appear to be operative in the land tenure practices of many Sea Islanders. [13]

A census of the Smith compound, as documented in Figure 3 and Table 1, reveals it to be a four generational localized extended family comprising 19 members who live in a cluster of six households. The consanguineal core group around whom the family is built consists of 5, 7, 10, and 19 who are males, and 9, who is a female. Each core member is the head of a household unit within the compound. And each core member is related through paternal genealogical linkages. Thus, in the first generation, 1 and 3 (now deceased) were brothers. In the second generation, the brothers 5 and 7 are the offspring of 1 and are therefore the paternal cousins to 9 and 10 who are the offspring of 3. In the third generation is 19, whose father and paternal grandfather are respectively 10 and 3. The only core female member, 9, is a middle-aged divorcee who has reaffiliated with her natal compound and has become the head of the household once occupied by her now deceased parents, 3 and 4.

It is important to reiterate that the "blood" related adult males who make up the core of the compound trace their kinship to one another, predominantly though not exclusively, through paternal linkages. In some Sea Island families, there are occasional instances in which the adult males of the core are "recruited" *via* maternal kin linkages. Two such potential cases exist in the Smith family. When 16 and 21 become married adults, their continued residential affiliation with the extended family of this compound will accrue through their mothers, 9 (a divorcee) and 15 (an unwed mother at the time of 21's birth). Of course, the bilateral flexibility in what is basically a paternally linked core does not contradict the fact that the core of the extended family compound is in essence made up of "blood" related males. The one exception in the Smith family is 9.

Genealogical lore is particularly important in regard to mate selection. The interviews and casual conversations with Sea Islanders (as well as genealogical charts constructed for various families, including the Smiths) throw into relief that neither marriages nor non-marital sexual relationships between "blood" kin, related paternally or maternally, are sanctioned on Wadmalaw. In those instances where this normative exogamous practice is contravened, the persons concerned may even deny that a kinship link exists between them.[14] This bilateral kin exogamy observed on Wadmalaw has also been reported for the residents of St. Simon Island, Georgia, who in their attempts to discourage an "incestuous" marriage between distant relatives hyperbolize: "The farther the blood goes, the thicker it is" (Reid 1956: 77). This adage would certainly be understood on Wadmalaw.

A cursory examination of the census for the Smith family also should make clear that its post-marital residence pattern is virilocal. On Wadmalaw and other islands, when the males born and/or reared in a given compound become married adults, they are expected to bring their wives to live among the males' extended family. And when females born and reared in a given compound become married adults, they will typically leave their natal home to reside among their husbands' extended families.[15] As descending generations become adults, they repeat the virilocal pattern.

The post-marital residence ensures that it will be normative for children to be born and reared in a domestic setting where the bonds of paternal kinship are emphasized. One's family of orientation is not the conjugal household idealized in urban Euro-America, but literally the total membership of one's natal compound. The virilocal residence practice then, functions to foster, strengthen, and reflect the solidarity of consanguines, especially the co-resident adult males. It is within the compound that a man first seeks one who will provide assistance in repairing a house or car, advice concerning a significant venture, small scale loan, or partnership in recreational activities. Of course, the adult males by virtue of their co-residence, have activated their rights to maintain households on family land. Their usufructuary rights to land is especially visible in those cases where they are collectively engaged in agricultural-related economic pursuits. However among those kinsfolk where both large scale cultivation has ceased and extensive migration of adult males has taken place, an erosion of the localized extended family compound seems inevitable. This erosion of the compound occurs in part because the post-marital residence pattern does not facilitate a continuance of the multihousehold settlement by females (Demerson 1974).

Whereas the male living on Wadmalaw appears to be intensely involved in his natal compound throughout this life cycle, the female is likely to be significantly involved in two compounds—one affinal and the other natal. Virilocal post-marital residence, while involving a bride in a new set of roles and relationships in her husband's compound, does not extinguish her roles, relationships, and rights in the compound of her birth. A woman's contributions to the social and economic well being of both her affinal and natal kinsfolk are various, including among others: babysitting, counselling youth, temporary or permanent fostering of minor relatives, caring for the infirm, assisting the elderly, contributing to ritual expenses (funerals, weddings, graduations, church and school programs, family reunions, etc.), gift-giving, and participating in the family business (Agbasegbe 1976b).

The men and women—and children too—who co-reside in a compound have roles, relationships, and rights that transcend the household. Thus virtually each person is involved in a constant face-to-face interaction with the members of *the family*, i.e., the localized extended family. It should not be surprising therefore that the household among African Americans of Wadmalaw, although significant, may not mirror the ideal household of urban Euro-America. Indeed the composition, headship, functioning, and relative self-sufficiency and autonomy of households on Wadmalaw vary considerably.

As noted for the Smith family in Table 1, household composition frequently, but not always, follows the model of the conjugal family. Census data collected on various localized extended families on Wadmalaw further reveal that while households may contain a virilocal couple and the offspring of that union, household boundaries are not rigid. Household boundaries are in fact "elastic," thus allowing for the temporary and permanent absorption of both minor and adult relations.

In several of the localized extended families on Wadmalaw, households formed around consanguineal rather than conjugal bonds are by no means uncommon. The developmental histories of consanguineal households may be related to several factors including for example: the death of a husband/father whose household is occupied by his surviving wife and children; marital dissolution in which the divorcee residentially reaffiliates with her natal compound in a household she occupies along with her children; the migration of young parents who entrust their child to the care of a widowed grandmother who formerly lived in a household by herself; and the assumption of some or virtually all aspects of the husband/father role configuration by an already married man whose "outside" children and their mother occupy a household in the setting of the woman's natal compound.[16]

A consanguineal household with one of the aforementioned developmental histories obviously has no resident adult male in the role configuration of husband/father. Nevertheless because the consanguineal household is not isolated, but found within the context of the localized extended family, it may draw upon adult males in the compound who provide wide ranging instrumental and expressive support, including monetary and various other material gifts, transportation services, household repairs, and affection and disciplining of minors. Quite importantly, these adult kins*men* also provide role models for young males, thereby ensuring sex role development of the youth in accordance with norms of the Sea Island communities. Because of the foregoing reasons, consanguineal households found within the context of the compound should not be characterized as "disorganized," "broken," and/or "matrifocal" families. The consanguineal households B and D in the Smiths' compound illustrate some of the issues noted above.

After her children became married adults and after the death of her husband, 2 became the sole occupant of household B. Her sons and daughters (some of whom no longer live on the island) provide her with periodic financial gifts, thereby adding significantly to her resources. And over the years she has received a great deal of support, (i.e., in kind gifts and services) from her resident sons, 5 and 7. Shortly after her son's unmarried daughter, 15, gave birth to 21, her household grew to include them. Thus 2 was able to relieve the overcrowding of household A while at the same time providing an inexperienced mother with assistance in caring for a baby. The young mother's limited resources from her part-time employment outside the home were hardly sufficient to meet all the needs of her household. While various members of 15's kin network, inside and outside the compound, occasionally contribute items of clothing or provide babysitting services for her son, she relies significantly on her parents. Not surprisingly 5's financial and decision making roles in household B increased such that he in essence is the head of two households, A and B.

Marriage in the Sea Islands is a long-lasting institution ending with the death of a spouse, and in rare cases, with divorce (Agbasegbe 1976b: 128; Moreman 1974; Reid 1956: 76). Of course the phenomena of widowhood and divorce may affect the residential status of women and their minor children. A woman has rights to land use and ownership in her natal kin group. She does not have ownership to the family land of her husband's kin group (even if her children are heirs).

On St. Helena it has been observed that: "Several compounds had resident widows who had lived with their husbands on the husband's compound for 30 to 50 years; when the husband died, they returned to the patrimony they had left as brides" (Moerman 1974: 83). On Wadmalaw elderly widows seem less likely to reaffiliate with their natal compounds. Indeed it is hard to imagine adult sons sending their mother back to her natal compound on the grounds that she has no ownership rights in her affinal compound (Agbasegbe 1976b). In the case of the Smiths, 2 did not return to her natal compound when she became widowed.

However, when 9 and her spouse divorced, she along with her minor son, 16, moved back to the Smith compound. The child continues to see his father and regularly interacts with his paternal kinsfolk while simultaneously being more fully integrated into the paternal kin group of his mother. Regularly employed outside the home, 9 appears financially self-reliant as she heads household D once occupied by her parents who are now deceased. The rearing or socialization of children to a great extent occurs within the context of the compound. Therefore just as 9 depended upon the adults in her affinal compound to help socialize her son and provide him with socio-economic security, so too does she depend upon the adults in her natal compound to do the same. This mother and son, then, do not belong to a broken family. Both of the extended families in which the son continues to interact are indeed intact. Marital disruption, therefore, is not synonymous with "broken family" in the Sea Islands, as would be the case in urban Euro-America where the autonomous conjugal household is defined as *the family*.

Not surprisingly the head of the extended family is often the eldest male of the consanguineal core around whom the co-residing kin group is formed. This male, moreover, sometimes has distinguished himself as a leader within the church, as an owner of a visible business within the community, or as one of the spokesmen for the community on issues of economic development with "off island" political officials and industrialists. Among the Smiths, after the deaths of males in the first generation illustrated in Figure 3, and after the migration of other older males of the second generation (not illustrated in Figure 3), a man of late middle-aged years, 5, became the acknowledged head of his extended family. In comparison with the many extended family leaders who are of advanced age, 5 is rather young. Suffice it to say, however, that Sea Island community norms do not force disengagement upon those of advanced age. Indeed within Sea Island extended families (and communities also) there continues to be a significant emphasis on respect for elders and their moral authority.

A CROSS-CULTURAL VIEW: CONTRASTS AND COMPARISONS

The foregoing ethnographic portrait of some aspects of kinship, land tenure, and residence in the Sea Islands compels the examination of family life in this region in a cross-cultural context. In so doing the point may be easily made that family structure among the African American Sea Islanders differs markedly from the ideal family structure of urban European Americans. The following are chief points of contrast.

The defining characteristic of the Sea Island family is that it is built on bonds of consanguinity rather than bonds of conjugality, as is the case in Euro-America. Post-marital residence is virilocal in the Sea Islands, yet in the wider American society post-marital residence is neolocal; i.e., a married pair and the offspring of that union live in a household apart from either spouse's relatives. Thus in African American communities in the Sea Islands, the family is a multigenerational and multihousehold localized group. This group, moreover, is structured around and identified by reference to a core made up of adult males related through paternal consanguineal linkages. By contrast, in European American urban communities of the mainland United States, the ideal family is a two generational household. Sea Island households, although exhibiting various degrees of self sufficiency and autonomy, are nevertheless interdependent in fulfilling many of the functions that Westerners see as the responsibilities of so-called "nuclear" families and governmental agencies. For African Americans of the Sea Islands, household is not synonymous with *the* family, whereas for European Americans, household and family are the same. Given the aforementioned differences, it is understandable that marital instability as evidenced by divorce is not to be characterized as a "broken family" in the Sea Islands. However in Euro-America, where the conjugal household is autonomous in relation to the households of other kinsfolk, it seems inevitable that divorce will be taken as evidence of a "broken family." Finally, both African American Sea Islanders and European Americans have bilateral kinship systems; however in the Sea Islands the localized or co-residing extended family is skewed in the direction of affiliation with paternal relations.

While the normative domestic group of these rural African Americans certainly contrasts with that of urban European Americans, family life in the Sea Islands bears a remarkable resemblance to that of African peoples elsewhere. More to the point, the phenomenon of residential clusters of close kin constituting one family, an extended family, has been documented for peoples of African descent in various eras and geographic locales. In precolonial and present day Africa, the normative domicile for the extended family was and is the compound (see e.g., Sudarkasa 1980). For the period of enslavement in North America, one could again document the presence of multihousehold extended families within the confines of a single plantation, as well as kinship networks that stretched across several planters' estates (see e.g., Gutman 1976; Kulikoff 1977; and Webber 1978: 111-17 and 157-79). And in twentieth century rural, urban, northern, and southern United States, the residential propinquity characteristic of African American extended families, has likewise been documented (see e.g., Aschenbrenner 1975; Frazier 1939; Mitchell and Mitchell 1978; Shimkin, Shimkin, and Frate 1978; and Stack 1974). Moreover, one may witness the presence of multihousehold extended family structures among African descendants in Central America, South America, and the Caribbean (see e.g., Gonzalez 1969; Köbben 1973; Laguerre 1978; and Mintz and Price 1977).

Parallels certainly could be drawn between the communal purchase of plantations by the former captives in the Para region of Suriname (Mintz and Price 1977: 36) and those in the Sea Islands. Moreover parallels could be drawn between land ownership and non-unilineal descent in post-emancipation Jamaica (Mintz and Price 1977: 39) and land ownership and bilateral kinship in the post-emancipation Sea Islands. And on the surface one even could, despite the contrasts, draw a number of striking comparisons in an examination of the kinship and residence patterns of the North American Sea Islanders, the Caribbean Haitians, and the West African Yoruba (Agbasegbe 1975 and 1976a). For example, in each of the three societies, genealogical recognition is extended to the kinsfolk of one's father and one's mother. And while the Sea Islanders and the Haitians have an observable emphasis on paternal kin linkages, the Yoruba by contrast have full-fledged patrilineages. Built around a core of consanguines and headed by the eldest male of that core, the multifunctional localized extended family in Yorubaland, Haiti, and the Sea Islands is residentially based in a compound. Furthermore, virilocality is the common post-marital residence in each ethnographic setting. Polygyny, while culturally sanctioned in Yorubaland and Haiti, is not *formally* practiced in the Sea Islands. Of course in none of these settings is marital instability to be equated with a "broken family" since a consanguineal rather than a conjugal basis undergirds the familial institution in these societies. Suffice it to say, a further examination of the ethnographic data on sex roles (although not the focal points of this paper) in the Sea Islands, Haiti, and Yorubaland, would continue to yield some striking comparisons.

The genealogies of many Sea Islanders and Haitians are no doubt traceable to the Yoruba of West Africa. Obviously, however, highlighting the readily observable resemblances in these three settings is not meant to imply that the Yoruba were extraordinarily able to preserve virtually intact their kinship, familial, and marital institutions in the Sea Islands or Haiti. What is more important to emphasize is that these societies share a fundamental emphasis on consanguinity which reflects, shapes, and reinforces observable social structures, values, and behavior patterns that in some ways are basically similar. This fundamental emphasis on consanguinity was also part of the "cultural baggage" that Africans brought with them to the Sea Islands as they struggled to recreate (while obviously adapting) their social structures, values, and behaviors within the given historical, political, economic, and ecological contexts.

Thus the early Africans in the Sea Islands could draw from the patrilineal Yoruba as well as the matrilineal Ashanti in reaching the understanding that *the family* was ideally an extended institution built around a core of "blood" relatives. Whether from the patrilineal Igbo or the matrilineal Kimbundu, the early residents of the Sea Islands could also be socialized to view the inheritance of properties as a right associated with consanguines rather than with spouses. Cultural memories deriving from the virilocal Mandinka and the uxorilocal Bijogo, notwithstanding the different post-marital residence practices of the two societies, nevertheless could provide African descendants in the Sea Islands with an understanding that the establishment of an independent conjugal household was not culturally preferred behavior. The Bamileke, the Fanti, and the Wolof, as well as the aforementioned Ashanti, Igbo,Kimbundu, Mandinka, and Bijogo, among several other ethnic groups, each in the formative years of the African-derived Sea Island culture could provide a model of extended family structure and a set of behavioral codes which ensured that this institution was a mutual aid society meeting the needs of all members. (See Murdock 1959 for other cultural summaries.) Thus, while the Sea Islanders have particular structural resemblances to the Yoruba and the Haitians, so too do they share on some very fundamental levels linkages, for example, across the Caribbean to the Garifuna of Belize, Central America, and to the Djuka of Suriname, South America; and across the Atlantic to the Ashanti of Ghana, West Africa.

It should perhaps be reiterated that the *contrasts* drawn between the rural African American Sea Island family and that of the urban European American are traceable to the emphasis on consanguinity in the former and conjugality in the latter. Moreover, the *comparisons* of the Sea Islanders' family to that of African peoples elsewhere in the world are traceable to the shared cultural heritage of an African emphasis on consanguinity (cf. Sudarkasa 1980, 1981).

SOME FINAL COMMENTS: THREATENING SOCIAL FORCES
This discussion has sketched traditional rural African American extended family life on Wadmalaw, one of several Sea Islands found along the coastlines of South Carolina and Georgia. This article, moreover, has outlined the Africanity undergirding Sea Island family life by means of cross-cultural allusions to West African prototypes and Caribbean and South American counterparts.

Today on some islands, urbanization, migration, corporate tourism, industrial development, and other forces instigated by non-African Americans are adversely affecting the resident Sea Island African population. These African Americans are facing continual underdevelopment and virtual extinction on some islands. The threatening forces, as one regional planner has stated, "impact . . . upon a declining breed, the rural Southern black family" (Thomas 1980: 1). One of the ways this impact is seen is in both the threat and the reality of the expropriation of African American-owned lands.

Challenging tasks are now before the Sea Islanders. Not only must they outline ways in which threatening forces are impacting and may impact on co-residential kin groupings; they must also propose ways in which localized extended families may become agents in a plan for the social growth and development of the Sea Island communities. Careful scrutiny of the social changes in the Sea Islanders' prototypical West African societies and their Caribbean counterparts may give clues as to the direction planned change in some communities of the Sea Islands may take. Similarly the close scrutiny of those Sea Island communities already devastated by relatively recent changes offer an unpleasant warning of what may occur if preventive measures and indigenous planned change are not instituted (Moore and Washington 1970; Thomas 1977, 1978, 1980). One cannot overemphasize that the very cultural survival of a people is at stake.

NOTES
[1]This account is based on anthropological field research directed by Dr. Niara Sudarkasa and conducted under the auspices of the Center for Afro-American and African Studies at The University of Michigan. The spring and summer of 1971 were spent collecting data on Wadmalaw Island in Charleston County, South

Carolina. While Wadmalaw served as a residential base, visits to other islands in Charleston and other counties were also made. (The term "today" when used in the text obviously refers to 1971.)

The comparative data on African, Caribbean, and South American Blacks are based primarily on a perusal of the anthropological literature and complementary field observations among the West African Yoruba in the summers of 1972 and 1973 and among the people of Haiti in the spring of 1974. Funding for the West African field trip in 1972 was provided in part by a grant from the Department of Anthropology made possible through the efforts of Dr. William G. Lockwood *and* a grant from the Max H. Coutchen Fund of the Honors Council, both of The University of Michigan. The Center for Afro-American and African Studies at The University of Michigan provided financial assistance for the field trip to West Africa in 1973.

This article summarizes much of the information on Sea Island family life presented in a series of the author's published and unpublished reports (see: Agbasegbe [Demerson] 1975, 1976a, 1976b, 1977, 1978, 1980; Demerson 1973, 1974, 1982). Parts of this article, including Figure 3 and Table 1, have appeared previously in 1982 in "Some Aspects of Contemporary Rural Afro-American Family Life in the Sea Islands of Southeastern United States," *The Western Journal of Black Studies* 6(2):60-65. Of course several scholars have contributed to our understanding of twentieth century family life in the Sea Islands region. Therefore one may wish to consult: Cooley (1926); Derby (1980); Guthrie (1977); Kiser (1932); Moerman (1974 and 1980); Reid (1956); Smith (1973); and Woofter 1930).

Gratitude is expressed to the Sea Islanders, the Yoruba, and the Haitians, whose interests and cooperation made the field research efforts valuable experiences. Many thanks are also extended to Dr. Niara Sudarkasa whose insights into African and African American ethnology in general, and family life in particular, have been instrumental in providing parameters for the ethnographic portrait of Sea Island family life documented herein. Especially enlightening have been her discussions of the principle of consanguinity, a transatlantic linkage, underlying African and African American families (Sudarkasa 1975, 1980, and 1981). Of course, responsibility for the demerits of this article rests solely with its author.

[2]The Slave Trade Act of 1808 was a Congressional prohibition making the intercontinental trafficking in human cargoes illegal in the United States. Nevertheless captives imported directly from Africa continued to arrive on the shores of the United States for another half century. The unique geography of the isolated islands made it easy for "slavers" to elude the authorities as they continued to profit from their violation of the law and lack of concern for human suffering. As a consequence, in 1858—just three years before the beginning of the Civil War and just five years before the signing of the Emancipation Proclamation—a human cargo of some four hundred Africans were disembarked from the ship *Wanderer* on Jekyll Island, Georgia. (See: Jackson, Slaughter, and Blake 1974: 33-34; Turner 1949: 1; and the sources cited in both.)

South Carolinian and Georgian planters evidently preferred those captives imported directly from Africa over those who had been "seasoned" and/or born in the West Indies and other parts of the Americas. Indeed they feared that the newcomers from Africa would be dangerously infected with the "misconduct" of rebellious and/or runaway captives from various Western Hemispheric regions. Thus by eighteenth century legislative decrees, South Carolinians and Georgians sometimes either barred the entrance of captives from some areas of the Americas, or they levied heavier duties on those not coming directly from Africa. It is not surprising, therefore, that the Sea Islands would have a high incidence of directly imported Africans and descendants of those Africans born and reared in this region. Likewise, the Africanity of the region should come as no surprise. (See: Jackson, Slaughter, and Blake 1974: 33-34, Turner 1949: 2-5; and the sources cited in both.)

[3]The comparative data in this article, as mentioned in n. 1 above, are based primarily on a perusal of the literature complemented with field observations in West Africa. The essays by Sudarkasa (1980 and 1981) are critical readings for anyone exploring the relationship of "traditional" African family structure to African American family structure. In addition to the studies on extended family life in Africa cited in this essay, one may wish to consult the synoptic reports found in Murdock (1959) and the relevant sections of the ethnographies indexed in the Human Relations Area Files.

[4]Societies in Africa and elsewhere may also prefer that spouses belong to the same "in group" defined on the basis of territoriality, social status, and some cases kinship. Such marriage patterns may be characterized as endogamous. Of course some endogamous marriages permitted in Africa are not a part of the norms extant in Euro-America or Afro-America because the kinsfolk to be wedded might be considered "too close."

[5]On Wadmalaw, the residents use "off island" in reference to a visitor or one who is not a native to the region.

[6]As the studies cited will confirm, the attempts by Africans to achieve and retain landholding status were not without numerous stumbling blocks. While a few had become relatively prosperous farmers, most cultivators according to Rose (1964: 382) "were living, in the years just after the war, on a subsistence basis, raising their own vegetable crops, with enough cotton to produce a little ready cash to pay the taxes."

Not every freedman became a land owner in the early 1860s. Those plantation owners who had reclaimed their estates after the Civil War, allowed Africans to continue living on the estates with the stipulation that the landless enter into contracts for leases and wages as tenant farmers. For descriptions of tenant farming conditions see Blackman (1880) and Lander (1960).

[7]An eighteenth century watercolor painting of Mulberry Plantation (Chase 1971: 60) and an early twentieth century photograph of the antebellum quarters on the Friendfield Plantation (Joyner 1984: facing 127) provide visual documentation of "the street" on such pre-Civil War Southern estates. Although the Africanity of the "vernacular architecture" is not the focus of this essay, it has been suggested by Chase (1971: 60), Joyner (1984: 118-20), Vlach (1978: 122-38), and others. An archeological record of the captives' habitations on the antebellum plantations

provides yet another dimension to our understanding of pre-twentieth century African life in the Sea Islands and elsewhere (see e.g.: Fairbanks 1984; Otto and Burns 1983; and Salwen and Gyrisco n.d. [circa 1877]).

[8]Some dwellings are perhaps more labyrinthic than duplexes and therefore may be triplexes (or even quadruplexes). As much is suggested by Smith (173: 19) who has observed that some houses are in fact "units with *multiple* extensions" (emphasis supplied). Smith (1973: 3) moreover has explained that the "long term economic deprivation where Blacks could not afford new houses . . . in part contributed to . . . the [inter]generational building habit of constructing newer dwellings either close to or as extensions of existing houses." Without discounting Smith's economic explanation underlying household/compound construction in the Sea Islands, one must also consider the Africanity that is the basis of the kinship, land tenure, and residence patterns that have emerged in this region.

[9]Collecting oral histories about social organization during captivity was not a preeminent concern at the time of fieldwork in 1971. Nevertheless, the impressions developed from some of the conversations with elderly Sea Islanders suggest that this is an important area for immediate fieldwork. Juanita Jackson, Sabra Slaughter, and J. Herman Blake (1974: 34) in their discussion of "African survivals and slavery," convey a sense of urgency by noting: "There are still many elderly blacks in the Sea Islands whose parents or grandparents were slaves and who can provide us with a good understanding of the latter years of slavery from the point of view of those who went through that experience . . . [Each has] an extraordinary story to tell, one which will be available for only a few more years."

[10]Moerman's (1974) study contains very useful ethnographic data on present day extended family life in the Sea Islands region. He states, "In general, there is little evidence on the actual structure of family life among ante-bellum slaves"; and "There is no evidence to suggest that the situation on St. Helena was any different . . . It seems fair to say that in 1860, St. Helena blacks had little family worth the name" (Moerman 1980: 29). These assertions, however, are not based on any research efforts. Moerman (1974 and 1980) attributes no African basis to the present day family life in the Sea Islands and views the "complex and ornate structure of family relations" on St. Helena within the rubric of "adaptations to marginality." In fact he characterizes the Sea Islanders as "masterful marginals" (Moerman 1980)! Even worse is Albanese's (1976) pretense of "scholarship" on antebellum plantation life in the Sea Islands. Albanese's (1976) outrageously antiquated view is essentially a frail effort to resuscitate U.B. Phillips.

It must be emphasized that the 1970s research by historians has drawn significantly on primary sources about South Carolina, Georgia, and the Sea Islands region. Sudarkasa's (1980) assessment of those writings points the way for continuing research into the primary documents utilized by historians. When coupled with oral historical research as suggested above in n. 9, our understanding of antebellum African family life should be enhanced.

[11]Throughout the Western Hemisphere, those Africans and their descendants who refused to be slaves were derisively labeled by the Europeans in terms of derogation. Indeed, a Eurocentric bias continues to be evident in the rubric utilized

in present day scholarship. Thus the freedom seeking and self-determining former captives, whether living together in small bands or in complex states they created, were called *maroons*. (See various contributions to Price 1973). Derived from the Spanish *cimarrón*, a term in the Western Hemisphere that was originally applied to livestock that had escaped to the hills, *maroon* by analogy was extended to captive Africans who had escaped to the natural (and often severe) environs. Like the livestock they were no longer "domesticated"; hence *maroon* connotes "uncivilized," "untameable," "unbroken," "wild," "ferocious," "savage," and "feral" (see among others Gove 1971: 406 and 1384; and Price 1973: 1-2).

[12]This issue is one that needs continued research. Indeed the collection of oral histories, the construction of genealogical charts, and the examination of documents in the Register, Mense and Conveyance office (in Charleston) for various kin and domestic groups on Wadmalaw and other islands would add immeasurably to our understanding of family life and family development in this region.

[13]A point made earlier should be reiterated: The evolutionary development of clusters of related households, along with their landholding histories, has not been neatly and carefully preserved in (or for) each family. Thus land tenure patterns have yet to be adequately documented. In addition to continued research along those lines mentioned above in n. 12, land as the subject of legal disputes among kinsfolk is another area of investigation that should not be ignored.

[14]One woman, when questioned about her genealogical linkage to her lover, explained: "We're not related, he's my mother's [distant] cousin."In regard to similar reactions given on St. Simon Island, Georgia, see Reid (1956: 77-78).

[15]Virilocality is the normative, but not the only, post-marital residence practice observable on Wadmalaw. Regarding uxorilocality I have explained: "In . . . rare cases, a couple will live among the extended family of the wife's father. When this does occur, often the husband is 'off island.' Also this . . . residential practice may represent for persons from the Island only a temporary domestic setting until the husband and wife move into their own household usually among his kinsmen" (Agbasegbe 1976b; 126).

Neolocality, the establishment of a household apart from either spouse's extended family, also occurs on Wadmalaw. Of course, close ties and generalized reciprocity among members of the neolocal household and members of thse spouses' natal compounds continue. I have also remarked: "Depending upon the amount of land owned by a given neolocal couple, their residence over a period of time would become a compound of several households, the core of which would be comprised of a group of partrilaterally related males" (Agbasegbe 1976B: 126-27).

[16]Although the Sea Islanders recognize and tolerate the fact that some men fulfill some aspects of the husband/father role configuration in more than one household, this plural mating pattern does not have full community approval. Having noted that "The Rabbit and the Partridge" in the Carawan and Carawan (1966: 120) collection on the Sea Islands is "one of the only places in African American folklore that polygamy shows up," Twining (1973: 59) mentions further: "It [polygamy] is practiced on the island as a *de facto* institution, of course, as it does not fit with the white man's law." Around mid-century, King (1947) documented the presence of a

"polygynous family-farm system" in rural Alabama which contrasts with the
pattern of plural mating seen in the Sea Islands. It may be further noted that the
descriptions and analyses of urban African American plural mating patterns has not
been without controversy (compare e.g., Scott 1980 with Allen and Agbasegbe
1980).

REFERENCES

ABBOTT, Martin. 1967. *The Freedmen's Bureau in South Carolina: 1865-1872.*
Chapel Hill: The University of North Carolina Press.

AGBASEGBE [DEMERSON], Bamidele. 1975. "Ethnographic Notes on the
Domestic Structures in a 'Gullah' Sea Island Community, with Comparisons from
Haiti and Yorubaland." Unpublished paper presented at the Seventh Annual
Conference of the African Heritage Studies Association, Washington, D.C.

AGBASEGBE [DEMERSON], Bamidele. 1976a. "Social Change and Extended
Family in the Black World: A Report on Research in Progress," *Michigan
Discussions in Anthropology* 2(Fall): 46-54.

AGBASEGBE [DEMERSON], Bamidele. 1976b. "The Role of Wife in the Black
Extended Family: Perspectives from a Rural Community in Southern United
States." Pp. 124-38 in Dorothy G. McGuigan (ed.), *New Research on Women
and Sex Roles.* Ann Arbor: The University of Michigan Center for Continuing
Education of Women.

AGBASEGBE [DEMERSON], Bamidele. 1977. Contemporary Rural Black
Family Life." Unpublished paper presented at the Ninth Annual Conference
of the African Heritage Studies Association, Wayne State University, Detroit,
MI.

AGBASEGBE [DEMERSON], Bamidele. 1978. "The Acquisition and Alienation
of Land in the South Carolina and Georgia Sea Islands." Unpublished paper
presented at the Eighty-second Annual Meeting of the Michigan Academy of
Science, Arts and Letters, Eastern Michigan University, Ypsilanti, MI.

AGBASEGBE [DEMERSON], Bamidele. 1980. "Males and the Patrifocal
Complex in the South Carolina Sea Island Family." Unpublished paper
presented at the Sixty-fifth Annual Conference of the Association for the Study
of Afro-American Life and History, New Orleans, LA.

ALBANESE, Anthony G. 1976. *The Plantation School.* New York: Vantage
Press.

ALLEN, Walter R. and Bamidele Agbasegbe [Demerson]. 1980. "A Comment on
Scott's 'Black Polygamous Family Formation.'" Pp. 375-81 in Noel A.
Cazenave (ed.), *Black Alternate Lifestyles.* Special issue of *Alternative
Lifestyles* 3(4).

ALLEN, Walter, Richard A. English, and JoAnne Hall (eds.), 1986. *Black
American Families, 1965-1984; A Classified, Selectively Annotated Bibli-*

ography. Bibliographies and Indexes in Afro-American and African Studies, No. 16. New York: Greenwood Press.

ASCHENBRENNER, Joyce. 1975. *Lifelines: Black Families in Chicago.* New York: Holt, Rinehart and Winston.

BASTEIN, Rémy. 1961. "Haitian Rural Family Organization," *Social and Economic Studies* 10(4): 478-510.

BLACKMAN, J.K. 1880. "The Sea Islands," *News and Courier* (Charleston, SC newspaper 22 April): 354-61.

BLASSINGAME, John W. 1972. *The Slave Community: Plantation Life in the Antebellum South.* New York: Oxford University Press.

BLESER, Carol K. Rothroch. 1969. *The Promised Land: The History of the South Carolina Land Commission, 1869-1890.* Columbia, SC: The University of South Carolina Press for the South Carolina Tricentennial Commission.

CARAWAN, Guy and Candie Carawan (eds.). 1966. *Ain't You Got a Right to the Tree of Life: The People of Johns Island, South Carolina—Their Faces, Their Words and Their Songs.* New York: Simon and Schuster.

CHASE, Judith Wragg. 1971. *Afro-American Art and Craft.* New York: Van Nostrand Reinhold Company.

COOLEY, Rossa B. 1926. *Homes of the Freed.* New York: New Republic.

DEMERSON, Bamidele Agbasegbe. n.d. "Afro-American Society and Culture in the South Carolina and Georgia Sea Islands: A Bibliographic Introduction" (work in progress).

DEMERSON, Bamidele Agbasegbe. 1982. "Some Aspects of Contemporary Rural Afro-American Family Life in the Sea Islands of Southeastern United States." *The Western Journal of Black Studies* 6(2): 60-65.

DEMERSON, W. [Bamidele Agbasegbe]. 1973. "Household, Compound, and Family in the Sea Islands: A Study of Domestic Organization in a Rural Afro-American Community." Undergraduate honors thesis in anthropology. Ann Arbor: The University of Michigan.

DEMERSON, W. [Bamidele Agbasegbe]. 1974. "Household and Compound: Domestic Structures in a Rural New World African Sea Island Community." Pp. 1012-24 in J. Sherwood Williams and Walter G. West (eds.), *Sociological Research Symposium IV.* Richmond: Virginia Commonwealth University Department of Sociology.

DERBY, Doris A. 1980. "Black Women Basket Makers: A Study of Domestic Economy in Charleston County, South Carolina." Ph.D. dissertation in anthropology. Urbana-Champaign: University of Illinois. ["Abstract" in *Dissertation Abstracts International: The Humanities and Social Sciences* 41(6) :2668A-2669A.]

DU BOIS, W.E.B. 1908. *The Negro-American Family.* Atlanta: Atlanta University Press.

FADIPE, N. A. 1970. *The Sociology of the Yoruba.* Edited by Francis O. Okediji and Oladejo Okedijo. Ibadan, Nigeria: Ibadan University Press.

FAIRBANKS, Charles H. 1984. "The Plantation Archeology of the Southeastern Coast", *Historical Archeology* 18(1): 1-18.

FORTES, Meyer. 1950. "Kinship and Marriage among the Ashanti." Pp. 252-83 in A. R. Radcliffe-Brown and Daryll Forde (eds.), *African Systems of Kinship and Marriage*. London: Oxford University Press.

FRAZIER, E. Franklin. 1939. *The Negro Family in the United States*. Chicago: University of Chicago Press.

GENOVESE, Eugene D. 1974. *Roll, Jordan, Roll: The World the Slaves Made*. New York: Pantheon.

GONZALES, Nancie L. Solien. 1969. *Black Carib Household Structure: A Study of Migration and Modernization*. Seattle: University of Washington Press.

GOVE, Philip B. (ed.). 1971. *Webster's Third New International Dictionary of the English Language Unabridged*. Springfield, MA: G. & C. Merriam Company.

GUTHRIE, Patricia. 1977. "Catching Sense: The Meaning of Plantation Membership among Blacks on St. Helena Island, South Carolina." Ph.D. dissertation in anthropology. The University of Rochester. ["Abstract" in *Dissertation Abstracts International: The Humanities and Social Sciences* 39(3); 1967A.]

GUTMAN, Herbert. 1976. *The Black Family in Slavery and Freedom: 1750-1925*. New York: Pantheon.

HOFFMAN, Edwin. 1956. "From Slavery to Self-Reliance: The Record of Achievement of the Freedom of the Sea Island Region." *Journal of Negro History* 41(1): 8-42.

JACKSON, Juanita, Sabra Slaughter, and J. Herman Blake. 1974. "The Sea Islands as a Cultural Resource," *The Black Scholar* 5(6): 32-39.

JOYNER, Charles. 1984. *Down by the Riverside: A South Carolina Slave Community*. Urbana and Chicago: University of Illinois Press.

KERRI, James N. 1979. "Understanding the African Family; Persistence, Continuity, and Change." *The Western Journal of Black Studies* 3(1): 14-17.

KING, Charles E. 1947. "A Polygynous Family-Farm System in Bullock County, Alabama," *Rural Sociology* 12()2): 174-76.

KISER, Clyde V. 1932. *Sea Island to City*. New York: Columbia University Press.

KÖBBEN, A. J. F. 1973. "Unity and Disunity: Cottica Djuka Society as a Kinship System." Pp. 320-69 in Richard Price (ed.), *Maroon Societies: Rebel Slave Communities in the Americas*. New York: Anchor Press/Doubleday. Reprinted from *Bijdragen tot de Taal-, Land- end Volkenkunde* 123: 10-52.

KULIKOFF, Allan. 1977. "The Beginnings of the Afro-American Family in Maryland." Pp. 171-96 in Aubrey C. Land, Lois G. Carr, and Edward C. Papenfuse (eds.), *Law, Society, and Politics in Early Maryland: Proceedings of the First Conference on Maryland History, June 14-15, 1974*. Baltimore: The Johns Hopkins University Press.

LAGUERRE, Michel. 1978. "Ticouloute and His Kinfolk: The Study of a Haitian Extended Family." Pp. 407-45 in Demitri B. Shimkin, Edith M. Shimkin, and Dennis A. Frate (eds.), *The Extended Family in Black Societies*. The Hague: Mouton Publishers.

LANDER, Ernest M. 1960. *A History of South Carolina, 1865-1960*. Chapel Hill: University of North Carolina Press.

MARSHALL, Gloria A. [Niara Sudarkasa]. 1968. "Marriage: Comparative Analysis." Pp. 8-19 in *International Encyclopedia of the Social Sciences. Vol. 10*. New York: The Macmillan Company and The Free Press.

MARTIN, Elmer P. and Joanne M. Martin. 1978. *The Black Extended Family*. University of Chicago Press.

MINTZ, Sidney W. and Richard Price. 1977. *An Anthropological Approach to the Afro-American Past: A Caribbean Perspective*. ISHI Occasional Papers in Social Change, No. 2. Philadelphia: Institute for the Study of Human Issues (ISHI).

MOERMAN, Daniel E. 1974. "Extended Family and Popular Medicine on St. Helena Island, S.C.: Adaptations to Marginality." Ph.D. dissertation in anthropology. Ann Arbor: The University of Michigan.

MOERMAN, Daniel E. 1980. "Masterful Marginals: Black Life on a Carolina Isle." Forthcoming in Merle Black (ed.), *Social Science Perspectives on the South: An Interdisciplinary Annual*.

MOORE, Colin and Robert Washington. 1970. *The Island Colonies: A Profile of Rural Poverty*. Prepared for the United Methodist Church. n.p.

MURDOCK, George P. 1959. *Africa: Its Peoples and Their Culture History*. New York: McGraw-Hill Book Company, Inc.

OKEDIJI, Peter A. 1975a. "A Psychosocial Analysis of the Extended Family: The African Case," *African Urban Notes, Series B* 1(3): 93-99.

OKEDIJI, Peter A. 1975b. "Developing a Measure of Extended Family and Kinship System." *Nigerian Journal of Sociology and Anthropology* 2(1): 75-79.

ONWUEJEOGWU, M. Angulu. 1975. *The Social Anthropology of Africa: An Introduction*. London: Heinemann Educational Books Ltd.

OTTO, John S. and Augustus M. Burns III. 1983. "Black Folks and Poor Bukras: Archeological Evidence of Slave and Overseer Living Conditions on an Antebellum Plantation." *Journal of Black Studies* 14(2): 185-200.

OWENS, Leslie H. 1976. *This Species of Property: Slave Life and Culture in the Old South*. New York: Oxford University Press.

PEASE, William and Jane H. Pease. 1963. *Black Utopia: Negro Communal Experiments in America*. Madison; The State Historical Society of Wisconsin.

PRICE, Richard. 1973a. "Introduction; Maroons and Their Communities." Pp. 1-30 in Richard Price (ed.), *Maroon Societies: Rebel Slave Communities in the Americas*. Garden City: Anchor Press/Doubleday.

PRICE, Richard. 1973b. *Maroon Societies: Rebel Slave Communities in the Americas*. Garden City: Anchor Press/Doubleday.

REID, John D. 1956. "The People of St. Simon: A Social Psychological Study of a Contemporary American Subculture." Ph.D. dissertation in sociology. Chicago: The University of Chicago.

ROSE, Willie Lee. 1964. *Rehearsal for Reconstruction; The Port Royal Experiment*. New York: Bobbs-Merrill Company.

SALWEN, Bert and Geoffrey M. Gyrisco. n.d. [circa 1977]. "Archeology of Black American Culture: An Annotated Bibliography." Washington, DC.: United States Department of the Interior, Heritage Conservation and Recreation Service.

SCOTT, Joseph W. 1980. "Black Polygamous Family Formation: Case Studies of Legal and Consensual 'Wives' ". *Alternative Lifestyles* (3(1); 41-64.

SHIMKIN, Demitri B., Edith M. Shimkin, and Dennis A. Frate (eds.). 1978. *The Extended Family in Black Societies*. The Hague; Mouton Publishers.

SHIMKIN, Demitri B. and Victor Uchendu. 1978. "Persistence, Borrowing, and Adaptive Changes in Black Kinship Systems; Some Issues and Their Significance." Pp. 391-406 in Demitri B. Shimkin, Edith M. Shimkin, and Dennis A. Frate (eds.), *The Extended Family in Black Societies*. The Hague: Mouton Publishers.

SMITH, Franklin O. 1973. "A Cross Generational Study of the Parental Discipline Practices and Beliefs of Gullah Blacks of the Carolina Sea Islands." Ed. D. dissertation. Amherst: The University of Massachusetts.

STACK, Carol B. 1974. *All Our Kin: Strategies for Survival in a Black Community*. New York: Harper & Row.

SUDARKASA, Niara. 1973. *Where Women Work: A Study of Yoruba Women in the Marketplace and in the Home*. Anthropological Papers No. 53. Ann Arbor: The University of Michigan Museum of Anthropology.

SUDARKASA, Niara. 1975. "An Exposition on the Value Premises Underlying Black Family Studies." *Journal of the National Medical Association*. 67-2-: 235-39.

SUDARKASA, Niara. 1980. "African and Afro-American Family Structure: A Comparison." Pp. 37-60 in Johnetta B. Cole and Sheila S. Walker (eds.), *Black Anthropology: Part II*. Special issue of *The Black Scholar* 11(8).

SUDARKASA, Niara. 1981. "Interpreting the African Heritage in Afro-American Family Organization." Pp. 37-53 in Harriette Pipes McAdoo (ed.), *Black Families*. Beverly Hills: Sage Publications, Inc.

SZWED, John F. and Roger D. Abrahams. 1978. *Afro-American Folk Culture: An Annotated Bibliography of Materials from North, Central and South America and the West Indies. Part I — North America*. Philadelphia: Institute for the Study of Human Issues (ISHI).

THOMAS, June Manning. 1977. "Blacks on the South Carolina Sea Islands: Planning for Tourist and Land Development." Ph.D. dissertation in urban and regional planning. Ann Arbor: The University of Michigan.

THOMAS, June Manning. 1978. "Effects of Land Development on Black Land Ownership in the Sea Islands of South Carolina." *The Review of Black Political Economy* 8(3): 266-76.

THOMAS, June Manning. 1980. "The Impact of Corporate Tourism on Gullah Blacks: Notes on Issues of Employment." *Phylon* 41(1): 1-11.

TURNER, Lorenzo D. 1949. *Africanisms in the Gullah Dialect*. Chicago: University of Chicago Press.

TWINING, Mary A. 1973. "Shared Images in Yoruba and Afro-American Folklore: An Open Question for Further Research." Pp. 53-62 in John M. Vlach (ed.), *Studies in Yoruba Folklore*. Bibliographic and Special Series No. 11 of *Folklore Forum*.

TWINING, Mary A. 1975. "Sources in the Folklore and Folklife of the Sea Islands." *Southern Folklore Quarterly* 39(2): 135-50.

VERNEY, Kevern J. 1983. "Trespassers in the Land of their Birth: Blacks and Land Ownership in South Carolina and Mississippi during the Civil War and Reconstruction, 1861-1877." *Slavery & Abolition* 4(1): 64-78.

VLACH, John M. 1978. *The Afro-American Tradition in Decorative Arts*. Cleveland: The Cleveland Museum of Art.

WEBBER, Thomas L. 1978. *Deep Like the Rivers: Education in the Slave Quarter Community, 1831-1865*. New York: W. W. Norton & Col., Inc.

WOOFTER, Thomas J. 1930. *Black Yeomanry: Life on St. Helena island*. New York: Holt and Company.

CHAPTER SIX

Time is Like a River: The World View of the Sea Island People*

Mary Arnold Twining

The integrated and insular world view of the Sea Island people can be seen in an examination of their relationship to their environment, which consists of land, water, and the rest of the natural world around them. This investigation must also include their relationships with their own family and kin, the broader community and the dominant society. Consciously or unconsciously, people relate to—indeed, are largely conditioned by—their environment. We have noted the relative isolation of the Sea Islands from the United States mainland and will discuss later some of its implications. It is appropriate at this point, in treating of the Sea Islanders' world view, to remark on their sense of their homeland as expressed in typical statements.

Many of the people on the Sea Islands purchased land after the Civil War, which some of them still own despite the continued attempts to cheat them out of it.[1] These land acquisitions established these people as peasants on the land to which they had previously been attached as slaves (Rose 1960). Like all peasants, they have in the main continued to be bound to the land and to relate intimately to it, their sustenance procured from the soil and the waters by their toil and sweat.

This sense of relationship of the self to the soil and its produce, all linked by human labor, is well expressed by John Pinckney (Johns Island) in his

---

*This article was first presented as a paper at the Annual Symposium on Language and Culture in South Carolina at the University of South Carolina, March 1977.

use of the biblical allusion "under my own wine (i.e., vine) and fig."[2] Individuals often construe their identity and personal characteristics in topographical context. Mr. Case (Johns Island) remarks the uniqueness of Sea Islanders in these terms: "I am a country man; I eat my grits hard. A city man eats his sof'; he don' have the same muscles a country man have." (Mr. Case emphasized his assertion by an exhibition of arm muscles to indicate strength.)

Sea Islanders marketed their produce in Charleston or the nearest city where other goods might be purchased with money obtained at the open market. Chickens were too valuable to be eaten at home but were raised mainly for market, before the mass chicken farming practised nowadays.

Most of the people remember starting work fairly early in life. Sea Islanders rely on themselves and family members for the hard labor required for the production of food, fishing and the raising of stock. Even the very young children go into the fields at harvest time; at the ages of six and seven they will work together picking and will be paid by the basket. Ms. Alice Wine had told me of her life of labor from her childhood to the present. Guy and Candie Carawan have recorded this quiet-spoken lady's prideful reminiscences of how "we do everything for weself" (Carawan 1967).

Waterways, which separate the Islands from one another and the mainland, prove a rich source of food and provide transportation routes to the mainland and other islands. Although they make their domiciles on particular islands, the people see all the islands together as a regional entity. The archipelagan consciousness is documented in frequent statements by the Islanders about fishing, oyster picking and other activities on the creeks and rivers (Carawan 1967). Joe Deas, an old fisherman on Johns Island, displays his understanding of the geographical situation of his home as he outlines the route he was accustomed to take in order to find the best fishing: "We go to Hut Creek, Willis Creek, then out to the sea. Great Lord, that's miles and miles out there—way out past the place they call Kiawah, then go to the south."[3] (Carawan 1967)

The children learned early about the hazards and exertion involved in traveling by water between the islands. Leigh Richmond Miner's (1971) photographs taken in the 1920s in *Face of an Island* show children going to school in a boat, a scene documented in the film, "With All Deliberate Speed," the story of Reverend Delaine's fight for equal schools in South Carolina.[4] A crucial event in the action was the accidental death of a child by drowning while boating to a segregated school which had no budget for a school bus. Many of the expanses of water are now spanned by bridges, built since the 1930s under the Works Progress Administration. The water barriers were the frontiers of Sea Islanders' lives, represented for the younger generation by the bridges. These limits mark the physical parameters of their world, even as social and racial attitudes form less tangible but no less real barriers—and gateways—to material success and personal fulfillment.

While it is possible to express a people's world view by means of actual statements of individuals, such as those given above; so great and various is the totality of acts and facts, situations and circumstances comprising a people's world view, that it is in the social and cultural aspects of life that the world view is most reliably enunciated. This is particularly true in the study of the folk experience. Much of the African American world view in general, and of the Sea Islanders in particular, is observable in their religious belief and practice. But there are other forms of societal behavior—such as ways of maintaining familial and group integrity, and attitudes toward socio-economic conditions—which also convey a sense of the Sea Islanders' conception of themselves and their place in the world.

While not bitterly outspoken about social injustices visited upon them as African people in white America, they are quite aware of their situation. One Johns Islander, Bill Saunders, in the mid-1960s offered this assessment: "I believe that we all need each other—without the whites the Negro couldn't make it and I believe without the Negroes the whites couldn't make it." He commented on the economic discrimination: "But the intimidation, I think, has been bad as far as the white is concerned. Like making a person feel like he might not have a job tomorrow. This is something that bothers the Negroes a whole lot." (Carawan, 1967). Joe Engels has remarked when discussing his time overseas in the Second World War that he finds it curious that the people in Europe were so different in their attitudes from Euro-Americans who are so over-concerned about "race." He reminisced that it was quite a jolt to come back to the conditions in the United States after the social atmosphere he enjoyed in Europe.[5]

Religion is one of the most important factors in the lives of the Sea Islanders, together with kinship. The ranking of individuals in organizations within the community, such as the church, lodges and burial societies, is to a considerable extent determined by kinship ties; and while these groups are not all religiously connected, the underlying reason for their existence is to maintain social order, offer ethical direction, and provide economic succor and some measure of emotional security. These societies, in this dimension of their existence, recreate to a certain degree the work of the secret societies in the African cultures from which many of these people came.

Although Sea Islanders are proud of their ability to endure, such songs as "Better Days Are Coming Bye and Bye," couched in the Christian evangelical tradition, express their clear longing for their life conditions to improve. The song "Better Days" goes on to say: "When I reach that city on the other side," possibly leading the literal minded to expect that Charleston, Beaufort, Savannah or whichever city was nearest, might provide relief from the poverty endured at home on the Islands. Often these cities, still essentially Southern, did not ameliorate Sea Islanders' lives enough and they continued on north to New York, Chicago, Detroit, ever hopeful that they might not have to wait for "bye and bye." For those left at home comfort was still sought in songs and stories to make bearable the waiting for the wanderers to return, or the "bye and bye" to come.

On the Islands, if someone says he will be there "in a few minutes" or "a li'l wile," the waiting may last from one to four hours. This different sense of time is seen in the many voluntary associations of both religious and secular character. Time is a quantity measured when something is happening and left to pass of its own accord otherwise. Most public occasions, such as church services, prayer meetings, or ushers' reunions last a great deal longer than similar functions of the majority culture. Ironically enough, the preachers, either ordained ministers or "jackleg" preachers, begin their sermons saying, "I won't take much of your time this morning..." This phrase, which propels the waiting congregation into two or three hours of preaching, certainly engages the willing suspension of disbelief and acts, as do opening formulas such as "once upon a time..." in folk stories, to close out the real world and bring on the effects of suspended reality.

Not all dispensers of the Gospel display the prudent solicitude of one preacher on St. Simon Island whose exhortations were so lengthy that his congregation would become uncomfortable and restless from the pangs of hunger. At last he would conclude his sermon, go outside the church and throw open the back of his large station wagon. Then, at twenty five cents a portion, he would serve sweet potato pie and chicken he had cooked himself.

The Islanders sing a song, "Time is Like a River and Time is Winding Up." It indicates that the Islanders have a strong sense of the passage of time and that one may get passed by if one is not awake. It was reworked by Guy Carawan to take on the meaning of warning to various Southern politicians that Bob Dylan's "Hard Rain" might fall on them if they didn't become aware of what people were feeling.

Social intercourse ranks high on the list of favorite occupations and ways to spend time. Groups of Sea Islanders can almost always be seen socializing in aggregations under the trees, a common sight in West Africa. They also lean against cars in convenient spots and gather in the little stores, "grab-alls" and "piccolos", for talk and occasional dancing or beer drinking.[6] Set occasions for parties are not as important as the ongoing, more or less continuous, casual contact which characterizes Sea Island social life. Face-to-face dealings on all matters of any importance whatever are the preferred mode of handling church, school, community or business affairs. The display of verbal agility exhibited at these junctures establishes one's reputation in the surrounding neighborhood, and the chief opportunity for men and women for such oral pyrotechnics is the church which affords a showcase for the virtuosity of its members in this respect.

Sea Islanders are gracious and welcoming toward outsiders particularly if they perceive them to be interested in them as people. Most of them feel that if you come in peace and goodwill those sentiments will be returned to you. The song "Ain't you got a Right to the Tree of Life" includes foreigners or off-islanders in a list of people including themselves who "got a right to the Tree of Life."

NOTES
[1]As documented in the work of the Black Land Bank, Penn Center, Ladies Island, Frogmore, South Carolina.
[2]MICAH IV, 4. The Bible.
[3]Kiawah Island has been purchased by Kuwaiti Arabs and recently developed by the Sea Pines Development Company who also developed Hilton Head Island. It is an expensive resort rhapsodically reviewed in the New Yorker.
[4](New York): This film was shown on national television in July, 1976.
[5]Personal communications, 1966.
[6]"Grab-all" because it grabs all your money. "Piccolo" means "jukebox" or an establishment which has a jukebox in it. Mary LaRoche, Johns Island, South Carolina, personal communications.

REFERENCES
CARAWANS, G. & C. (1967) Ain't you Got A Right To The Tree of Life. New York: Simon and Schuster, pp. 61, 66, 31, 32.
CARAWANS, p. 31. For a number of testimonials to the hardness of life and toughness for the Islanders see Chapter I "Days Past" in Guy and Candie Carawans, pp. 9-53.
CARAWANS, op. cit., p. 150.
GUTMAN, H.G. (1976) The Black Family in Slavery and Freedom 1750-' New York: Pantheon. Corroborates these and other points about th~ ness of the Afro-American family..
HERSKOVITS, M.J. (1941) Myth of the Negro Past. Bosto~ 187.
HORTON, R. (1970) African Thought and Western Scie Row, pp. 131-171.
JONES, B. & HAWES, B.L. (1972) Step It Down. New

MINER, L.R. (1976) Face of An Island. Columbia, S.C.: South Carolina Bicentennial Commission.

PARSONS, E.C. (1923) Folklore of the Sea Islands, South Carolina. Cambridge, Mass.: Memoirs of the American Folklore Society XVI. The American Folklore Society: p. 22.

PETERKIN, J. (1934) A Plantation Christmas. Cambridge, Mass.: Riverside Press, p. 12.

POWDERMAKER, H. (1966) Stranger and Friend. New York: W.W. Norton.

ROSE, W.L. (1960) Rehearsal for Reconstruction. New York: Vintage.

CHAPTER SEVEN

Singin' 'bout a Good Time*
George L. Starks, Jr.

> Good time, a good time,
>   We gonna have a time,
> Good time, a good time,
>   We gonna have a time.
>
> Singin' for a good time,
>   We gonna have a time,
> Good time, a good time,
>   We gonna have a time.

Music has traditionally played an important role in life on the Sea Islands and nowhere can this be better seen than in connection with religious activities.

The words above from a favorite spiritual sung on the Sea Islands express the important role that music plays in the worship service. If one asks a Sea Island resident how he or she enjoyed a church service, the most likely response is, "We had a good time."

In an early printed collection of Afro-American songs, *Slave Songs of the United States* (Allen et al, 1967), the largest body of songs from any one particular locale same from the Sea Islands. A number of articles on Afro-American music which preceded or which were written around the time of the publication of *Slave Songs*, also dealt with the Sea Islands (McKim

1862; Spaulding 1863; Garrison 1862; Higginson 1867). The major portion of the songs appearing in these writings were of a religious nature; there is no question, however, that other types of songs existed. Religious songs were the ones made most available to these early writers, or were the songs which they sought out. One important reason for this is that many of these early writers were or had been engaged in religious work.

The statements of several writers, in addition to the songs which appeared in print, offer additional evidence as to the extent to which religious tunes were heard. James Miller McKim (1862), a former Presbyterian minister, wrote of Sea Islanders: "Their songs are all religious, barcaroles and all, I speak without exception. So far as I heard or was told of their singing, it was all religious."

Henry George Spaulding (1863), a Unitarian minister stated:

> Apart from these religious songs there is no music among the South Carolina freedmen, except the simple airs which are sung by the boatsmen, as they row on the rivers and creeks...The joyous, merry strains which have been associated in the minds of many with the Southern negro, are never heard on the Sea Islands.

Higginson (1862), a Unitarian minister, declared: "I never overheard in camp a profane or vulgar song. With the trifling exceptions given, all had a religious motive...."

The most important of these songs grew out of the everyday existence of the people. The reply given McKim (1862) by a black man when McKim inquired as to the source of black songs in the Sea Islands makes this clear:

> Dey make em sah. . . . I'll tell you, its's dis way. My master call me up and order me a short peck of corn and a hundred lash. My friends see it and is sorry for me. When dey come to de praise meeting that night dey sing about it. Some's very good singers and know how; and dey work it in, work it in, you know, till dey get it right, and dat's de way.

This quotation gives important insight into the manner in which early Afro-American songs were created.

Sacred music has continued to play an important role on the Sea Islands until today, and church and church-related activities remain a vital part of Island life. Though tradition is strong on the Islands, the passage of time has brought changes in the method of conducting worship services in Island area churches, including many of the more tradition-rooted churches. In many instances, the order of service as determined by the particular denomination is producing change, while in others what is often referred to as "coming up to date" is the motivating factor. In the face of this, however, are musical traditions still to be found and practices which have been in existence for many years and others which are closely related to the older traditions.

Remnants of long-standing practices involving music and dance can be seen in many churches during the time of collecting the offering. In such churches, members of the congregation bring their offering to a table located at the front of the church and the money is counted as it is deposited there. This portion of the service is festive and ceremonious. After the congregation, the choir and the ushers make their offering. The congregation usually walks to the table, whereas the choir and ushers march. Traditional songs have long been sung while the offering is being taken.

When the choir members leave their seats behind the pulpit to begin the march around the table, they are at their musical and kinesthetic best. As their voices resound through the church, their walk becomes a dance-like sway. As the choir comes around the table singing, its members move in accordance with the tradition that the feet are never crossed in church. Each left foot slides along the floor until it is brought alongside the right foot and vice versa. In addition to the movement of the feet, holy dancing is also recalled by the swaying of the body, moving to the right or to the left, in rhythm with the music.

The ushers follow the choir and take the lead in the singing as they march. The marching style of the ushers is the same as that of the choir, and the marching and singing of the combined groups spotlights a musical characteristic that is widespread in many black neighborhoods, expecially in the rural South. There are so many good singers that it appears that everyone in the community has at least an adequate voice. There is almost never a diminution in the quality of singing as the principal role shifts from choir to ushers, or from congregation, to choir, to ushers, for that matter.

In some churches, collection practices have been changed and a basket is now passed for the collection of the offering. This practice is among congregations tending to deviate from traditional denominational order. Another interesting reason which I was given for the modification of this practice is that when a basket is passed for the collection instead of marching, "no one will know if the worshipper put in a nickel or a dollar." If a person remains seated, the amount of his offering is less likely to be observed.

Praise meetings were of great interest to the nineteenth century writers referred to earlier. According to the information obtained and passed on by McKim, new songs were created at praise meetings. Of particular interest to nineteenth century commentators was the "shout" with which these meetings culminated.

Closely related to the old praise meetings are the prayer services of today.

Prayer meetings are now often held on Sunday, frequently in lieu of the regular worship service. Tuesday and Thursday were prayer meeting nights on the Islands, with meetings also being held on Sunday night. Prayer meetings are remembered as being the source of strength that sustained the people when times were hard or when their troubles seemed insurmountable. As is still true, the singing, praying, and "shouting" had a therapeutic effect upon the worshippers which they could find nowhere else, then or now. A minister told me, "The people would sing and they would pray there and get spiritual strength, and they come church on Sunday, they would be strong."

The importance of the prayer meeting can be seen by taking a look at Daufuskie Island. Because homes were widely separated on the island, and because travelling was difficult, Daufuskie had a prayer house in each community although those who attended these all belonged to the same centrally-located church.

From a musical standpoint, with the decline of the prayer meeting came a decline in the pure "shouting" song as opposed to the "shouting" spiritual. Worshippers still use prayer meeting time, however, to sing, pray, and testify. As "the spirit rises," everyone in attendance, young and old, rises or kneels to offer his or her testimony.

Song remains a significant part of the prayer service and a vast store of old and "older" religious songs manifest themselves in a service of this type. Evidence of the vital role played by singing in this type of service can be seen in that a song rises following each testimony or prayer. The testimonies and prayers are almost without exception powerful pronouncements; but after each, a rousing, emotion-filled song always follows in order to give the feeling of completeness that only the tuneful employment of the human voice can provide.

Immensely popular today on the Sea Islands is gospel music. This music is often popularly confused with spirituals and the terms are frequently incorrectly interchanged; or often one or the other label is used to cover the spectrum of Afro-American religious music. Although the roots of gospel music lie in the spiritual which goes back to the days of slavery, Afro-American gospel music is primarily a twentieth century form which has been influenced by the total history of the Afro-American musical tradition. Spirituals were passed along as a part of the Afro-American oral tradition; and while there are gospel songs which have been created and passed along in the "folk" sense, the composers of many gospel songs are known and these composers have often published their work.

It seems very likely that most spirituals were performed *a cappella*, while gospel songs traditionally feature instrumental accompaniment (although *a cappella* gospel singing is not uncommon). Melodically and harmonically, spirituals draw from the early days of the Afro-American musical tradition while gospel melody and harmony show evidence of the twentieth century origin of music.

Much of the confusion in making distinctions between the two styles comes from the fact that gospel singers often perform spirituals. Characteristics of the gospel style, however, most often dominate these performances even though both idioms share traits reminiscent of West African music, such as call-and-response, hand clapping and improvisation.

Afro-American music has traditionally been an important means of self expression for its creators. It is very important to observe in this regard that the textual context of spirituals and of gospel music differ because they both take their subject matter from the concerns of the people at the different times they were created.

Gospel music is often performed by groups frequently referred to as "quartets" whether there are four, five, or six members. College groups such as those from Tuskeegee and Fisk helped popularize the quartet concept in black religious music early in this century. A predecessor of gospel groups on the Sea Islands was the St. Helena Quartet of Penn School, and just as the famous Fisk Jubilee Singers toured to raise money for their institution, the St. Helena Quartet toured in order to raise funds for Penn School. This group also provided much of the material on which Nicholas Ballanta-Taylor (1925) based his very important *St. Helena Island Spirituals*.

Of the religious musics heard in the Sea Island area today, next to hymns, gospel music reflects the greatest amount of "outside" influence. Recordings, radio programs, television programs, and live appearances featuring gospel groups from around the country are tremendously popular and have had a strong influence. Nevertheless, gospel music also has been infused with the spirit of the older religious music native to this area. In some instances local groups attempt to render carbon copies of recorded material. In other instances, these same songs, introduced to the people from records and radio, are then sung by church congregations, audiences at various types of gatherings, some organized groups, and people just sitting around the house, in a style very much like that in which their parents and grandparents sang spirituals. This style includes unison singing and freedom in vocal improvisation along with the complex hand clapping that usually accompanies spirituals.

The guitar is commonly found as an accompanying instrument in gospel music and its popularity among gospel groups is part of the overall gospel influence to be found on the Islands. At a program I attended which featured a young gospel group from Yonges Island, the guitarist for the group was absent from the performance; as a result, the hands and feet regained their place as the principal accompanying instruments and the voices found freedom which would not have been possible with a harmonic accompaniment. This, too, was a clear demonstration that the old and the new can coexist.

Change has taken place on the Sea Islands as it has in most places in this country with the passage of time. This change is reflected in the music heard on the Islands, as well as in the traditions with which music is associated. The songs of the Islands have always reflected the lives of the people, and the old and the new of every day existence have found their way into the musical heritage.

There are many cherished traditions on the Islands which are alive today, and which probably will be alive for many years to come. On the other hand, new or different practices which an Islander encounters, and which he feels will make life better for himself, and for those to come, become a part of his way of doing things and are reflected in his music.

The old spirituals are often sung in the same worship service as the hymns which are becoming more and more part of church services. The gospel songs heard on the Islands are sung with the same fervor as the older religious songs, and are capable of bringing on "shouting" just as readily. When these songs are performed a cappella, there is often no difference between the "gospel" and the "spiritual" sounds.

Special religious events call for particular songs and therefore ensure the existence of these vocal creations for some time to come. Christmas, Easter, Communion, and Baptism, for instance, demand certain songs. Many other "special occasion" musical pieces, which are favorites and are sung at any time, will continue to be heard even with the modification or demise of the practices with which they are most closely associated. That these songs are indispensable is evident. During a church service I attended in the community of Red Top, a close neighbor to Johns Island, the minister said, "You know, I love singing so much." A member of the congregation, himself a former minister, replied, "That's the foundation."

REFERENCES
ALLEN, W.F., WARE, C.P., GARRISON, L.M. (1967) Slave Songs of the United States. New York: A. Simpson.
BALLANTA-TAYLOR, N. (1925) St. Helena Island Spirituals. New York: Schirmer.
GARRISON, L.M. (1862) Songs of the Port Royal Contrabands. Dwights Journal of Music.
HIGGINSON, T.W., COL. (1862) Negro Spirituals. Atlantic Monthly: p. 20.
HIGGINSON, T.W., COL. (1867) Negro Sprirituals. Atlantic Monthly. These journals, excerpts or articles from the above can be found in BERNARD

KATZ, ed., The Social Implications of Early Negro Music in the United States. Arno Press and the New York Times; New York, 1969. Future citations in this text refer to this reprint.

MCKIM, J.M. (1862) Negro Songs. Boston: Dwights Journal of Music: p. 2.

SPAULDING, H.G. (1863) Under the Palmetto. Continental Monthly, p. 8.

CHAPTER EIGHT

Christmas Eve Watch on Johns Island

Guy Carawan

It is a long time ago now since I first attended the Christmas watch meeting. The year was 1959. I had gone to Johns Island that year to learn about Sea Island folklife and to work with the Highlander Folk School Literacy Program which had been started on the suggestion of community leader, Esau Jenkins. It was for me a unique opportunity and privilege to witness the service, for I was the first white person to do so. I treasure the experience as one of the most moving and unforgettable of my life.

Esau Jenkins and I arrived at Moving Star Hall about 11:00 P.M. It was a clapboard building with only a pot-bellied stove for heat and light. Older people were beginning to arrive and take their seats along the wooden benches. They walked through the pitch-black night outside from their farms in the surrounding area. The bright flickering flames from the stove threw off an orange glow that lit up many faces—some of deep black, reddish brown and golden tan. Shadows danced on the walls to the accompaniment of all the friendly greeting going on amongst the arrivals. I sat there in the dark next to Esau taking it all in and feeling like I was in heaven.

When the singing started I knew I was. Some woman with a thick, rich low alto started off in the corner and very soon was joined by some deep, resonant male "basers" from another corner. The falsetto wails and moans sailed in to float on high over the lead. By the time the whole group of about sixty worshippers had joined in, each freely improvising in his or her own way, the hall was rocking and swaying to an ecstatic "Savior Do Not Pass

Me By." This is a relatively modern hymn of white origin, but their style of singing it was as old as any black religious singing in America today. All sorts of overlapping parts and complementary sounds wove and blended together to produce a breathtaking whole full of rough beauty. I'd never heard such colors in the human voice before. Some people did things with their voices that I don't think anyone could duplicate unless they had grown up in that tradition.

Song followed song with different people taking turns leading off as the spirit moved them. I couldn't understand half of what was being sung because of the thick local speech.

After a while different individuals began to pray and give personal testimony while everyone else hummed, wailed, moaned and answered fervently in response. That sound was the strangest and most beautiful of all. Every person seemed to have special musical twists, turns and vocal colorings which expressed his or her deepest feelings and said things that words couldn't say. The total sound was beyond description. As the fervor mounted at the end of each prayer or testimony, the congregation would soar back into song, sparked by the testifier or by someone who felt a particular song at the moment.

Then the preaching came, with different people telling in their own words the Nativity story as found in the Bible and expressing their special Christmas feelings. (The many versions of the Christ story told in the Gullah speech that night, some of them in contemporary terms and settings, would make a beautiful book of Sea Island folklore.)

I could hear a single foot tapping in response to the preaching, sometimes rising and falling to a hush, sometimes increasing in tempo, stopping, or changing to a rapid double time. It punctuated the sermon and added excitement. The tapping came from different parts of the hall but I rarely heard more than a single foot at a time.

From the moment the watch started with the first song, heads and bodies began to sway, feet to tap, and hands to clap in time to the singing. The people sang with their whole bodies. Their motions increased in abandonment as the evening went along until finally the "shouting" started. Someone stood and started rocking back and forth doing a special rhythmic step and hand clap in time to the singing. Others followed, and by the end of the song the whole group was on its feet singing, dancing and clapping a joyous noise to the Lord. The whole building was rocking in time. Three different rhythms were carried by the hands, feet and voice. (I felt like a motor moron when I tried to do it.)

The watch went on from beginning to end in a seemingly informal fashion but with a near perfect sense of timing for a change of mood and pace. Everyone seemed able to sing, lead a song, pray, preach or give testimony when the spirit moved them, always in a very beautiful way that contributed to the whole. *It was truly a group product and form of expression.*

This highly developed folk form of worship, body of songs and style of singing are in danger of complete extinction in another generation or so. Most of the younger generation in this area have lost them to a great extent already. The combined forces of the schools, the organized churches, and the mass commercial culture with its control of radio, records, TV, etc., have been too much for the young people to resist. The finer aspects of their parents' folk culture get practically no recognition from these institutions that play such a large part in their education. Local schools and most churches here usually take no responsibility for helping keep them alive. The young people are losing a valuable part of their heritage.

The older people will never lose this heritage, I mused then in 1959. It is already too much a part of them. The main place they have to express themselves in this older form of community religious celebration is Moving Star Hall, but it is the last such place on the island and without the support of other institutions there is a question how long it will last.

The meeting house, Moving Star Hall, today in 1987, is no longer being used for the old-time meetings. In many island churches, like Wesley Methodist just down the road from the old hall, there is a very vigorous contemporary black religious culture with gospel choirs, wonderful organ accompaniment and a powerful preacher. But the older, more spontaneous forms of expression—raising a song by the spirit, taking it into a shout, testifying and preaching when moved by feelings—are not so easily integrated into the more formal structure of the service. There is the feeling from some of the younger people that it will be no great loss if this older level of expression dies out completely.

On the other hand, a small group of singers from Johns Island continues to travel and share the old ways. Mrs. Janie Hunter of the Moving Star Hall Singers was honored in 1984 with a National Heritage Award from the National Endowment for the Arts and she has been featured in two national television programs focusing on different aspects of coastal culture this past year. When Wesley Methodist Church commemorated its 117th anniversary in the fall, a photographic display of many of the older community members was hung and nightly discussions were held about the history of the island and the passing of traditions.

There's still the possibility and the challenge of carrying some of the treasures of the past into the future in Sea Island communities.

CHAPTER NINE

A James Island Childhood: Africanisms Among Families of the Sea Islands of Charleston, South Carolina*

Janie Gilliard Moore

I am a Sea Islander who for many years did not recognize that my religious practices, beliefs and customs—so many things, in fact, that made up my very being—were African. My discovery of this has generated my interest in comparing African culture with that of the Sea Islanders, with results which I have found astonishing. The similarities are numerous.

It is appropriate here to express sincere appreciation to Lydia Nku August, Michael Mawema, and other continental Africans who took the time to talk with me about the commonalities between the culture of their individual countries and that of the Sea Islands. Since the Sea Islands have strong remaining Africanisms, their culture can play an important role in the development of our sense of identification with the African homeland. Africa's heritage can be shared, studied and preserved by all African Americans. Thus I hope these observations by a Sea Islander can shed some light on the situation.

For many years of my childhood I lived, believed in and loved this Sea Island experience, but at that time, like most Sea Islanders, I did not

---

*This article appeared previously in the *Journal of Black Studies*, Volume 10, Number 4, June 1980.

consider it unusual. We did not see ourselves as a unique group of people with a rich surviving African culture; we did not know that our way of living was so African, for we were just being ourselves.

I grew up on Yonges Island, S.C., where I lived and believed as my parents and community encultured me. But as I progressed through high school and afterward college, I "discovered" (as I thought) that many of our practices were simple, superstitious and ignorant. Educated people, I came to feel, simply did not believe and act as we did. So I began to disregard some of these customs and practices and they receded to the back of my mind. However, some practices were maintained out of habit. For example, after combing my hair I still would not carelessly discard the combings, but would burn them.

With the Civil Rights Movement, Blacks became more concerned about their ethnic roots and authenticity—their African heritage and culture. Thus arose the desire to relate to everything which is African. And so it has come about that new attention is focused on the Sea Islands. For we are that unique group of people, that remnant which has maintained to the highest degree evidences of ethnic authenticity, of African cultural continuity. This was my first awareness of our uniqueness. I still did not fully realize just how African we Sea Islanders were until I enrolled at the Interdenominational Theological Center in Atlanta. I came into contact with other African students, from the continent, and had the opportunity of discussing the various customs and practices we shared. The similarities were overwhelming. For example, while I was telling about a practice one day, an African American student asked, "Is this Africa?" He did not realize these events could be happening today in the United States of America.

All of the African students with whom I have engaged in discussions find the similarities amazing. Michael Mawema, a South African student at Interdenominational Theological Center who has visited the Sea Islands, declared: "Janie, you are pure African"—meaning that concepts and some of my experiences as a Sea Islander are such that my manner of relating to things is truly African.

For me, too, the similarities between Sea Island attitudes and customs and those of the African continent have been astounding. Even some of the quite minute practices are the same—which proves that four hundred years of the "diaspora" have not decultured us as a people.

The discussion around African cultural retentions in the United States has gone on for some time. Did the American experience completely eradicate all remaining African heritage? E. Franklin Frazier (1963) stated that

> In any phase of the character and the development of the social and cultural life of the Negro in the United States, one must recognize from

the beginning that because of the manner in which the Negroes were captured in Africa and enslaved, they were practically stripped in their social heritage . . . the capture of many of the slaves in inter-tribal wars and their selection for the slave market tended to reduce to a minimum the possibility of the retention and transmission of African culture."

He further contended that the traditions could not survive because the majority of the earlier slaves brought to these shores were males who are "poor bearers" of the cultural heritage. On the other hand, Melville J. Herskovits cast a different light on the situation in his book *The Myth of the Negro Past* (1941):

It is seen that the African past is no more to be thought of as having been thrown away by those of African descent than it is to assume that the traits that distinguish Italians, or Germans, or Old American or Jews or Irish, or Mexicans or Swedes from the entire population of which they form a part, can be understood in their present forms without a reference to a preceding cultural heritage.

Roger Bastide in *African Civilizations in the New World* (1972) gives this reason for the remaining African tradition in the New World:

The slave-ships carried not only men, women, and children, but also their gods, beliefs, and traditional folklore. They maintained a stubborn resistance against their white oppressors, who were determined to tear them loose, by force if need be, from their own cultural patterns, and acclimatize them to those of the West . . . Revolts they engineered bore witness to their determination to escape the economic exploitation of which they were the victims, and hideous working conditions; but this by no means was their only motive. Such rebellions also hint at their struggle against being dominated and swallowed up by an alien culture. It should come, then, as no surprise that in America we find whole enclaves of African civilization surviving intact, or at least to a very substantial extent.

As indicated by Herskovits, Bastide and many other sociologists and anthropologists, it has been researched and proven that there is retention of Africanisms in the New World. Where is that retention? For the Africans in America this is a burning issue. It is essential that we not just discover, but recapture this evidence of continuity from the past into the present, and project its import with pride.

The doubters and those searching to regain their heritage must go to the

Sea Islands of South Carolina. There live a people who are Africans in the traditional sense. One might say that the area is a "living museum." The Blacks of the Sea Islands of Charleston, Wadmalaw, Johns and James Islands are among that group whose mannerisms, ways of life and beliefs are African.

Herskovits (1930) wrote:

> . . . we realize that all of African culture has not by any means been lost to them. Next on our table [of African survivals] we should place such isolated groups living in the United States [as] the Savannahs of southern Georgia, or those of the Gullah Islands off the Carolina coast.

One of the most notable African traits of the Sea Islanders is the language (or dialect, as it used to be called). "Gullah" is the word used to designate the Sea Island speech, which is derived from a West African people, the *Angola*, from among whom came some of the Africans who were enslaved on the Islands. "Angola" was shortened to "Gola," and later corrupted further to Gullah. To the outsider it seemed that the Islanders had total disregard for English grammatical structure, plurality, and so forth. The Gullah tonality and enunciation sounded strange to them; hence the Sea Islanders were labeled ignorant, backward, and they were considered merely as speaking bad English. In an article published by the University of South Carolina, Reed Smith (1926) wrote:

> What the Gullahs seem to have done was to take a sizeable part of the English vocabulary as spoken by the inhabitants from 1700 on, wrap their tongue around it, and reproduce it changed in tonality, pronunciation, cadence, and grammar to suit their native phonetic tendencies, and their existing needs of expression and communication. The result has been called by one writer (Trowbridge 1866), "the worst English in the world."

Gullah speech would certainly seem to have a fair claim to that distinction if one is expecting to hear "accepted standard English." To understand it requires a trained ear, and at first brush with it, it is equally unintelligible to white and Black people alike. Smith goes further to say:

> . . . the shapes of the words are strange; they are the residuum of language literally worn away by use; the phonology is archaic; the engaged grammar a mystery; to the wit and to the acute phonetic sense of the reader much must inevitably be left.

The notion that the pattern of speech might be African was not recognized for decades. Many African American scholars, as well as whites, held the view that Gullah was not African influenced. Thus Carter G. Woodson (1958) wrote:

> The Negro African language was lost here for the two reasons that the imported Negroes were compelled to learn the language of the enslavers, and the Africans brought from various places speaking different tongues did not find themselves always in contact with fellow members of the same stock.

Linguists have studied the Gullah speech and have proven this view to be invalid. After extensive research, the linguist Lorenzo D. Turner demonstrated that Gullah is fundamentally African. In his book entitled *Africanisms in the Gullah Dialect* (1949), which presented convincing and previously unknown information, he revealed that the Islanders' speech is not "bad" English but a creole language developed during the slave trade. He discovered a significant number of African words still being used by the people.

> These survivals are most numerous in the vocabulary of the dialect but can be observed also in its sounds, syntax, morphology, and intonation; and there are many striking similarities between Gullah and the African languages in the methods used to form words.

Scholars are increasingly referring to Gullah not as a dialect but as a language in its own right. Thus, Richard A. Long, director of the Center for African American Studies at Atlanta University, states definitively: "Gullah is a creolized language."

We turn now to some Sea Island beliefs and the practices associated with them, especially those relating to the role of the traditional healer. Among African peoples the belief is widespread that there exist forces or spirits which influence nature and man. These forces can be used for good or evil. This concept is still in the consciousness of the Sea Islanders, although it may be somewhat modified due to the change in the historical situation. The traditional healer in Africa, or the "root doctor" in the Sea Islands, is the agent who is able to manipulate these forces. These practitioners are highly respected and valued. Four hundred years of exile from the motherland had not eradicated this concept and practice; in other words, the Sea Islanders have that firm consciousness of mystical powers common to all Africans according to John Mbiti's (1969) statement:

> . . . the whole psychic atmosphere of African village life is filled with belief in this mystical power. African peoples know that the universe

has a power, force, or whatever else one may call it... To my knowledge, there is no African society which does not hold belief in mystical power of one type or another.

The function of the root doctor is diverse. As a counselor, he advises on matters spiritual; as a healer, he provides medicine (herbal) for various illnesses, natural or unnatural. The individual periodically consults the root doctor to find out what to expect in a new situation, to investigate the possibility of what can be done if one is "fixed"—the state or condition resulting from the fact or belief that evil forces have been used to cause excruciating pain, sickness, sudden catastrophe, insanity, or even death to an individual. Not all root doctors are alike. The "Christian" doctor believes his power is a gift of God to be used to help mankind; therefore, he will never invoke evil power to do harm to a person. However, he can release someone from a spell. And usually he prays, seeking God's guidance before interpreting situations. In contrast, there is the root doctor who specialized in "fixing." Individuals who are vengeful seek out the service of this root doctor.

Since there is always the danger of getting "fixed," then some counter measure must be devised. Here is where "protection" comes into play. "Protection" is a small bag with substances in it which are supposed to neutralize destructive forces used against one. In order for this "protection" to be effective, it must be worn on the body at all times. Usually it is worn around one's waist, or in the case of men, in the wallet. In Africa there is also personal protection; Parrinder (1970) wrote:

Very common are small objects, which are called amulets or talismans. A leather packet, often worn around the neck, may contain dried leaves, or texts from the Quran.

Parrinder further states:

... nails, hair, spittle, sweat, urine, washing-sponges and water, sleeping-mats, dirty clothes, are all intimately connected with the body and so may be used in preparing offensive charms against the people to whom they belong. Therefore, great care is taken in the disposal of these things...

The identical concept is operative among the Sea Islanders. One never leaves one's clothes overnight on the clothesline. After combing the hair, those left in the comb are burned. Non-believers may say, "How can you be so stupid? It is only superstition." But is it? There are persons who will vehemently say they have been helped or cured! I use the initials of these individuals so as not to reveal their identity.

Mr. B. owned a grocery store on Yonges Island. His business was prosperous. Mr. B. recalled seeing his neighbor, Mr. K., moving around his house one night. At that time Mr. B. said he did not think too much about the incident. Several months later he became seriously ill. His body was infested with sores. He could not lie down. Mr. B. stated that he went to a doctor (medical) who prescribed medicine and other treatments, but his condition instead of improving only worsened. Mr. B. said he was in this condition for about five or six months with no release from his agony. The physicians were unable to diagnose his case. Finally a friend suggested that his illness was not "natural" (meaning not caused by God or nature) and took him to see a root doctor who told him he had been "fixed" by a jealous neighbor. He proceeded to describe the person who had "fixed" him. The description was of Mr. B.'s neighbor, Mr. K. The root doctor mixed herbs for Mr. B. to use daily and after several visits Mr. B. was cured. The root doctor gave him a "body-guard" to protect him, so no one could "fix" him in the future.

There is the case of a Wadmalaw Island woman, Mrs. C., who said she had "lost her mind" and was going around saying "weird things." Her mother took her to a root woman who cured her. And ever since, she said, "I have not lost my mind."

A Johns Island man related this story: One night a group of white boys molested and killed a thirteen year old black boy. The mother, crying at her son's funeral, swore: "Those who have done this will not go free. The law don't have to do nothing!" She (to use the local expression) "dressed the coffin." A month later the three white boys were dead. Two were killed in automobile accidents and the other was found dead in his bed.

That certain individuals can make themselves invisible, is a belief found in Africa. Our Sea Island counterpart is the hag. A hag is usually an old woman who comes out of her skin at night to suck the blood of a sleeping victim. The victim usually cries out in his sleep for help. My father seems to have been one of the hags' favorite victims, I recall. Many times while sleeping he would cry out in his sleep. Shaking my father, my mother would say, "Leave my husband alone." An incident I remember is this: One day a lady, who was suspected to be a hag, came to visit at my house. This day we youngsters decided, as mischievous children will, to prove this matter. We placed a broom across the door, for it was thought that a hag would never step across a broom. That day she visited for a long time. As long as the broom was across the door she did not make any effort to leave. Finally, late that evening, we removed the broom and she left immediately thereafter. Was she indeed a hag?

Among the customs which are dying out, but which were formerly practiced a great deal among the Sea Islanders, was this one—that the burial services were performed, but the sermon was preached weeks later. Herskovits indicates that this, too, has its origin in Africa. Also, Africa has the custom of placing utensils, chairs, and other items related to the deceased on the grave of the departed (Puckett 1926).

Today in the Sea Islands we still pass small children over the coffin of the mother or father just before burial. It is thought that the parent may return for the children, so the passing of the child is intended to prevent this from happening. According to Herskovits (1941), "The custom of passing young children over the coffin has not been reported for West Africa, but something that is closely related to it has been witnessed among the Bush Negroes of Dutch Guiana."

The Sea Islanders have the concept of "the living dead"—that is, they believe in a continued relationship between the dead and living. There are many accounts current of individuals who claim their mother or wife or father appears to them in their dreams, and by this means these relatives communicate. It is contended that they only appear when there is impending danger, and he or she comes to warn the family. For example: In 1953, after our father died, one of my brothers was becoming a delinquent. One morning he came to my mother frightened. He said he had seen our father during the night. My mother told him, "Leonard came to warn you about your behavior." Needless to say, my brother was a changed person after that incident.

Every effort is made that the wishes of the dead should be carried out conscientiously, for it is believed that if this is not done, then the dead person will haunt the family or individual responsible for going against his wishes. If the deceased said he wanted to be buried in a certain suit or a particular place, this must be done.

There is also the belief that the dead look out for their loved ones. As an illustration, I will use my own experience. As a child I was terrified of the dead. But once my father died I lost my fear of the dead because I believed that since he was among spirits he would look out for me, and would not let a ghost bother me.

The significance of "signs" plays an important part in the lives of the Sea Islanders. For instance, if a dog howls or a rooster crows in the doorway, it is a sign that someone will die. If a small child takes a broom and begins to sweep, this is a sign that a relative not seen for a long time will be coming to visit soon. The itching of the right palm of the hand indicates that a letter or money is on the way.

I can recall during my childhood that there was great fear of being "marked" or "cursed" by an old man or woman, who could curse you by the very word uttered. Children would tremble in fear if an old person pointed his finger at them and said, "You will *butt* the rest of your life"; that is, "You will have a very difficult and miserable life" (Smith 1950). Mbiti (1969) states:

> There is a mystical power in words, especially those of a senior person to a junior one. The words of parents, for example, carry "power" when spoken to children: they "cause" good fortune, curse, success, peace, sorrow, or blessing especially when spoken in moments of crisis.

Sea Islanders believe that when an individual is asleep his spirit leaves the body. So if you harass him and he wakes up before his spirit has returned, he will die. There are parallel African concepts which involve spirits out of the body for a variety of reasons. The Ibo believe that if the inert form is turned 180 degrees while the soul is absent, the returning spirit will be unable to reenter the body and the person will be found dead in the morning (Arize 1975).

Deserving of mention is yet another African concept which is found in the Sea Islands: the relationship between God and nature. I think that this belief, as held by Sea Islanders, is not Christian but African. Sea Islanders believe that when it thunders it is God talking. During this occurrence one must be totally silent in reverence to God. I can recall during my childhood that when it was raining, lightening and thundering, we children were made to sit down in a corner and were admonished to be quiet for God was talking, and if we were playful or naughty He would strike us dead. John Mbiti, in his book *Concepts of God in Africa* (1970), points to an analogous practice:

> The Herero, Kuku, Lokoiya, Suk, and Zulu say that God produces *thunder*. For many, thunder is the manifestation of God or of His power. Thus, by the Badiwa, Bawbuli, Bavenda, Bena, Ewe, and Illa, thunder is taken to be the voice of God.

MY PERSONAL REFLECTION

Numerous other African practices and customs still exist in the Sea Island region. They include using salt to prevent spirits from bothering one; putting salt or sulphur in one's shoes to guard against picking up roots put down by one's enemy; customs associated with the rearing of children, and the lore of women who make remedies to render a woman fertile so that she may become pregnant; and notions as to how snakes play a significant part in the practice of "fixing" an individual. From these African practices, perhaps we may also say that there are African theological implications. I have not attempted to prove this, but I suggest that these implications exist; for the theology of a people, that is, their understanding of God, comes out of their existential situation. Further, if those aspects of the culture which I have discussed remain, why not also African theological ideas? This area of study can probably be undertaken by scrutinizing the Sea Islanders' prayers, sermons, "testimonies," and folklore.

GLOSSARY OF TERMS USED IN THE SEA ISLANDS

BUTT—Misfortune that befalls one cursed by an older person.

FIXED—Spell cast on an individual; it can be in the form of great disaster in one's life or illnesses.

SEEKING—The process of going into the woods to pray at night or early morning.

ROOT—The practice of witchcraft..

ROOT DOCTOR—One who practices witchcraft.

PROTECTION BAG—A bag containing ingredients which is used as a means of protection.

GULLAH—This term is used to denote the language of the Sea Island people, and the themselves.

GEECHEES—This term is applied to "the people who eat rice daily for dinner." (This is a name used for Sea Islanders with the pejorative connotation of "country" or "hick." The term has its origin in "Kissy," the word in the Mende language for the country Liberia. Ed. note)

REFERENCES

ARIZE, C. (1975) Personal communication.

BASTIDE, R. (1967) Les Amériques Noires. Paris: Payot (original publication).

BASTIDE, R. (1972) African Civilizations in the New World. New York: Harper Row.

FRAZIER, E.F. (1963) The Negro Church in America. New York: Schocken Books :4.

HERSKOVITS, M.J. (1930) "The Negro in the New World." American Anthropologist :32.

HERSKOVITS, M.J. (1941) The Myth of the Negro Past. New York: Harper :355.

MBITI, J.S. (1969) African Religions and Philosophy. New York: Frederick A. Praeger :197.

MBITI, J.S. (1970) Concepts of God in Africa. New York: Frederick A. Praeger: 739.

PARRINDER, G. (1970) West African Religion. New York: Barnes and Noble, Inc. :161.

PARRINDER, G. (1970) West African Religion. New York: Barnes and Noble, Inc. :163, 164.

PUCKETT, N.N. (1926) Folk Beliefs of the Southern Negro. Chapel Hill: University of North Carolina Press, (ed.).

SMITH, E. (ed.), (1950) African Ideas of God. London: Edinburgh House Press :220.

SMITH, R. (1926) "Gullah." Bulletin of the University of South Carolina, 190.

TROWBRIDGE, J.T. (1866) The South. Hartford, Connecticut: L. Stebbins: 538.

TURNER, L.D. (1949) Africanisms in the Gullah Dialect. Chicago: The University of Chicago Press :15.

WOODSON, C.G. (1958) The African Background Outlined. New York: Negro University Press :170.

CHAPTER TEN

Growing Up On Johns Island:
The Sea Islands Then and Now*
William C. Saunders

A s a kid growing up on the Islands in the 1930s and '40s, there really was no need for money. A lot of us now (1980) in our thirties and forties are realizing we weren't so bad off then. When we were young, we looked at things as being awful. Now that attitude has changed. When I was a kid we grew our own rice, we had our own grits grinder, we made our own pestle and mortar to clean our rice with.[1] We had our own smokehouse, killed our own meat, and we ate everything that was in the river in season. This time of year now you can go anyplace and buy oysters. People then never ate oysters after April. Crab wasn't eaten in the winter. All of these things replenished themselves during that time. Now we destroy them by eating them all the time.

Most of our clothes were made of material from feedbags or things that something had been bought in. We made our own mattresses, pillows, and so forth. My grandfather used to build roofs out of something that now I can't find anyone to make, or any of the old fellows to even discuss; they made roofs out of "palin'."[2] They had an instrument they made that would slice through pine and cut it into very thin stripping like paneling, and they would overlap these strips on the roof. You could see right through it, but it wouldn't leak when rain hit it; it would just swell up. We made chimneys out

---

*This article appeared previously in the *Journal of Black Studies*, Volume 10, Number 4, June 1980.

of clay on the Islands. We took the clay, grass and other things and would do coloring with it. We used to make beautiful floors from rubbing colored clay onto church brick.

Most people needed to hold onto money for their nickel and dime insurance. Most illnesses that came up, someone had a remedy for it; we called it root medicine. They would take roots and things and boil them into a medicine.[3] We would also pack open wounds with sand or sugar. Nowadays you get a little cut and you go to the nearest hospital emergency room. There were so many things to be done and work was hard. We worked from "can see to can't see," from sunup to sundown. We were independent and didn't recognize it. We are more dependent now than we have ever been. Most of us my age now are re-looking at the past and looking at the present and saying maybe we need to go back to some of the things we came through that we didn't like too well. Even up to the late 1950s. I used to bring two live chickens to the market (which is now a flea market) and sell them for $2.50 to $2.75 apiece (since they were very expensive back then) and use the $5.00 to buy all the extra things our family needed. Three or four years ago I was in a house where they had sesame seed candy, and I didn't recognize it, because we used to grow it, but we called it benne. We'd take benne and syrup and mix them together for candy.[4]

I think the chemicals that have been put into the land in fertilizers and such here hurt it. Maybe I'm wrong. When I was a kid, we used to take cabbage and fry it just like a pork chop, and it would turn pretty and brown. Now you can't do that; the way it's grown now, it just turns to water. The fertilizer we used was from cleaning our horse stables, chicken houses, etc. The U.S. government back in the 1940s had a really good program which should be reinstated. They used to bring a truckload of lime and dump it in a certain place and everybody would get their horse and cart and get a load of lime and spread it in their fields. The agriculture people came by and told you what crops were best to plant and how to plant.and when to do it. Summertime, the government used to come through and spray houses for mosquitoes and flies, and since we didn't have any screens, we didn't have to close our doors. They had people to go from house to house to help canning. We had 300 to 400 jars of food preserved this way. They brought pressure cookers from house to house and put things together. In October when things were slow everyone in the community got together and went from house to house and helped each other make quilts. This way they caught up on gossip and socializing they couldn't get in the summertime due to too much work. The people, the white farmers who most Northerners feel to be real racists, most of us would just consider them honest folk that had a feeling about where they stood and where we stood; but as far as help it was altogether different than, for instance, a Northern white man. The Southern white man is considered an honest man. When the seasons were slow, they'd go to the river and catch fish and just come through the community and pass it out. None of those things happen anymore.

The children in my age bracket have mostly spoiled our own children by not wanting them to go through anything we did when we were kids. We have not really involved them in the world of work. Like right now, out of my nine kids you could probably ask three of them what I really do for a living and they would not know. People learned from their parents, or uncles, or from someone close. During the age of television there's a lot we've lost. Most of the housewives of the Island today really don't want anything unless it comes out of the supermarket. We still grow turnips, collards, tomatoes and stuff like that, but my wife went to the supermarket and brought back four cucumbers when there were some still in the field. She likes it that way. Or frozen green packaged. I think the system itself has had a bearing on the people. Everybody wants to live like the TV housewife or something. Very few people jar anything anymore. When I was a kid we had a large grape, plum, fig orchard. Grapes still grow wild on the Island, but people still buy them in the market. Now you owe everybody! You owe the furniture store, vacuum cleaner store, and the rest. You name it, you owe it! And the finance companies loan money to people for any reason. A guy from the Island comes to the city and meets a chick from the city. He figures he needs to be slick, so he borrows $100 to do it, and he blows it. All he has is a good time, but he's left in trouble. These things happen. Why? Well, for one thing, it's different. We're not used to it. To a lot of people credit has been a way of life. On the Islands we never had access to this kind of thing. We have the Watkins man who sells any and everything you can use. So everybody had a little credit with the Watkins man who came by once every two weeks. That was about it. Well, we did have our nickel and dime insurance, but that was a way of providing for a future need. Nickel, dime and quarter insurance was where you joined the whole family often for a nickel a week for each member of the family. You paid it for the rest of your life, 70 or 80 years, and you got $30.00 when that person dies. Really a rip-off insurance, but it's still going on. That's where the insurance man comes to your house every two weeks and collects. You really don't get anything out of it at all, but a lot of people felt secure if they had it.

A lot of people say that alcoholism is a problem on the Island because of the lack of things to do. There isn't any recreation on the Island, no movies, no nothing, and they say people drink a lot because of that. I think we have a lot of alcoholics among the poor people period, not necessarily just on the Island. One thing that is seldomly mentioned about Island people is moonshine. You always hear about how the people are so sweet and full of heart and took it all to God. This just isn't so. The biggest trade there's ever been on the Island is moonshine. Most of the blacks that have gotten started in it did so because it was the only thing you could make money on. You always had access to a lot of drinks, and it's been free most of the time. Having this kind of access and not handling it properly is, of course, a problem, but it hasn't just started. A man could make a good bit of money on moonshine, on the Islands or even in the city. The big ones used to do both, selling it to the people on the Islands and also to people in the city.

People from the universities have been writing about these Islands, about African heritage and all that. I would say that as far as the Islanders were concerned, I don't think that there was much pride in heritage in the past, but that they were proud, period. I don't think that they used to connect themselves with Africa, you know, *"Roots"* type stuff, but they were and are just real people that show their heritage. My grandfather and many people I know never had anything, but they were so independent; they were proud of what they were not going to do. They were just beautiful people. Between 1945 and 1960 we lost that. So many things changed in that era that caused a lot of people to lose sight of being proud. I really feel personally that a lot of government giveaway programs have taken away that pride.

I think the people don't work quite as hard. Some of them have tractors now, and they have motors on boats instead of oars. I think it's different with them. But that's the thing a lot of people have problems understanding. I can take you where two blood brothers live, one in a little farm of about thirty years and the other not more than one mile away living in a $65,000 house. But that's what they chose. One chose to go all out with two jobs, lots of money; the other stayed with his small farm and he's probably happier that way. He'll probably even live longer.

I think that there's really not that much interest in the past at this particular point, simply because most of us didn't bring our children up when what was happening during the 1960s, and during that time we did a lot of things. But you couldn't teach your kids and fight for what we considered the way at the same time. I think the Black and Beautiful thing has taken a bad twist. There are so many blacks shaking hands and all, with really no concept of what is needed. There are so many things that have been so commercialized that they feel "Black and Beautiful" should automatically give them a job. That somebody owes them something. The ones I'm talking about, my grandfather and those of his time, never ever felt like anybody owed them anything and they're the ones that had the right to feel that way. They didn't.

My grandfather lived on a master's plantation and had a cousin or something that was free. And this cousin went out and bought a parcel of land for each of the families, and no one really knew until they moved off the plantation that they had houses. My grandfather never had any formal education at all, yet he was a surveyor for people on the island where I lived; and every parcel of land that he surveyed back in the 1920s and 1940s— right now you can get any surveyor to go out to it, and it's right. Yet we don't have one black surveyor in the state of South Carolina today.

There's something else that links to that that no one thinks about anymore (but there's always been a chain)—In the age of Tarzan, most of us hated Africa because of the way it was presented to us—that everybody was stupid and it took one white man to whip 200 or 300 of them at any stage in history. My grandfather was not exposed to that kind of thing, so he had a better outlook on Africa than I did when I was a child. I took a real positive view on Africa about 1960.

My own children, now, have very much interest in Africa, more than I did. Before, they knew very little about Africa, but in the 1960s in many ways it reached a new proportion. They now know where so many raw materials came from, more about Africa possibly being the Mother of the World. There's a lot of scientific things that they know that we didn't. So they have a lot more interest in Africa. They have a chance even to interact with people from Africa now. They have a better sense of their being connected with Africa, and it's growing more and more, even though we don't like people calling us "Gullah." It's a derogatory word, supposedly meaning the way we talk or our language. That is just how black people talk.

People used to make fun of the way blacks talk, but the whites that I grew up with spoke the same way we did. There are whites on the Island now and for them their language is the same as ours.

Getting into this, there are certain expressions I've become aware of, like talking about the weather in terms of "he"—"He's gonna shine tomorrow." Is that an expression you're familiar with? At one stage in our history we never used "she," everybody was "he." I started using she when I was in the Armed Forces. But before that, everybody was "he." That's mostly dying out on the Islands today. I don't know if that's good or bad. I really don't see any reason to put a value judgment on it, that's us just the way it was for some reason which I think will eventually be known. Dr. Marianna Davis and another person have gotten together on some scientific facts about those kinds of things and how those things renew themselves.[5] One of the things that fascinated me was that people from different Islands spoke differently. We used to say they "spoke bad" and they said the same of us. People from Wadmalaw Island use, for instance, "lee" instead of little. They'll say, "That lee boy or that lee girl." They go to college and come back and say, "That lee little boy." Most of them don't ever drop the "lee," they just add another word. I've been doing some research of my own, and I've found some people up around and above Summerville who also use "lee little," and I've tried to connect the two.

There are records of our talk that you can buy made by whites, and if you hear them, the way they sound is pretty genuine. People ask me what I think about these records and the stories on them, supposed to be about us blacks. Well, I say the talk is a good imitation, and the stories are funny, very funny—to whites. But then, if you go to the Slave Market in Charleston you'll find out that slavery wasn't bad and everybody but the slave enjoyed it. But blacks don't get involved in protests about that kind of thing. There are some whites who have gotten involved. It's not whether or not you care; this country is run on power. They have the power to do what they're doing. Like some whites flying the Confederate flag. I don't see any of it to be a real important issue. If they want to fly their flag, let them. It just shows some kind of sickness as far as I'm concerned. There are more important things to be dealt with. There's housing, jobs, economics and all that. Take schools, for example. When I was a kid we were looked upon on the Island as country folk. Whenever we came to Charleston, we were really put down. I went to Berk High School there. That's one of the reasons why I'm against bussing today. I'm against it, but can't say so publicly. I passed right by the school where my son is now the president of the student body, but I couldn't go there. I had to be bussed by a bussing system set up by white leadership. When we got to school, we were really treated awful.

In Charleston, whites had buses but blacks up through the eighth grade had to walk to school. We Islanders had a bus to ride only to bus us the fifty miles, but that was the only time. Blacks would be walking and the white school bus would just come right by. It could be raining hard, and they'd just whiz by splashing us with mud and water. The Progressive Club came along in that era. That's when we bought the school building and turned it into the Progressive Club. Even the schools were painted dark like black. We never had any lights in it when it was a school.

Starting in 1945, there's been a lot of things going downhill. It would have gone a lot worse if it wasn't for Esau Jenkins. Esau held together a pretty tight-knit situation, especially on the Islands. He had special political meetings on each island, set up organizations, and lots of people got involved. The thing I can't really relate to is that I can't say that it was a *sense* of pride before 1945, because nobody that I know said, "Yes, this is what we want to do;" it just happened. I almost have seen an organized effort after 1945 to make people dependent. I see the welfare system was designed to fail. I don't see any way it was made to help people. So many of the other programs have built-in failures. They are allowed to build people up to a point, where they could be destroyed. If you live so close to the ground you can't get destroyed. Getting to my own case, there's a lot of interest and requests for checkbooks, that all of a sudden have grown in the last three or four years. The auditors are going to come in here to COBRA

(Committee on Better Racial Assurance) from DSS (Department of Social Services) and audit the last three years. Anything they want to do to me then, I'm vulnerable to. If I'd stayed with my situation that I was with, it wouldn't happen.

But then, today, there is a lot of movement. There is movement in and out of the Islands, mostly out to the cities. Black people from Charleston used to regard us Islanders as country people. They used to look down on us. They still do somewhat, but not as much as in the past. Yet a good many of the people who own anything are from the Islands. A lot of blacks owning businesses in the city are from the Islands. People leave the Islands and come into Charleston and go as far as New York. Most of the people from the Sea Islands that are in New York are together somehow. They have their times to get together. Getting together is the only way they could have a good relaxed time. Most people up there won't even own up to the fact they're from the Islands. Even when I was in the Army, I told people that I was from Charleston. When they have those kind of gatherings and stuff, there's a chance for them to let their hair down and reflect on their old life. But other than that, they live in an unreal world. Once they get the group together, it's a different story. I still live on the Island. I'm forty-two years old, and out of my whole life I've spend maybe three nights in Charleston. My grandfather had a saying that I always tried to live by—"You should always live far enough away from people so that if you and your wife have a fight, nobody knows." I have never lived in an apartment and don't think I could. Not with someone on top of me, beside me, or under me. Let me tell you something that might make you understand better my view. Most of the property on the Islands is "heirs property." I don't know if you know anything about that or not. That's a very serious problem to a lot of people in the Islands in the sense that although you pay taxes on the land, you don't own it and can't build a house on it or anything. We ran into a real stumbling block in terms of building houses, so we got together with a contractor who bought up a lot of land and built houses on a minimum amount of land per each house. So each house was on about a half acre lot. People went into those houses, but they wouldn't pay their notes, and what we realized was that they were just too close for the people. Now the younger blacks who've been to Vietnam and school and out around are taking those houses, but the older people just won't live that close.

Many of us who were born on the Islands live there all our lives. Some of us who have gone to other places in the States, and even gone overseas, come back to settle down. Esau Jenkins has a son, Abraham, who is Administrator for the Sea Islands Health Center on Johns Island. That's something we are really, really proud of that we created.

Abraham Jenkins is right near fifty. He retired as a Major in the Air Force after twenty-one years of service; he's been working here for the last four or five years. He had some friends on the Island, Robert Fields, Frederick Fields, and many people. The Fields brothers have been very outstanding; two of them stayed with the farm and they have probably the largest farms going of black people. The other one has a dry cleaning business chain of laundromats, and so on. He lives on the Island too. Everybody I'm talking about lives on the Island. They are very interested in the Island and have a lot of pride.

Truth is, I guess, we all have a lot of pride. People still say, "Bill, that's a nice suit," and I say, "I'm just a country boy," and they say, "A country boy don't wear no suit like that." They're saying the only way you can wear a nice suit like that is to be from the city. I used to go to Atlanta University and other places to make talks and I would be really, really country. I'd make my clothes country, my accent too. Most people would take one look at me and hear me and automatically say I was stupid, because they think if you speak country, then you're automatically stupid. And I was making fools of all of them. Now they've caught on to that; I've got to change my tactics. But then, there's changes in everything.

There was a time when there was just one way of life on the Islands. Now numerous ways of life are found, and they range from those of the 1940s and 1950s to any type of modern living you could name. You can find some black people making $2,000 a year at most, and also others (blacks) making $150,000 a year or more. There's a basic meeting place for these people. Even though one may have more material things than the other, that particular thing exists still. You may find a lot of people working for someone they grew up around. You may find many young people now have a college degree; I have a son who is an engineer. What brings us together is that we're still Islanders, and we are proud when we see one of our people being a success.

In conclusion, I would like to say that in the Islands today, the feelings and attitudes that dominate most are the same feelings and attitudes that dominate America. The biggest concern is survival through new changes such as the Kiawah Beach Company which is bringing new employment in. We were able to get them to fund a community school program in which the schools on Johns Island are being used to train people for those new professions they have not been acquainted with yet. I think the attitude now is that a lot of things must change and are changing.

NOTES
[1]The mortars were often made of tree stumps and hollowed out for the rice to be

pounded in them. The pestles were carved of wood and in the existing illustrations are shaped just as they are in Africa. For illustrations see:

PARRISH, L. (1942) Slave Songs of the Georgia Sea Islands. New York: Farrar and Strauss.

PENNINGTON, P. (1913) A Woman Rice Planter. New York: Macmillan.

[2]The shingles were made with in instrument called a draw shave and a wooden mallet. The wood split down the natural grain when it was cut. As the shingles swelled up in the rain, the water drained down the natural grain lines of the wood surfaces.

[3]The older people on the Island can tell you of the medicinal uses of plants growing there such as "Life-Everlasting" for colds.

[4]"Benne" is sesame seed which was brought from Zaire. It is one of Africa's contributions to the New World's cuisine.

[5]See TURNER, L.D. (1949) Africanisms in the Gullah Dialect. Chicago: University of Chicago Press.

CHAPTER ELEVEN

Baskets and Quilts:
Women in Sea Island Arts and Crafts*
Mary Arnold Twining

The roles of women in family life as mothers and wives, sisters and grandmothers, are almost taken for granted in a discussion of family functions. These roles, along with housework and cooking, are taken to be the women's unpaid and economically unremarkable contribution to society. On the Sea Islands, however, the women's economic contribution has been much more extensive. The women plow and plant, shock, sheave and harvest, as necessity dictates. They fish, working alongside the men with drop and drag nets, seining in the creeks up to their hips in water. They also line fish, and while they enjoy the activity, its main purpose is fish for dinner. Those families who are able, freeze the excess catch; others send somebody around among the houses to sell fish. Occasionally they will go into Charleston and hawk the fish on the street, making it seem that not much has changed since the times made famous in the opera "Porgy and Bess." This intensive economic involvement of Sea Island women is readily reminiscent of the "mammy traders," women entrepreneurs of West Africa.

BASKETRY

Basketry and quilting are two Sea Island crafts which have had little

---

*This is the first publication of this article which was written especially for this volume.

attention paid to them because they are domestic in nature originally, elements of the culture which are not immediately visible to the outside observer. These domestic arts are integrated into the life of the family and, by extension, into the community, radiating outward from the family core in a network of social intercourse and exchange which helps to guarantee the survival of its members and of the crafts they make. Embedded in the familial core of the society, these domestically-oriented crafts provide bedcovers for family and neighbors, receptacles and utensils for various needs within the community, and utilize the tourist trade to increase the cash flow.

BASKETRY: FAMILY AND ECONOMICS

The main basketry style surviving today is that of the coiled variety made by the women of Mount Pleasant, South Carolina. The craft continues in that locality as a result of the suggestion of a WPA worker during the depression, who encouraged the people to develop a home industry by selling baskets to tourists on Route 17 (part of the New York to Florida highway).

Mount Pleasant, through which Route 17 runs, is a coastal community east of Charleston, South Carolina. There is a high retention among the townspeople of not only the physical characteristics, but also of the cultural customs of their West African ancestors. Social institutions such as the family, residential patterns, burial and insurance societies and lodges, and forms of artistic expression such as music and dance styles, clearly define this area of Afro-American culture. The factors which preserved other culture traits here, as well as elsewhere in the Sea Islands, have operated to preserve basketry as a family activity and industry.

The traditional Sea Island families in Mt. Pleasant live in enclaves where several generations occupy houses in close proximity with a common, open area among them. The residence pattern closely approximates its West African counterparts, with allowances for difference climates. African cooperative work patterns foster productivity in the traditional mold.

The baskets are handmade by one of the oldest groups of African American artisans to hand down the art of basketmaking from person to person. In Mt. Pleasant, the transmission of the art of basketmaking is often from one woman to another, or from one woman to her children. Sea Island men also are basketmakers, as is the case in Western African societies, where men can be seen making mats and woven (as opposed to sewn) baskets. The children all join in the family industry of basketmaking once they are old enough to hold and manipulate the materials; the boys relinquish the practice at about the age of ten, when they declare it "women's work."

In the 1930s, a Works Projects Administration (WPA) worker came down to the Islands to effect a revival of this craft which was no longer widely practiced. An older woman in the community claimed she was the only one making baskets at that time and, from her, the rest of the Mt. Pleasant women learned the skills of basketmaking again. This is probably an oversimplified version of what happened. It is perhaps more likely that the WPA person helped the women understand that their baskets would sell and that it would be worthwhile to set themselves up at the stands at the roadside. Today, the basketmakers are seen in a hundred or so roughly built stands along Route 17. Some of the women live right by their stands, while others commute a short distance to tend them. The returns from the basketmaking are hardly sufficient to support the manufacturers of them; mostly the makers have small incomes from other sources which they augment by sale of the baskets. Most of the stands are tended by older women who learned the trade from their aunts, grandmothers, or mothers a long time ago. They are often accompanied by members of their family, not all of whom live in the aggregate residence, who sit around making baskets and enjoying joking and telling stories while they work.

In days past, baskets served useful functions in the plantation economy. The rice fanners were used for harvesting nuts and winnowing grain (Dabbs 1971). Corn or rice rations for the families of the enslaved Africans were handed out in baskets on the plantation. Sewing baskets, flower baskets, and special little baskets for children's toys, were made for the "big house." Some of these items manufactured by enslaved Africans and African Americans can be seen in the Old Slave Mart Museum in Charleston (Chase 1971).

Today basketry is a distinctive feature of the Sea Island culture. Though it may have enjoyed a wider spread throughout the Southeastern United States in the past, it probably had its strongest manifestion in this location, which was one of the points of Africans' first contact with this country. The geographic conditions would encourage people to continue their African practices. The riverine marshes of South Carolina are similar to those of the Senegambian region in West Africa. It is not, however, the geographic/climatic conditions alone which determine the production of these items. They are also produced in the arid western section of Senegal where the climate is extraordinarily dry and different sorts of grasses are used to create the same style of coiled basketry.

The continuance of family association patterns as work groups sitting out in the open, as their ancestors did and as their contemporaries do in West Africa, helped to ensure the flow of continuity in the basketmaking art.

Conversations with Mary Manigault have revealed that she worked hard during her life in more physically demanding employment, and turned to basketmaking only when she was no longer strong enough to do heavy agricultural labor. Basketmaking at this juncture provided an opportunity to put her home and family associated skill to profitable economic use. She taught her daughter and granddaughter to make basketry in the traditional way. She also learned from elder female relatives in her time. We can see Ms. Manigault's fine craftmanship reflected in the statements of her cousin, Louise Jones, who quickly spots and criticizes loose, flabby construction as a sign of a poorly and hurriedly made basket, remarking that her relative, Ms. Manigault,[1] in contrast, sews with a tight stitch and that the resultant baskets are tough and hard and lasting. The sea grass, palmetto and pine straw (needles) tend to dry out and fade to a yellow and brown pattern from their original color; and to cause baskets now sewn tightly enough to loosen and weaken.

Ms. Manigault has indicated the importance of color in her use of the palmetto, sea grass and pine straw. The sea grass forms the base for the basket, the palmetto is the binding thread, and the pine straw gives color variation. The materials for the baskets are harvested by the makers themselves, but there is no proscription against having others do it for them. Often, the male members of any age in the family go to the areas known for the presence of all three necessary materials. As far as we know, there is no ownership of trees or areas, but family members will keep a good harvesting spot secret for as long as they can. The baskets are built in many different shapes and sizes. The rice fanner is an old type of basket not made anymore except by special order.

The big fanners Ms. Manigault makes today are made of a rush called *Juncus Roemerianus Scheele*, which is larger and stiffer than the sea grass and grows in the salt marshes which reach their northern limit in South Carolina. Ms. Manigault and her husband gather the rushes and put them to dry on the roof of a shed so that the material gets both sun and air. The harvesting is seasonal, mostly during the summer and fall months, and is dependent on the weather. July and sometimes June are extremely rainy and this slows the drying process. The basketmakers try to keep a good selection in their stands at all times, but variety fluctuates with sales and the women's ability to produce at a fairly consistent rate. Other members of the family help out, either making baskets or minding the stand.

In the past, the baskets were used for a variety of practical purposes by the family in the home and community, such as fanning rice, winnowing corn or other grains (Dabbs, 1971), measuring food allotments, traveling, harvesting, sewing, collecting money in churches, and so on. The church-offering basket, which looks like a small fanner, is still an integral part of the culture. As stated above, the designs are now determined according to buyers' demands. Knitting and sewing baskets, wall vessels, purses, bread trays, mats, glass trays, waste baskets, and flower baskets, are among the shapes which consistently reappear.

Peter Weil reports from his work with the Bambara-Djula people in Mali, that the coiling techniques used by the Mount Pleasant people are found in Africa as well.[2] In Mali, they use coiling for bowl covers made to fit down inside the bowl on top of the food carried by family members to the men working in the fields. The covers keep the food hot and the bugs out. The coiling technique is also seen in the flat face masks worn by the newly-circumcised boys when, as part of their coming-of-age ritual, they run through the village beating their sisters and other women in revenge for childhood spankings in a show of their changed status. The African masks are very similar in construction to the mats from South Carolina, but have holes for eyes and a loop or handle at the side, executed in exactly the same way as on the South Carolina baskets either for use as handles or for decoration. Among the Bambara-Djula people, the basket containers are associated with females and their roles in the society; particularly, the containing function of the baskets is equated with the women's ability to hold and carry children. There is an obvious connection in the Mount Pleasant community as well, between women and basketmaking.

From the research which I conducted in West Africa, it would appear that the model for the coiled basketry found in the Sea Islands came over chiefly with the enslaved Africans from the Senegambian area of West Africa. Coiled basketry, one of humans' oldest patterns, is easy to find in many societies. In the Sea Islands and the Senegambian region, however, we are dealing with groups whose genetic, historical, and linguistic links are known, so the basketry merely adds one more piece of evidence that cultural patterns have been transmitted along the same routes as the people.

In the "Man in Africa" exhibit at the Museum of Natural History in New York City, organized by Colin Turnbull, there is a section entitled, "The New World Experience," which is illustrative of the African and African American basketry analogs. In it are four coiled baskets—two from the modern period and two winnowing baskets from an earlier period. The two large winnowing baskets were dated before 1860 from South Carolina, and circa 1900 from Angola. The two modern baskets were marked as having come from Senegal and South Carolina. Each of the two sets of baskets is similar in materials of manufacture and style of execution. They are a silent demonstration of the persistence of traditional material culture between West Africa and the United States.

These likenesses are a testimony to the continuity of families and the crafts they practice on both sides of the Atlantic. On the American side, the Sea Island communities are like the traditional West African villages, often isolated, tightly-knit and closely interrelated, where artisans sit outdoors making their baskets and socializing. The substance of family is diffused throughout the community. This extension of family makes shifts in the nuclear family less of a disaster than it is for European American families which tend to stay more isolated.

The crafts, therefore, remain within a closer circle and the practice of them is reinforced by the presence of teaching models. It is these early and lifelong impressions that formed the mental templates the people brought with them in their enforced migration.

The late Alan Merriam conceived of a scheme which encapsulates the process of transmission of artistic experience within any given societal group. The original concept of the artifact feeds into the activity, which results in the completed product. The use and continued presence of the product in the group reinforces its input back into the concept. Thus the culture carries on its typical designs and customs as each enters the aesthetic process and stands the test of repetition in action and product.

This pattern of artistic behavior in human societies is observable in regard to the Sea Islands baskets. The basketmakers conceived of ideas for new baskets within the framework of their traditional culture as well as through stimulus from the outside world. With the materials found in their new environment, they fashioned implements using the templates of their home cultures. The products of this cultural reaffirmation in turn reinforced the remembrance of their own or their parents' home, and carried forward the crafts learned in a similar agricultural setting by teaching them in the retained African family context. The survival of the crafts ensured by the families thus demonstrates the integrity of the sense of family in the African American context—the crafts being a symbol and evidence of the unity of their makers' family groups.

QUILTING

Quilting is regarded as a peculiarly American speciality in the domestic arts and crafts. It did, however, come originally from England and Holland in some form familiar to early colonists. Economic necessity was a factor that forced housewives to use every piece of valuable material, no matter how small. Aesthetic considerations were also important in the making of quilts, not only in regard to the satisfaction of viewing the finished product, but also in relation to the actual process of placing the pieces of cloth in the quilt top, known as "setting together." In this operation, symmetrical patterns were deliberately organized, or "crazy" patchwork arrangements were incorporated into quilt designs.

Another important factor, also, is the social aspect of quilting. Among the early English and Dutch colonists, an individual woman often made her quilt top while at home; then the women and the other members of their families and of the community at large would gather for the "quilting bee." Sewing on quilting frames for the expert seamstresses, cooking for the women with other talents, socializing and courting, seemed to be ingredients for the "quilting bee." All of these factors—social, economic and aesthetic—are essential aspects of the complex behavior surrounding the making of bed covers.

Subjected to a new and colder climate than either Africa or the Caribbean, the enslaved house servants replicated for their own family use the warm covers they helped make for the comfort of the big house dwellers, following the European American models as to structure. There was, however, a notable difference between the designs of the tops of the bedcovers made for the European Americans and those African Americans made for themselves. The European American patterns were characterized by centrality and symmetry in the colors and shapes of the design units. The African American quilt designs, by contrast, were arranged in patterns which featured a staggered, "syncopated" strip formation, and utilized differences in color to achieve the effect of highlights placed in dramatic dispersion on the quilt top (Wahlman and Torrey 1983).

Quilts of other designs are found in other African American groups; what distinguishes Sea Island quilts is the "strip" formation. These quilts are an integral part of Sea Island family life and culture. At the same time they illustrate most remarkably a recognizable continuity in aesthetic heritage, linking continental and diasporic Africans.

The women who make these quilts live on the Islands in South Carolina and Georgia. Their quilt patterns have a quite varied range, including some basically European American styles such as "log cabin," "handkerchief corner," and "step" pattern. These European American patterns are rectangular, that is, linear, squared-off and centrally organized. More distinctively, the Island women also have "patch" or "patchy" quilts which are made up of bits of cloth cut into rectangular shapes, these sewn together by hand or machine into long strips, sometimes running the whole length of the quilt except the border. Abrahams has termed these "strip quilts" because of the little strips which go together to form the long strips from which the quilt is fashioned.[4]

There is an African analog for these quilt top patterns in Ashanti Kente cloth which is woven on belt looms in strips; the strips, which consist of rectangular units, are sewn together. This relationship between Kente cloth and Sea Island quilts is part of the whole African design connection, because the design concept of these quilts extends to far-flung parts of the African world such as Surinam and African American communities in the Northern United States. The layered quilt form itself is a European culture trait. The design of the tops is our basis of comparison. The colors such as red, kelly green, and sapphire blue in some of the quilts compare to those of the Ashanti Kente cloth. There are quilts, however, which have much darker tonalities, and these have an analog in the woven cotton cloth made by the Ewe people, also called Kente, which combines darker hues in the same style as the Ashanti Kente cloth to make their patterns.[5]

Another consideration in the establishment of the origin of quilt design is the placement of the rectangular design units. In the Ashanti Kente cloth, the units are evenly lined up, and it is clear that the technique of the weaver determined where the units would be in relation to one another as the strips were sewn together. In the end zone, however, one can see the offset pattern of the border, which also follows a preconceived plan. In the Ewe Kente cloth, many of the rectilinear design units are offset, and it is that fact and the distinctive color tonalities of the Ewe cloths which corresponded to the darker quilts mentioned earlier, that indicated provenance other than the Ashanti Kente cloth. In a review of hundreds of slides of materials submitted for an exhibition of African material culture in New York City, I found many instances of the offset technique of the rectangular design features. This usage was not limited to Ghanaian materials alone, but was widespread among West African craftsmen.

The African American quiltmakers in South Carolina use any cloth they can obtain to make the quilts—old clothes, sewing scraps or material bought by the yard. They mix velvet, broadcloth, upholstery fabric, nylon, batiste, twills, woolens, rayon—all in the same quilts, sometimes without regard to what will wear well or endure washing. The surface texture is quite varied on those quilts where a variety of cloth types are used. Others are very smooth, as the material is uniform in surface texture.

Backing material varies on the quilts; some of them used pieced quilt tops on both sides, termed "old style" by Ms. Hunter of Johns Island, which may indicate simply that only cloth strips were available for use both as top and backing. The construction, as well as the design, was thus economically determined. Some quilts are backed with a muslin material called "Sea Island" from the cotton boom days. Rice bags are still used; the material of those is not much rougher than the "Sea Island" and lasts very well. Purchased yardgoods are also used as backing, which the women buy from the stores in the cities or from modern day peddlers who come around to the remote island areas.

Members of a family can identify the patches and can tell whose clothing, drapes, or household cloths they were before they did final duty in the quilt tops. Turning points in individuals' lives, certain favorite garments and bygone episodes associated with them come to light as they speak of the quilt and its maker. The quilts are cryptic chronicles, readable only by those who are initiated into the lexicon and context of the familial documents involved. They are an historical record, a primary source, coming directly out of the life of the family—only understood by them and possibly treasured all the more because of it. The African analogs of these fabric folios are possibly found in the distinctive cloths of the Fon of Benin (formerly Dahomey) in which appliqued figures represent personages and events in the history of this West African people. These cloths also relate to lineages and their histories and so constitute a family code which through artistic usage has become more widely known. The Yoruba drum language is also analogous since a knowledge of the appropriate proverbs and idioms is necessary both to transmit and understand this somewhat esoteric mode of expression. The cloth patterns woven on the belt looms in West Africa consist of rectangular units, many of which are named for a proverb. Although this underlying poetic significance was lost in the transfer from Ghana to the United States, the arrangement and usage of the rectilinear design units was reaffirmed and reinterpreted in the quilts as family documents and the more quotidian bedclothes. Such cultural transfers seem to tell us that in spite of the present day artisans' inability to recite Akan proverbs in conjunction with their manufacture of the designs, they retain the placement rhythms and the templates of what sewn cloth ought to look like. Therefore, we can reject the notion that if the makers of the patched cloth (or other material culture traits) do not identify the item as to its original function and designation, it is not then truly "carried over."

Sea Island quilts document African cultural continuity. The quilters themselves are apparently quite unaware of that historical aspect of their creations. They are deeply conscious, however, of another more immediate, more intimate significance of the quilts: that is, the communication of affection between family members and the celebration of their family history. Thus the quilts relate to family events as symbols of the continued caring from one generation to another. Rites of passage such as marriage, births of children, young people leaving home to go to school, are often signalized by the making or completing of a quilt which accompanies the departing family members to their new situation as a reminder of the ties of kinship which connect them to the parent family. The quilts symbolize to those departing their continuing membership in the family group, though their status may have changed and new family allegiances added.

In addition to their symbolism in the annals of life, the colors serve other functions in the designs assembled by these artists in the culture. The quilt artist takes the best advantage of these qualities inherent in the colors and puts them to work in the quilts. The colors red, blue, and white are very important in this culture. The red signifies danger, fire, conflict, and passion. Blue is a "good" color which is used on doors to repel negative influences, to "keep away the bad spirits," according to Sea Island belief. White is a color which suggests innocence and sanctity, which "makes you good," a color used in conjunction with solemn occasions such as weddings, funerals, and turnouts. Thus red, blue, black and white are the four colors mentioned in the courting game, "I've come to see Jenny" (Beckwith 1922). In this game, the children sing, "Red is for soldiers," obviously the conflict and passion motif. Red, blue, black and white are four important quilt colors; not only is there the effective use of the colors, but also there is their significance which connects to a deeper set of values and beliefs in the culture, which have meaning beyond the visual combination of colors which work well together.

Another interesting discovery which has come to light in the quilt researches is the cross quilt. In this quilt, by Ms. Robert Johnson of Johns Island, we see a huge cross made of large pink arms and a dark blue middle section somewhat off center in the whole quilt. The design is actually a very large nine-patch framed by strips. This short-armed cross symbol is one that appears often in the Americas. According to Thompson (1970) who has found it, the Caribbean and circum-Caribbean regions are areas where reaffirmations of West African culture are stronger and more obvious than in North America. The small crosses are found in one North American example, the Harriet Powers Bible quilt, at the Smithsonian Institute (Adams 1980; Fry 1976). It consists of biblical scenes and was manufactured in the 1800s in Athens, Georgia. The scene of Cain's birth has two of these crosses in it. The cross signifies a curse of bad vibrations according to Thompson, who found a cross in the work of a Surinamese carver. The carver's idea was: "If you don't like my work, stay away, or curses on you." Obviously Cain is a person involved in an archetypal curse situation; we are in the presence of evil. The cross is not a Christian cross, according to the residents of the island where Ms. Johnson's quilt was made. This cross design represents danger, evil and other bad feelings antithetical to a calm and peaceful life. The quilts are often made in dramatic colors of hot/cool, good/bad, safe/dangerous; these binary oppositions are some of the dichotomous predicates that make up the dynamics of human societies, and which, achieving certain degrees of cognitive elaboration, may be formulated into world views.

The view has been advanced that European Americans tend to think and react in squares and rectilinear forms in general; for example, the box step in social dancing. On the other hand, African Americans tend to be more curvilinear in their world view; e.g., undulating dance steps (Abrahams 1970). As it happens, the quilts illustrate this theory very well in the contrast between the centrality and symmetry of the squared-off designs made by European American quilt makers, and the curvilinear, uneven, undulating overall patterns of the African American quilt makers.

The mini-unit of strip quilting is the smallest strip which, with many similar strips, makes the next largest unit in assembling the pattern. This next larger unit is also a "strip" composed of such mini-units. These larger strips are then assembled to complete the top. Often, a border is added to create more area or to pull the whole design together. Sometimes part of the pattern will be a unit from another design sequence, usually used in the European American quilts, part of "log cabin" or "courthouse steps" (Ickis 1949). This part may be surrounded by pattern units more typical of the African American groups and bordered in their style.

The Sea Island quilters place their design units according to schemes of organization which show that the centrality and balance in a four square framework are not of primary importance to them. There are, therefore, visual analogs in the quilt designs to the spontaneity of invention, and the freedom of improvisation which are to be found in African American folk music such as blues, jazz and spirituals. In some quilts, it might be said that the evanescent forms of these dance, song, and verbal skills are caught in the material medium.

From the European American standpoint, the African American quilt does not conform to traditional design and, therefore, is without design. Organized as it is, however, from completely different aesthetic considerations and mental templates, the Sea Island quilt follows its own sense of order, which relates to the African analogs amongst the Ewe and Akan. The undulating lines may correlate with the indirection in personal contact as well as the oblique modes of speech well known in African and African American communities.

Some quilts made by African Americans are made in the Anglo- or European American style tradition; we are discussing quilts done by African Americans working within their own tradition. As with other aspects of African American culture, we are concerned with a phenomenon known nowhere else—the syncretistic American experience. The construction of quilts as a culture trait is European, no doubt, but the pattern of the tops is within the transatlantic continuum from West Africa to the Southeastern United States. It is the combination that gives us the uniqueness of the African American cultural syncretism.

The coiled basketry comes from the Senegambian region of West Africa, and the strip quilt patterns point to the area of the Ewe and Ashanti speakers in Ghana. I believe that this kind of folklife research has implications for the eventual location of the origins of African-descended peoples (Haley 1974). The people who make the basketry and the quilts interact in family-oriented groupings. African American women, in their roles as commemorators of family events and teaching and practicing artisans, act as conservators of the ethnic culture. They are at once responsible for the preservation of the African traits which have survived, and for the adaptation of these traits to the American situation. Just as linguists take linguistic clues to guide them in their research, so folklorists and family researchers can use material and non-material culture traits as indicators in their research. These folkloristic and family clues exist anywhere in the United States; they are to be found in their purest form in the Sea Islands, the richest area for Africanisms in North America. The role of Sea Island women in the preservation of African American culture is unique and incalculable.

NOTES
[1]Ms. Mary Jane Manigault was the recipient of a National Heritage Fellowship Award from the National Endowment for the Arts, 1984.
[2]Professor Peter Weil, University of Delaware, personal communication, 1970.
[3]A. Merriam, personal communication, 1966.
[4]ABRAHAMS, R. (1970) Personal communication.
[5]See KENT, K.P. (1971) West African Cloth. Denver: Denver Museum of National History, Figure 32.

REFERENCES
ADAMS, M.J. (1980) "The Harriet Powers Pictorial Quilts," Black Art Vol. 3, No. 3, pp. 12-28.
BECKWITH, M. (1922) Folk Games of Jamaica. Poughkeepsie: Vassar College.
CHASE, J.W. (1971) Afro-American Art and Craft. New York: Van Nostrand Reinhold.
DABBS, E.M. (1971) Face of an Island. New York: Grossman.
FRY, G.M. "Harriet Powers: Portrait of a Black Quilter," Missing Pieces: Georgia Folk Art 1770-1976. A. Wadsworth ed. Atlanta: Georgia Council for the Arts and Humanities, pp. 16-23.
HALEY, A. (1972) "My Furthest-Back Person—the African," New York Times Magazine Section, Sunday, July 16, pp. 13-16.
ICKIS, M. (1949) The Standard Book of Quiltmaking and Collecting. Greystone.
PENNINGTON, PATIENCE (1913) A Woman Rice Planter. New York: MacMillan, p. 375.
THOMPSON, R.F. (1983) Flash of the Spirit. New York: Random House, p. 222.
VLACH, J.M. (1978) The Afro-American Tradition in Decorative Arts. Cleveland: The Cleveland Museum of Art.
WAHLMAN, M.S. and TORREY, E.K. (1983) Ten Afro-American Quilters. Oxford, Mississippi: Center for the Study of Southern Culture, the University of Mississippi.

CHAPTER TWELVE

Leadership Patterns in a Sea Island Community*

Simon Ottenberg

M any studies of African Americans in the rural South deal with caste and class, others consider general economic and social problems, and still others are concerned with the civil status of the rural African American in the South. In general these studies lack a sense of what for rural African Americans constitutes a community, and they usually do not show an interest in the analysis of rural African American leadership, except within the framework of relations between African Americans and European Americans. Surprisingly little has been published on African American leadership activities carried out within their own rural communities (Kaufman 1954). This is perhaps because in some Southern rural areas there is no distinct geographic area of purely African American settlement and thus such communities might appear not to exist; or because African American leadership might be seen to play such a minimal role, as a consequence of the caste system, that leadership could be said to be absent or to be concerned mainly with intercaste relations. This paper presents an analysis of a single African American community in order to indicate the extent to which the community leadership is present and changing.[1] In a number of ways the community is atypical of Southern rural African American communities. It is geographically distinct, non-agricultural, and

---

*This article was first published in *Phylon*, Volume 20, Number 1, 1959, and has been slightly edited for appearance in the present work.

not far from a large urban center. Yet, a comparison of the data from this community with published information suggests that many of the basic patterns found here are also present in other African American areas of the South where ecological factors and social groupings differ.

Shrimp Creek,[2] an unincorporated community of some four hundred persons, is located about fifteen miles south of Savannah. One of a number of African American communities found in an area of bays, tidal creeks, and marshes, its houses are scattered along or near a road which leads north to Savannah. South of Shrimp Creek the road ends at a bay where there is a dock used by European American sportsmen and fishermen, while to the north there is an area of interspersed European American and African American residences extending toward Savannah. The community lacks a central meeting place, though at one point on the road there is a concentration of houses, two churches, and a small store, which serves as a central area. Five independent small wooden Baptist churches serve the community, none of which has an active membership of more than seventy or eighty persons.[3] Two small taverns are located a short distance from the main road.

The ancestors of most of the present residents of the community came from the Georgia Sea Islands after the Civil War.[4] The way of life on the islands was similar to that on the South Carolina Sea Islands, being characterized by extensive plantations with large populations of enslaved Africans, small numbers of European Americans, and considerable isolation of the African population from the mainland (Johnson 1930; Woofter 1930; Georgia Writer's Project 1940; Bascom 1941; Turner 1949). When they moved into the Shrimp Creek area they obtained small plots of land and built their own houses, and today many persons still own their own land and homes. They found farming small plots unrewarding and gradually shifted to fishing for shrimps, crabs and oysters. Today, except for some gardening, virtually no agriculture is practiced, and farming is generally viewed with disdain. The fishing is generally performed by the men, either singly or in pairs, in small boats in the nearby estuary and bay. Some of the seafood is sold to a cannery in a neighboring community and some to Savannah markets, but a considerable amount is hawked on the streets of Savannah on Tuesdays and Fridays. No cooperative fishing or marketing organizations exist in the community. The general economic level is low, most persons falling roughly into the range from lower lower class to lower middle class in terms of the Warner type of classification (Davis and Dollard 1940; Davis and Gardner 1941).

As a result of the decline in fishing in recent years, due to large-scale white commercial competition, some persons have taken up positions of manual labor in Savannah or work as servants—in either case still generally residing in Shrimp Creek. These occupations always attracted a few persons even when the fishing was very good. Others have migrated to New York, Philadelphia and other Northern areas. Yet fishing remains a major economic activity for many persons, particularly members of the older families in the area, and a source of food and income for those who are temporarily unemployed. In the last fifty-odd years other African Americans, particularly from Savannah, inland Georgia, and South Carolina, have moved into the community, settling mainly in its north end. Though some of these persons have married into the older Shrimp Creek families, the newcomers rarely fish for a livelihood, finding that they are discouraged by the members of the older families and that their urban or agricultural backgrounds make this way of life a difficult one. They work mainly for European Americans in the countryside surrounding the community of Savannah.

The usual Southern caste relationships exist in the community, but no tense caste situation has developed in recent years. The people of Shrimp Creek have a feeling of considerable independence from the European American population. Not only do many own their own homes and land, but few are deeply in debt to European Americans. Except for an occasional salesman or bill collector, few European Americans visit the community, and contacts between the two ethnic groups occur mainly in Savannah or elsewhere.

Integrative ideologies exist which make Shrimp Creek more than simply a collection of persons living in a common geographic area. The people consider it a distinct community with its own leaders and organizations, clearly differentiated from neighboring settlements. Most of its members share a heritage of life as an enslaved African population on the Sea Islands, the seasonal orientation of life in a fishing community, whether they themselves fish or not, and the tradition of private ownership of their homes and land. They are conscious of being Baptists with a common local ritual and ideology, and of lacking strong class or economic distinctions, in contrast to Savannah.

The community is crossed by a network of interpersonal relations, by ties of friendship, kin, and marriage, and those created through the adoption of babies (generally informally) by friends and relatives of the mother or both parents. Again, different social groups in Shrimp Creek are linked to one another by overlapping membership. Persons frequently belong to a number of local burial and insurance societies and to savings clubs, which brings them into social relationships with persons from different sections of the community. Visiting churches other than one's own is a common practice, facilitated by the fact that the services are generally held at the Shrimp Creek churches on different Sundays. The membership of any single church is not necessarily based on persons living in the immediate area of the church or exclusively belonging to certain families, and children and young adults sometimes join the church of their friends rather than that of their parents.

There are a few activities that bring large numbers of persons into face-to-face contact. Basically religious in nature, these are often considered to be the most exciting gatherings in Shrimp Creek, and it is mainly through these that Shrimp Creek visibly becomes a cohesive social entity. Each church has a week-long annual celebration in which members of other Shrimp Creek churches take part. Most of the adults and many of the children participate at funerals and revival ceremonies. In these religious activities the deacons and ministers of the churches readily cooperate with one another, and join together in organizing and carrying out the services. The initiative is taken by the deacons and ministers of the church where the religious service is being held, and the officials of the other churches gladly give support and aid. This cooperation is carried out on an informal basis without much urging from the leaders of the church concerned.

Only a few other interests or activities involve the community as a whole. Every few years the deacons of the five churches join together to clear the main cemetery of the community. There have been sporadic discussions by community members of the possibility of establishing one large community church in place of the present five, but this has never taken the form of a widely accepted movement. In former times a community grammar school served as a focal point for community identification, but since the establishment of a consolidated district school in a nearby community in the early 1930s, this focus has shifted outside the community. Recent attempts by a few of the more prominent deacons and their wives to have the old school building repaired for use as a community center have not succeeded.

The common ideological identification of the people of Shrimp Creek, the informal network of social relations surrounding kin, marriage, and friendship, the interlocking relationships associated with the activities of the churches and the burial and insurance societies, and the face-to-face contact of large numbers of the community at church anniversaries, revivals, and funerals, give Shrimp Creek its focus as a community. It lacks any formal legal and political organization of its own; it has no established cooperative labor groupings, no secular educational institutions, and only a few types of voluntary associations;[5] and it is not the center of highly organized commercial activities. It is a community only for certain limited purposes and activities. Shrimp Creek itself is enmeshed within the larger political and social organization of the county and of Savannah, but without significant representation within these groupings.

Though there is no formal government organization in the community, and the community carries out only limited activities, effective leadership does exist. The leaders are, with one exception,[6] the deacons of the five Baptist churches. There are about thirty deacons in all, ranging in age from about thirty to over eighty years. Almost all of them are descendants of the older, well-established families, and all are married or are widowers, marriage being a requirement for deaconship. Some of them earn a living by fishing, and some work as servants or unskilled laborers. Many own their own houses and though a few are poor, they mainly fall roughly into the middle or upper range of the economic level of the community. Some financial stability is necessary since they are expected to dress reasonably well and to contribute generously at church services.

They are permanent leaders since once they are selected by their church they hold the position for life. Brothers from the same family may occasionally become deacons, but the community leadership seems to come from a broad sample of the older families. They are nominated to deaconship by the board of deacons of their church and approved by their congregation. The selection is noncompetitive in that only one person at a time is nominated and there seems to be little rivalry to secure nomination.

No formal hierarchy of offices exists among the leaders, though the most senior are generally the chairmen of the boards or deacons of their churches. Two or three of the older chairmen are considered to be the most influential in the community, but they do not strongly dominate the other leaders. Their position is based not only on age—for seniority alone does not secure them their special position—but also on continuous active interest in church and community. Associations and contact with prominent European Americans seldom directly strengthen a man's leadership potential, since European American contacts are generally removed from the community, and European Americans show little interest in it (Lewis 1955). Some deacons are quite withdrawn and retiring, while others are highly vocal and directly manipulative of other persons.

The deacons are in charge of church collections and finances, and they organize prayer services, picnics, and other activities. If cooperative activity between two or more churches is to occur, it is the deacons of these churches who make the initial arrangements. They act as "spiritual fathers," or religious advisors, to those seeking a "vision" or a "call" to join the church. Though any church member may be selected as spiritual father by a potential candidate or his parents, generally the person chosen is a deacon, whose task it becomes to advise the candidate on any dreams or visions that he has had, to give him some rudimentary religious instruction, and to sponsor him when he is prepared to join the church. The role of spiritual father is considered an important one by many persons in Shrimp Creek. Much of the responsibility for religious guidance and teaching at a critical stage in the individual's life rests in the deacon's hands.

Each church holds a regular communion service with its minister once a month. There are four ministers for the five churches, two of them being served by the same person. All of the ministers live in Savannah where they also serve other churches. Some also have churches in other outlying communities near Savannah. The ministers are the nominal heads of the churches, but they are not, in fact, its actual leaders. None of them are on fixed contracts, and their services can be terminated on short notice by their congregation. They do not actively participate in the life of the community, but generally come from Savannah only once a month for the Sunday service (twice a month in the case of the minister who has two churches). They rarely attend the monthly church meetings of the board of deacons of their church, and if communication with them is needed, it is sometimes made by telephone. Many people in Shrimp Creek do not wish to have their ministers living in the community, for they feel that they would be "too close" and would see too much of what was going on. Problems concerning the church, and those arising from sexual promiscuity, unmarried mother-hood, alcoholism, vagrancy, and so on, are handled by the deacons. These are brought to the attention of the minister only if they need his approval or support in some action that they have taken or are contemplating.

The ministers sometimes differ with the deacons over theology and church practices, tending to use the urban church pattern as their model. They try to discourage too great an emphasis on possession, the role of the spiritual father and mother, and a long period of training before joining the church. Some ministers note that in the city churches the minister is sometimes a person of more influence than in Shrimp Creek. The deacons maintain control over the churches and are sometimes opposed to modifications of church practice. As one influential deacon said, "We built our own church and we can run it the way we want." The ministers are chosen by the congregation, following guest sermons, and the deacons play a most influential role in the selection process. The ministers are well aware of their position. Several commented that they had to be extremely careful not to be too critical of their congregation, not to interfere too much in church matters, and not to attempt to change church rituals. There is no open conflict between deacons and ministers, but a subtle play of authority between them.

Some rivalry occurs among the churches in terms of competition as to which church has the largest congregation, the best choir, the most skillful preacher, the finest physical plant and so on. These rivalries, which do not have theological or ritual differences as their basis, find expression in some covert jealousies among the ministers and deacons, but are not seriously divisive of the community.

The deacons dominate the burial and insurance societies, called "socials,"[7]—the other major type of non-kin grouping in Shrimp Creek besides the church,[8]—holding the major offices in these groupings. These societies, of which there are at least eleven, vary in membership from about twenty to more than one hundred persons, and may include either sex or both. Local in origin, and independent of one another (except for several women's groups that are auxiliaries of men's societies), they are not associated with insurance societies elsewhere. With only a few exceptions they carry out few purely social activities, but hold a meeting once a month to collect dues (usually less than a dollar a month), and to report on finances. Each society has a constitution based on church organization regulations and procedures. Almost all adults belong to at least one society, and many belong to two or more.

There are at least six offices in each society, and the more important positions are almost always held by the deacons—or in some cases the deacon's wives. Some deacons hold offices in a number of societies. The officers are supposedly elected on an annual basis, but elections are rarely held, and in practice a person holds office indefinitely. The selection of a new officer is generally noncompetitive, as in the case of selection of deaconship, there being only one candidate, usually nominated by the other officers. The more recent settlers are frequently members of the societies but have little voice in most of them.

The deacons administer these organizations and retain financial control over them, as they do the churches. The societies, like the churches, have regulations permitting the organization to expel those who cause trouble in the community. Thus the task of dealing with disputes, theft, minor assault cases, alcoholism, and so on, falls mainly to the deacons, who try to keep matters out of the hands of the police if possible. The settlement usually does not involve direct punishment imposed by the deacons themselves, but reconciliation of the parties concerned, with financial compensation when necessary. In these cases the deacons of the churches and the officers of the societies to which the individual or individuals involved belong meet with others concerned to reach a settlement. Such cases are in actuality rare. Almost every church and society in Shrimp Creek has at least one member who is a troublemaker in the community. The tendency is for people to comment on this a great deal both in private and in public, and for the deacons to try to stimulate the development of informal social pressures, but they take little formal action. Theirs is non-authoritarian leadership which is essentially conciliatory and non-punitive.

The deacons are considered to be responsible for controlling the community's behavior in the event that caste tensions develop. They are always on their guard against any infringement of caste custom, and they will reprimand persons who cause difficulties of this nature. Anxious to avoid trouble across caste lines, they accept the status quo in caste relations. Though deacons spend little actual time representing the community or its members in intercaste matters, this is always potentially a major area of action for them.

The role played by the deacon's wives in relation to the women of Shrimp Creek is similar to that of the deacons in the community as a whole. They control many of the positions open to women in the church congregations and hold most of the major positions in the women's burial and insurance societies. They also often act as "spiritual mothers" to candidates for church membership. Women who are relatively new in the community rarely marry deacons and have little access to leadership positions.

Thus, it is around the deacons, and their wives, that the basic network of community activities is organized. There is a distinct feeling among newcomers, whether by marriage or otherwise, that it is difficult to be fully accepted in the community and virtually impossible to become a leader.[9] The road to prestige and leadership for newcomers of both sexes lies through newer channels, generally secular in nature, such as holding offices in the Parent-Teacher Association of the District School, organizing or taking part in 4-H Club and agricultural extension activities, or through social groupings and organizations in Savannah. The newer settlers feel that the older families are restrictive; that they control the church and the burial and insurance societies, and community activities, and that they are against change and "getting things done." Those in older groups deny these accusations if they are suggested to them. The distinction between these two groups is not always clear since there is some mixture on a residential basis, some intermarriage occurs between them, and at least one old-time family is associated with the "progressive" elements among the later settlers. Yet it is clear that the older group maintains its key position in Shrimp Creek by its control of the positions of leadership and its exclusion of others from access to them.

The rewards of leadership in Shrimp Creek include prestige, deference, and outlets for approved activity, and occasional opportunities to go to church conferences away from home. For some leaders there is also the satisfaction of maintaining the continuity of the position of the older families in the community. Though officers of the churches and the burial and insurance societies receive no salary, in some of the societies the senior officers are exempted from paying monthly dues. Nevertheless, a few community members feel that the leaders sometimes appropriate money for their own use from the churches and societies—a charge which was impossible to verify. The major rewards of leadership, however, appear to be social and not monetary or material. The pattern of authority is thus social control by religious leaders from the older families, and by their wives. The leaders lack clear rank distinctions and are not strongly dominated by one or two men. They do not maintain a great deal of social distance from community members. Leadership positions are essentially noncompetitive. Social control by leaders is not authoritarian, and a wide range of behavior is permitted community members—and sometimes suspected of the leaders. Their control is largely ideological and moral. The leaders, outside of expelling misbehaving persons from the churches and burial and insurance societies, and keeping aloof from them, have no effective legal, property, or economic sanctions over them. The deacon's controls over the church and the burial and insurance societies give them controls over community ideology, over the major social organizations in Shrimp Creek, and over the collection, use and distribution of the financial resources of these organizations.

The influence of general American culture patterns is creating changes that are causing the disappearance of the community as a social entity. The most basic change is probably the decline in the fishing industry which is altering the basic economic pattern of the community. A second factor is the presence of the newer settlers who tend to be less isolated in general outlook than other community members. A third influence is that arising from contacts with surrounding rural communities. There has always been some such contact through marriage and through the employment of a few local persons in nearby settlements. To these can be added the influence of a consolidated school in a nearby community, which has led to increased contact of students with children from other communities south of Savannah and to an increased competitiveness among children who consider (or whose parents consider) education to be a means of social and economic advancement.[10]

Urban influences are increasing. Through the sale of seafoods the people of Shrimp Creek have had contact with Savannah for many years. Community members purchase food, clothing, and household goods in Savannah. They now rely on Savannah for doctors, dentists, and funeral homes, whereas formerly they used locally produced medicinal preparations, consulted midwives, and buried their dead themselves. Many youth find life more exciting in Savannah and complain about the lack of things to do in Shrimp Creek. There is a growing schism between some young people and some older community members based on differences in education and willingness to accept elements of urban and general American culture, such as secular music, using automobiles for pleasure, and generally taking part in Savannah urban life. The local Shrimp Creek taverns are for some young persons the closest emulators of the pattern of pleasure in Savannah. Some youths are not highly receptive to guidance by the deacons, but rather seek leadership in their own peer groups and emulate persons and groups in Savannah. The elders feel that the children are harder to control than formerly and that they are "weaker but wiser" than their parents were as children.

Other urban influences include the employment of an urban ministry, the occasional visits of choirs and other singing groups between Savannah and Shrimp Creek churches, and the presence in two churches of a Savannah Methodist choir director who is introducing new patterns of singing.

Migration to the North also acts as an urbanizing influence. When persons return to the community to visit or to stay they bring not only Northern and general American ideas of social behavior but also urban ones.

Thus Shrimp Creek is changing from a relatively isolated, highly religious, tradition-oriented, rural fishing community to a suburban area with weakening community ties. It is being drawn to social change as a way of life, to the patterns of social etiquette and customs of the city, to higher educational standards, and to a somewhat different conception of the role of the church and religion in social life.

New leaders, who emphasize educational qualifications, social class distinctions, and business and other economic activities, and who have as their field of operations the general area south of Savannah, and even the city itself, are beginning to appear among the newcomers' group and even among a few of the older families. It is still a diffuse and not highly organized leadership. The deacons, particularly the old ones, are conservative, but they realize that the social and economic possibilities are limited in the community and that they are greater in Savannah and elsewhere. They are not anxious for their sons to become fishermen. They have regrets about the passing of the old way of life, and most of them do not wish actively to engage in change, but only in two areas do they strongly oppose it: with regard to church ritual and procedure, where they oppose some of the interests of the ministers; and in their opposition to the newer settlers gaining positions of leadership in the community. Their conservatism in these areas is associated with their desire to maintain their position in the community and to direct the carrying out of normal community activities. The deacons thus accept change as long as it is not a direct threat to their position of leadership (in terms of being replaced by others), but they do not reject change that is leading to the eventual disintegration of the community. If anyone is to lead they wish to; but they are apparently willing to accept the likelihood that migration and and urbanization will eventually eliminate or further minimize their position.

Unlike many acculturation situations, there is no well-organized leadership within the community for change. The members of the newcomers' group hold little influence in the community, and their orientation is to a large extent beyond its borders. They are directing change through community organizations, rather than through leadership within specific communities, but even on this level they are not as yet very effective. In short, a characteristic pattern is that strong leadership or group organization for or against change in the community is lacking. Change occurs through broadening of neighborhood ties with other rural communities south of Savannah and through emulation of urban economic, social and religious patterns, and through family, friendship and work contacts. To some extent the lack of strong leadership is related to the caste system. Caste helps keep wealth and class distinctions small in the rural setting and precludes power controls over financial resources. There is greater potentiality for the development of power and class distinctions in the urban scene, and there we find more highly organized African American leadership. In the absence of caste in Shrimp Creek, we could not be sure that stronger leadership would have evolved, since it is frequently lacking in non-caste American rural areas; but the potentiality for its development would have been greater, particularly with the economic resources of shrimp fishing. The data suggest that in rural African American communities where caste is present, culture change will tend not to be strongly directed, but may still occur with rapidity despite this lack of leadership.

NOTES
[1]The research on which this paper is based was carried out using traditional anthropological field methods during the summer of 1950 with the aid of a grant from the Department of Anthropology, Northwestern University, Evanston, Illinois.

[2]This is not the real name of the community.

[3]A few Methodists live in the community, most of them fairly recent settlers.

[4]They came mainly from St. Catharines Island, but some also migrated from Ossabaw Island and Harris Neck. A few older persons living in Shrimp Creek at the time of the study actually were born on the islands.

[5]Lodges, fraternal organizations, political clubs, and self-improvement associations are all lacking. A few men, particularly some of the deacons, belong to such organizations in Savannah.

[6]This person is a Sunday School teacher, equivalent in social status to a deacon, who prefers not to become a deacon. A retired school teacher lives in the community but has little authority in it.

[7]These provide small sums of money for the ill and some care and attention from

fellow members. Members who die have a portion of their burial expenses paid by the society, whose members take part in the funeral.

[8]Several local savings clubs also exist in the community, some organized annually to provide money at Christmas time, and others on a permanent basis. These clubs are generally controlled by the deacons and their wives.

[9]Several of the deacons denied these statements or expressed the feeling that the newcomers were not readily interested in the community.

[10]Some members of the young adult generation have continued their education at Savannah State College, learning skilled trades in particular, though they are often able to obtain only laboring positions following the completion of their training.

REFERENCES

BASCOM, W.R. (January-March 1941) Acculturation Among the Gullah Negroes, "American Anthropologist, XLIII" pp. 43-50; Drums and Shadows: Survival Studies among the Georgia Coastal Negroes.

DAVIS, A., GARDNER, M.R. (1941) Deep South: A Social Anthropological Study of Caste and Class. Chicago.

DAVIS, A., DOLLARD, J. (1940) Children of Bondage. Washington.

GEORGIA WRITERS PROJECT (1940) Savannah Unit. Athens, Georgia: Works Progress Administration.

JOHNSON, G.G. (1930) A Social History of the Sea Islands. Chapel Hill.

KAUFMAN, H.F. et al (1954) Toward a Delineation of Community Research, Social Series No. 14. Mississippi State College: pp. 35-36. Studies of predominantly urban areas in the South have dealt more fully with these aspects of Negro life.

KISER, C.V. (1932) Sea Island to City. New York: Columbia University Studies in History: Economics and Public Law, No. 368. Almost every family from which a genealogy was collected had some record of movement to northeastern cities. Once a member of a family is established there, others often follow. The pattern of migration seems similar to that described by Kiser for the Sea Islands at an earlier time.

LEWIS, H. (1955) Blackways of Kent. Chapel Hill. pp. 168-71.

LEWIS, op. cit., pp. 190-193.

TURNER, L.D. (1949) Africanisms in the Gullah Dialect. Chicago: University of Chicago Press.

WOOFTER, T.J. (1930) Black Yeomanry. Henry Holt. New York. The older residents of Shrimp Creek still speak the characteristic Sea Island dialect and possess some customs of probable African origin.

CHAPTER THIRTEEN

The Sea Islands as a Research Area

Juanita Jackson, Sabra Slaughter,
and J. Herman Blake

The recent rise in black consciousness has created an extraordinary interest in the study of black heritage and the preservation of black culture in America. Many scholars and students are turning their attention to African American cultural patterns which have been long ignored and often scorned. Black people are realizing more and more that these patterns exemplify key features of their heritage and may offer not only clues into the past, but also provide guides to survival in the future. As this interest gains momentum, African Americans should look toward the American South, particularly to its rural and isolated areas where so many of the unique elements of contemporary black culture have their roots.

The islands off the coast of South Carolina and Georgia, known commonly as the Sea Islands or Gullah area, represent some of the most outstanding opportunities to black scholars for research and study.[1] The unique history and geography of this region have combined to produce one of the most distinctive reservoirs of African American culture in the United States.

The Sea Islands begin just north of Georgetown, South Carolina, and continue south to the Florida border. It is estimated that there are approximately 1,000 islands along the coast of South Carolina separated from the mainland by marshes, alluvial streams and rivers. Some of the islands are bordered by the Atlantic Ocean and are as far as twenty miles or more from the mainland. They range in size from very small and uninhabitable islets, to Johns Island, South Carolina, the second largest

153

island in the United States. They were probably formed by silt washing down from the coastal plains and thus their soil is extremely fertile.

Since the islands are separated from the coast by marshes, creeks and rivers, they have not generally been accessible, except by boat, until fairly recently. Until the end of World War I, none of the islands were connected to the mainland or causeways. Beginning about 1915, construction was started on bridges, but it was not until 1940 that most of the islands had direct access to the mainland. Turner (1949) found in 1932 that some Sea Islanders had never visited the mainland. However, even today there are still inhabited islands in this area which are unconnected and can only be reached by boat. Some of these are as far as 18 miles from the nearest public dock on the mainland.

From their earliest settlement by Europeans, the Sea Islands have been the basis of a very profitable agriculture. During slavery the long-staple cotton grown here was considered the best available anywhere and brought very favorable profits on the world market. Until the twentieth century, life in the Sea Islands was organized around two crops, rice and cotton, or as one analyst puts it, "Queen Rice and King Cotton."

In the antebellum period the economy of the region was based almost wholly on slavery, and because of the labor-intensiveness of the crops, very large plantations developed in this area. The available data show that from the earliest period, the blacks outnumbered the whites by a substantial margin. For example, in 1800 there were 2,150 whites and 12,400 slaves in the Georgetown district, and by 1840 the same region contained 2,200 whites and 18,000 slaves. Similar conditions were found in the other parts of the Sea Islands.

The large plantation was typical throughout the region. Some whites owned entire islands containing thousands of acres of land, and maintained hundreds of slaves to till the soil. On many of these plantations and islands the only white persons present were the owner and the overseer, and in some cases there was no overseer. The work of the slaves was directed almost entirely by slave drivers and in some cases slave overseers.

The isolation of the islands and the large numbers of slaves meant that the influence of American white culture upon African and slave culture was minimal. Further enhancing the development of a unique black culture, was the continual importation of slaves directly from Africa. South Carolina residents felt that slaves had frequently been sent there from other areas because of misconduct. Therefore in the early part of the eighteenth century, South Carolina legislators imposed an excessive duty on slaves not brought directly from Africa. Consequently, the overwhelming number of slaves entering South Carolina during the eighteenth century came directly from Africa. This practice of importing slaves from Africa did not end with the imposition of the Slave Trade Act of 1808, however, for the isolation of the islands made them a prime location for slavetraders to land illegal cargoes of Africans. As late as 1858, Africans were imported into the Sea Islands (Howard 1963).

The emphasis on African-born slaves plus the extraordinary number of slaves in comparison with the whites, together with the isolation of the Sea Islands, meant there was a geographical, social and cultural basis for the retention of many elements of African culture in the Sea Islands and for the development of a distinctive African American culture.

Although the Sea Islands area has been of perennial interest to white sociologists and anthropologists who have produced an extensive literature on Gullah culture, this area has been hardly touched by black scholars. Most of the available social science literature on the area was published a generation or more ago. There is no contemporary published research which gives a comprehensive view of present-day Gullah culture.[2] A review of the earlier research—even the worst examples—provides exciting insight into life in the Sea Islands and shows some of the rich resources yet to be tapped.

It should be of grave concern to scholars that two of the most recent publications on contemporary life in the Sea Islands have been done by white observers who were untrained social scientists—who lived among the people for a short time, gained their confidence to some degree, captured a limited portion of their lives and presented quite distorted images of the culture.[3] In both cases, these works have aroused some hostility among the local residents and made it difficult for others to do the kind of quality research needed. There are a number of areas of obvious interest to black people which could benefit from contemporary research and study in the Sea Islands. We would like to suggest some possible topics for consideration and then suggest ways in which scholars might conduct this research and also make positive contributions to the lives of the people studied.

AFRICAN SURVIVALS AND SLAVERY

The question of African survivals has been one of long debate in this country. Sea Island research can provide us with further enlightenment on this subject. During the slave period many of the customs the people developed clearly reflected African culture, and postbellum conditions enhanced their retention. In recent research we have found birth and naming practices, styles of dress among women, the use of gourds and shell, language patterns, and local crafts which reflect distinct African roots. In some cases these practices have been attenuated and altered by modern technology, but they are sufficiently distinctive to be noticeable. A systematic analysis of contemporary manifestations of African culture in the Sea Islands is very much needed and cannot be long delayed if it is to be effective. Social change has reached the Islands and is altering these patterns rapidly.

Memories of slavery are fading fast and there are only a few short years left to conduct oral history research of the slave era. There are still many elderly blacks in the Sea Islands whose parents were slaves and who can provide us with a good understanding of the latter years of slavery from the point of view of those who went through that experience. The child of a slave, we have found, was very often raised by grand- or great-grandparents, and in some cases, their accounts can go back two or more generations into the slave experience. Diligent oral history research has led us to a number of exceptional informants, and we believe there are many others in the latter years of their lives who have extraordinary stories to tell, stories which will be available for only a few years more.

We are particularly interested in locating descendants of those Africans who came into the Sea Island area on the slave ship *Wanderer* in 1858. Even though the foreign slave trade was ended by law in 1808, slave traders continued to unload their cargoes of slaves directly from Africa into the Sea Islands until the middle of the nineteenth century. The last ship recorded to have landed a cargo of Africans in this area was the *Wanderer* which came to Jekyll Island, Georgia, in 1858 with 400 Africans, most of them males between 13 and 18 years of age. They were unloaded to the Dubignon Plantation and later about half of them were taken to the Butler and Tillman plantations near Hamburg in Edgefield County, South Carolina. Although the Africans were scattered throughout the South, a number of them remained in Georgia and South Carolina, within a radius of some thirty miles from where they had landed.

In 1905 and again in 1930 and 1940, a number of these Africans were located and photographed and interviewed. It seems quite feasible that given the ages of the Africans when they arrived, their grandchildren and possibly even some children may still be alive in the Sea Island area. Their memories could provide some important understandings, and if they possess old artifacts they could be extremely revealing.

The *Wanderer* was only one of a number of slave ships landing Africans in various portions of the South, and a research project to identify and interview the descendants of Africans who came to the United States in the middle of the nineteenth century seems quite feasible. It is quite likely that a considerable number of these descendants could be found in the Sea Islands because of the unique geography and history.

Another project which might grow out of the oral history research is a critique of the slave narrative collections. The Library of Congress collection of slave narratives has been an important resource for scholars who wish to study the nature of slavery and its impact upon black people. Our own explorations have left us with considerable doubts about the emphasis some people place on these data. This is not to say that the ex-slaves did not tell the truth as they saw it. We wish to question whether those who collected the narratives were competent to understand what they heard and to report it accurately. Interpretations based on these data may be very faulty.

We have found that in order to adequately collect narratives and understand the people it is necessary to have a wide knowledge of the history and geography of the area. One must be familiar with bodies of water, places, political and social events, as well as major calamities such as storms, earthquakes or fires. Any name that might come up in an interview must be placed into some context. Failure to do so may mean that the descriptions of the respondent will seem to be nonsensical or the researcher will not know what questions to ask or what leads to pursue.

Two examples illustrate this. We were recently interviewing an old gentleman on an island in Charleston County, South Carolina, when we casually remarked we were headed for Beaufort. This led him into a detailed description of festivities blacks used to hold in Beaufort. We found that blacks throughout the state came to celebrate Memorial Day in Beaufort. They called it "Decoration Day," however, because it was the day for decorating the graves of the Union soldiers buried in the National Cemetery at Beaufort. There was always a parade and celebration with speeches from the podium in the cemetery. While the practice still exists, it was a major event for South Carolina blacks until the late 1950s. In a later interview with an elderly resident in Beaufort County, we learned that everybody went to Beaufort (Port Royal Island) on Memorial Day, while on the 4th of July all the blacks gathered at St. Helena Island for festivities. In another series of interviews we learned of special Christmas festivals slaves used to hold and found that in some places they are still observed.

Our search through the historical literature and slave narrative collections for this area shows no mention whatsoever of these events. Undoubtedly there are many other local customs which enter the mind of a respondent, and interviewers of the ex-slaves may have missed many of them. As black scholars learn what it takes to do effective oral history with blacks, we may develop a detailed and incisive critique of the slave narrative collection.

BLACK GENEALOGY
The study of genealogy can have an extraordinary impact on black consciousness. It will provide valuable insights into slavery and survival of

blacks in the United States. There are many cultural patterns and survival techniques which will be illuminated through genealogical research which not only penetrates slavery, but also the slave trade and the African past.[4] It may be possible to develop African roots by tracing some family lines back three or four generations. There are many records in Bibles, deeds of manumission, plantation records, property transfers, tax records and other sources which can open our understanding of the genealogical links of families. We have found that many of these records are still in the possession of Sea Island residents. The collection, preservation and analysis of these records is an eminently feasible research project.

CONTEMPORARY GULLAH CULTURE

An analysis of contemporary Gullah culture is very much needed, for the developments of the past 20 to 30 years have brought significant changes to the Sea Islands and altered many of the classic patterns studied by earlier scholars. The area manifests an extraordinary syncretism of African American, and slave patterns, plus an overlay of contemporary American life and culture. It is probably the most unique pattern of black culture to be found anywhere.[5]

A. The Shadow of Slavery

There is no question that the shadow of slavery is still to be found in some unusual circumstances and has a profound effect upon contemporary life. One of the issues that might be explored is the social and psychological effect of retaining slave names in the same places where that slavery was served. In one area we came upon an island which had the name of the planter who owned it. The plantation and mansion of the same name were still there, and throughout the area were many blacks and whites with the same name. As we observed black-white interaction in public places such as post offices and stores, we got the impression that the existence of a common name for blacks and whites with a slave history affected their perceptions of each other and their subsequent interaction. We began to raise questions about the degree to which contemporary interaction among blacks and whites might be structured by an historical consciousness.

B. Survival Patterns

Given the isolation and independence of the Sea Islanders, they had to develop survival patterns which can still be studied and which provide excellent examples of Gullah culture as well as insights into the ability of a people to conquer their circumstances. One pattern we have found most instructive is in the philosophy of time and the utilization of time. In many of the islands we have found that the older blacks have a different relationship to time than many younger and "up-to-date" blacks. In some places we find that the older people do not gamble or play cards, they rarely read and seldom spend time watching television. They do keep very busy fishing, hunting, working in the fields or doing household chores. When they are not engaged in these activities, however, we find that a major time-consuming mechanism is reminiscing and telling stories. Indeed, the raconteur provides an important form of pleasurable activity and is highly respected. In almost every community we have found at least one and usually several raconteurs—those who can take old accounts and stories and recount them in a distinctive fashion, usually acting out every part to the amusement of everyone else. Others will take almost any topic, historical or contemporary, and weave it into an incredible story spontaneously: waiting for a storm to pass so that they can go fishing, waiting for a meeting to begin, or the like. These long and elaborate stories are not only humorous, they also help pass the hours so that time does not hang heavy when people are waiting.

Other survival mechanisms are related to coping with the environment. One island we have studied is very isolated and until recently, there was no way of foretelling the weather even though the men went out in their small flat-bottomed rowboats to fish daily. One resident developed the ability to sense atmospheric changes and for over 25 years, made his living as a weatherman. He would go about the island with his daily report and the people would reward him with staples. We have found his reports to be generally reliable.

In seeking sustenance from the nearby waters, the people have developed the ability to attract wild porpoises and use them for fishing. Anglers will row their boats into the waters and then rap on the sides or bottom with a special rhythm which attracts porpoises to the boat, scaring the fish ahead of them. The porpoises will then circle the boat, feeding on the fish and keeping them in a tight bunch for the angler. When casting with a net, the men will attract the porpoises to scare the fish into the shallow waters.

During the winter when the water is often too cold or rough for fishing from a boat, a man will stand on the dock watching for porpoises to come swimming by in the river. When he spots some he will wait until they are a certain distance away and then cast his net into the school of fish fleeing in front of the porpoise. The abrupt arrival of the net scares the fish back toward the porpoises. The porpoises will then remain in the area for a while scaring the fish toward the man with the net while he scares the fish back toward the porpoises. It is a most efficacious style of fishing and produces a very good catch. When porpoises are in the area it is not unusual for a man to catch ten fish with each cast of his net.[6]

C. Socio-Psychological Issues

The social and psychological issues are profound, rarely articulated and little understood. We believe it would be insightful to study the consequences of growing up in an area where blacks have been a substantial numerical majority since the beginning of the country. Consequently they may have different self perceptions and attitudes as compared to blacks raised in other areas. Furthermore, Sea Island blacks have frequently owned their land since the years before Reconstruction. Many of them do not know what it means to pay rent or a mortgage, and to some the very concepts are meaningless. The ownership of land and the abundance of crop yields may have important psychological consequences which we have not begun to understand.[7] To add to these issues is the fact that the people were very isolated from meanstream culture until recently, and they could only survive by developing a posture of self-sufficiency and independence.

We would assert that the presence of black majority, the ownership of fertile lands from their first awareness, and the isolation and independence have created a unique psyche for blacks in the Sea Island area. Its nature and its social-psychological consequences are worthy of in-depth exploration and analysis.

We have seen their consequences in a number of ways in our research. We constantly encounter elderly blacks whose knowledge of and acquaintance with whites is very limited. They have not had to interact with whites or the majority culture in the same way as blacks in other parts of this country. Many of them have a fierce kind of pride and a lack of fear which is seldom seen in other places. The self-doubts and sense of inadequacy and inferiority often cited as characteristic of the black psyche are not found to the same degree in our Sea Islands research.

D. Protest and Political Activities

After the decline of cotton with the arrival of the boll weevil, many of the men left the islands to work on dredges in the nearby waters. We have talked with numerous men who have described labor strikes they organized because of the inequities they experienced. The same is true of the women who worked in the oyster factories and fishing industries which grew up in the islands. Well-organized and successful strikes were the rule whenever the people felt they were being treated unfairly. In one instance, we discovered a benevolent (preservation) society which was organized out of a strike and continues to exist with its own property and buildings for meetings.

A second example of pride and independence is to be found in the civil rights activism and political organizing of blacks in the Sea Islands. Some of the earliest support for the Civil Rights Movement of the 1950s and 1960s came out of the Sea Islands, and Martin Luther King developed some of his major campaigns during retreats to the area.

Our research gives preliminary indication that some of the local independence and activism has its roots in the Reconstruction Era and the black majority in the area. On one island we talked with an old woman who was considered the spark for a major campaign of black registration and voting back in the 1950s which has sent a number of people to the legislature. We asked her reasons for starting these efforts, and after some thought she pointed out that her first example of voting came from her father. When she was a child he would take the family in the wagon and journey to the polls and cast his vote in every election. This was at a time when the Reconstruction constitutions were still extant and blacks held many elected positions in the area. She said that she had no other examples of voting until she met some local leaders in the 1950s who began to press for integrated schools.

Enlightened by this insight, we then asked each elderly respondent when they first registered to vote. A large portion of them had registered before 1910 (when the constitution changed) and they had maintained their registration constantly over the years. When the Civil Rights and political effort began in the 1950s, many of the elderly people played very active roles, sometimes serving as temporary heads of committees and programs until the younger people had stepped in. The Sea Islands offer us an excellent opportunity to study the nineteenth century roots of contemporary black activism.

These are brief and preliminary observations on some of the cultural resources for black people which can be studied in the Sea Islands. Although similar issues can be researched with valuable results among black people wherever they may be found, we believe that the Sea Islands offer an unusual and unique opportunity to pursue such research.

BLACK SCHOLARS IN BLACK COMMUNITIES

We do not subscribe to the view that because a scholar is black his or her research will necessarily be in the best interest of the communities or people studied. While blackness may give access and some community acceptance, it does not guarantee non-exploitation. Therefore, we hold that blacks who are scholars should not be permitted to enter the community to do research simply because they desire to do so. There must be some way of verifying their integrity and the uses to which they will put their results, for research can also be used against the communities if we are not careful about what we do and how we use the data.

We submit that scholars who wish to study black communities should be held to a philosophy of service to the community through research; that is, in conducting research in any community, we scholars must work with the residents to assist them in meeting their needs as they perceive them. In so doing, we may gain the material we need for our research, but research should be coincidental to service.[8] We should no longer be satisfied with scholars generating statistics about communities in which the statistic that most concerns the people is their low income.

An efficacious way to conduct such research in black communities is in coordination with local agencies which are community-controlled and provide effective services to the people. Such agencies often have access to a wide variety of information about the community and can introduce the scholar to all the sources of information needed. At the same time, such agencies often have need for information and material in written form for funding or other purposes which the scholar can easily provide. The research of scholars in black communities should be "coordinated research" so that the agencies can get needed materials and data at the same time the scholars are getting the results that they seek. Such coordination, if handled well, will reduce the risk of community exploitation and produce short-range and positive results for the community.[9]

NOTES

[1]The initial research upon which this essay is based was supported by the Faculty Research Committee of the University of California at Santa Cruz. Subsequent research has been supported by the Kinte Library Project funded by the Carnegie Corporation and headed by Dr. Leonard Jeffries of California State University. We gratefully acknowledge the support of these agencies.

We have received helpful criticisms of earlier drafts of this material from Dilip Basu, Courtney Brown, William Clement, Jr., Myrna Davenport, David Franklin, Diane Lewis, M. Lee Montgomery, Douglas Perkins, William "Bill" Saunders, Carrol Seron, Janice Shroud, Nancy Turner, George Trask, Rita Van Lew and Janice Willis. Extraordinary clerical assistance has been given by Miss Sadie L. Brown. We are deeply indebted to our colleagues for their advice and criticism. Only the authors are responsible for the contents of this article and any errors it may contain.

²Willie Lee Rose has published an excellent historical account of the Port Royal Experiment of the 1860s in her *Rehearsal for Reconstruction*, New York: Bobbs-Merrill, 1964; and Peter Woods (1974) has an excellent history on blacks in colonial South Carolina, *Black Majority*, New York: Knopf, but there is still no good research available to the public on contemporary Sea Island culture.

³See: Guy and Candie Carawan, *Ain't You Got a Right to the Tree of Life?*, New York: Simon and Schuster, 1966; and Pat Conroy, *The Water is Wide*, Boston: Houghton Mifflin, 1972.

One of Carawan's respondents told us in 1967, shortly after the book was published: "I talked on a recorder once; I will never talk on a recorder again." Another gave us a very painful account of the deceptive ways some deeply personal material was elicited. Johns Island, the location of Carawan's work, is Dr. Blake's family home. While his book is accurate, it covers only a limited portion of the lives of the people. Therefore, it has created a hostility to research on the part of island residents. Even when they consent to interviews, they are rarely candid and open.

In recent visits (1973 and 1974) to Yamacraw Island, the object of Conroy's book, many of the residents spoke freely to us of their hostility to Conroy for his distorted characterization of their lives. One elderly resident leafed through a copy of the book, looked carefully at the pictures, and then commented, "Poor Conroy, sitting there watching them die, and nobody to testify." We have lived in the homes of the people of this island and worked with them since 1967. We find Conroy's characterization of the men of the island (pp. 86-95) to be shallow and distorted as well as inaccurate. This book is such a vulgarization of the lives of the people of Yamacraw that they asked the author to leave the island in the summer of 1972 when he came to present them with copies of the book.

In spite of the limited view of the people the book presents, it has been made into a major movie, "Conrack," staring John Voight and Paul Winfield. The movie, however, had to be made in another location because the film makers could not get any cooperation in the Yamacraw area.

Conroy has shared some of the profits of his venture with his subjects, however. Each student in his classroom received a thousand dollars on his or her eighteenth birthday.

⁴The extraordinary research of Alex Haley and the universal response to his story indicates the importance of genealogical research. A program of research has been institutionalized in the Kinte Library Project, funded by the Carnegie Corporation and a wide range of investigations are presently underway both in Africa and the United States.

⁵The term Gullah or "Geechee" is frequently used to describe the distinctive linguistic patterns of native blacks. The origin of the term Gullah is uncertain. It is generally believed to be a derivation of the Africa Gola or Gora, names of African tribes from Liberia, east of the city of Monrovia. Others hold it is a derivation of the African Angola, since many slaves were brought to the Sea Islands from Angola.

The word Gullah is also used to refer to the unique cultural patterns of Sea Island blacks. "Geechee," often used by blacks, comes from the Ogeechee River, one of the prominent waterways in the area. See: Turner, op. cit., and Mason Crum,

Gullah, Chapel Hill: Duke University Press, 1940, reprinted in 1968 by Negro Universities Press, New York.

[6]For a fascinating account of a similar phenomenon among West African fishermen, see: R.G. Busnell, "Symbiotic Relationship Between Man and Dophins," *Transactions of the New York Academy of Sciences*, Series II, 35 (February 1973), 112-131. We are indebted to William Doyle, Professor of Biology, University of California at Santa Cruz, for bringing this reference to our attention.

[7]We are grateful to Ike Tribble, Jr., of Mills College for bringing this significant point to our attention.

[8]Our position is similar to the concept of the "Involved Observer" developed by Kenneth Clark. See: *Dark Ghetto*, New York: Harper and Row, 1965. We take a stronger position, however, in that we hold that not only should the observer be involved, he or she must be accountable to the community. This is a very difficult position to maintain and do effective research in the community, but it is not impossible. We think that this position does not reduce objectivity but it does increase access and insight. However, it does place an extraordinary drain on the scholar. The rewards are even more extraordinary.

[9]The research described in this article is coordinated with Penn Community Services of St. Helena Island, South Carolina, under the directorship of Mr. John Gadson, and the Beaufort-Jasper Comprehensive Health Services, Ridgeland, South Carolina, under the directorship of Mr. Thomas Barnwell. We are deeply indebted to these agencies, their directors and staffs for their outstanding cooperation and support. However, there is no implied endorsement of these views by either agency.

REFERENCES

EASTERBY, J.H., ed. (1945) The South Carolina Rice Plantation. Chicago: University of Chicago Press, p. 8.

HOWARD, W.S. (1963) American Slavers and the Federal Law. Berkeley: University of California Press: pp. 144-146.

MONTGOMERY, C.J. (Oct.-Dec. 1908) Survivors From the Cargo of the Slave Yacht Wanderer. American Anthropologist, 10:pp. 611-623.

TURNER, L.D. (1949) Africanisms in the Gullah Dialect. Chicago: University of Chicago Press, reprinted in 1969 by Arno Press, New York: p. 5.

WELLS, T.H. (1967) The Slave Ship Wanderer. Athens: University of Georgia Press: pp. 86-87.

CHAPTER FOURTEEN

Selected Sources in the Folklore and Folklife of the Sea Islands
Mary Arnold Twining

L ong celebrated as a quaint, picturesque area with an air of exotic mystique, the Sea Islands have not been done justice in the literature. But sorting out the sources available to us, we can begin to put some of the old and new attitudes in perspective.

It is very easy to second-guess the works of the past and pass judgment on their glaring inadequacies from the safe vantage point of hindsight. We must, however, take into account the temper of the times which produced these earlier works and glean such information as we can from the texts in spite of the styles and attitudes of yesteryear.

Rehearsal for Reconstruction (Rose 1964) is an historical investigation of the persons who came to the Port Royal area to teach during the Civil War. Rose used primary sources to great advantage in illuminating the early Reconstruction era and showing how the foundations were laid down for some of the social and cultural conditions noted in the Johnson (1930), Johnson (1930), Woofter (1930), and Kiser (1932) group publications later on. Rose's prize-winning work illuminates a period and area little known in rigorous historical scholarship and brings together many scattered sources to do it.

The two oldest folklore collections are Jones (1888) and Christensen (1892). Jones, a member of a Southern plantation-owning family, seems to typify the paternalistic attitudes of that group. Christensen, on the other hand, came to the Sea Islands from elsewhere. She was an early member of the American Folklore Society, coming at the information from another perspective—note the use (1892) of the term "Afro-American" in the title of her work.

There are several linguistic articles in this list—Blok (1959), Hair (1965), Hall (1950), Johnson (1967), Krapp (1924), and McDavid (1964), which should be located together with some examples of more up-to-date works as a group of relevant readings. Krapp (1924) is at one end of the spectrum representing the exclusively European-oriented school of thought. Hair's (1965) article on the Sierra Leone idioms in Gullah would be on the other end as it stresses the African provenience of the Gullah language. Baird's (1980) article is a response to Johnson's (1967) views on the disappearance of Gullah. There have been a number of dissertations done more recently by Cunningham (1970), Nixon (1976), Guthrie (1977), Nichols (1975), and Vass (1971).

The Writers Project of the 1930s depression era brought *Drums and Shadows* which has been used over and over by subsequent scholars both for information about Afro-American folklore as well as the Sea Island area.

In the 1940s, Herskovits' book *Myth of the Negro Past* included many examples taken from Sea Island life. It is a major work for Afro-American anthropology as a whole and the Sea Islands in particular. It is still worthwhile as an introduction to the field in spite of its age, as it tackles the problem of attitudes. Whitten and Szwed (1970) edited the overall look at Afro-American anthropology since Herskovits; entitled *Afro-American Anthropology: Contemporary Perspectives*, the book includes only a brief look at the Sea Island area in three contributions to the picture essay. Abrahams and Szwed (1978) have done a comprehensive, two-volume bibliography of folklore in the African World which includes a number of entries on the Sea Islands.

The fictional sources are valuable in their own way. Peterkin (1924-1934), Simms (1859), and Heyward (1929) present major works about the Sea Island area. Peterkin includes a lot of folklife detail that actually makes her books useful mines of information. Heyward, famous for his book *Porgy* (1925), the basis for Gershwin's *Porgy and Bess* which takes place in the Lowcountry area, also wrote other material, using that area as background, one of which is *Mamba's Daughters* (1929).

A miscellaneous group of articles may be useful for background material and could add to people's understanding of the lives of the persons in the culture. In this group, Mednick (1956), Pollitzer (1964), Szwed (1970), and others are included. Szwed's (1970) article points out that the Sea Islands form a link with the African past in a review of the existing scholarship available to him at the time of writing. Mednick (1956) and Pollitzer (1964) are of interest to physical anthropologists, but also serve to lend scientific credence to subjects often treated with mysticism and doubt, as shown in Herskovits' discussion of the "myths" of the African past. The sickle cell phenomenon has only comparatively recently been recognized in the popular press, though the information has been available since 1956 at least. Pollitzer's information on blood types establishes the genetic or physical links with the West African population. It is useful to have documentation to validate attempts to extend the scope of the African-American continuum from the physical to the cultural.

Much of the research and the works resulting from it has been done on the Port Royal area, which includes St. Helena, Ladies Island, Dataw and many others. The more northerly islands around Charleston have been little dealt with. Guy and Candie Carawan (1967) lived on Johns Island for four years and produced, *Ain't You Got a Right to the Tree of Life*. This book is composed of the testimonies of the people of the River Road segment of Johns Island chiefly and fine pictures by Robert Yellin. The long sub-title, *The People of Johns Island, South Carolina—Their Faces, Their Words and Their Songs*, truly tells us what the book is about. The Carawan's book is one of the few sources that deal with these circum-Charleston islands. The first article in the bibliography under my name was written by my friend and mentor, W.C. Saunders and myself over a year's time. It was a cumbersome way to do it, but included the person-in-the-culture having input into the scholarship.

Betsy Fancher's *The Lost Legacy of Georgia's Golden Isles* (1971) is a mixture of useful information, mysticism, ecology, and impressions of the Georgia Sea Islands.

Fanny Kemble's (1961) book has the advantage of being written by a person outside our culture. Originally written in 1831-32, it gives us a different perspective on the plantation situation from her position as the wife of Pierce Butler, who owned two islands off the coast of Brunswick, Georgia. Her book provides useful information on conditions in the family lives of the enslaved Africans and the disruption in family continuity which could be caused by their owners in the pre-war South.

A handsomely published book is *Face of an Island* (Dabbs 1971). It is a fine collection of photographs, some of which were taken in the first decade of this century and a few somewhat later, around 1915-20. The glass plates containing the photos were hidden away for a long time and were discovered and assembled for publication by Ms. Dabbs in time for the bicentennial year 1976. It is a group of primary documents of some aspects of the lifestyle of the African American population on St. Helena, South Carolina, and surrounding islands.

Lorenzo Dow Turner's (1949) work really formed the watershed between the older European-oriented scholarship represented in Krapp's essay and the new Africa-oriented scholarship. Turner's book, which was not published for an unconscionably long time after it was finished, has been reissued; it is a very valuable work, not only for Sea Islanders, but Afro-Americans as well. He is criticized for his research methods or lack of them, but given an over forty years' lapse between the research and our present-day linguistic knowledge, it seems both justifiable and explicable. The historic value of his work remains undimmed.

Books having to do with African American families such as Billingsley (1968) and Staples (1978) do not deal specifically with the Sea Islands. Gutman (1976) in his massive work, does write about the Sea Island region as a locus of some historical development of the Afro-American family. The special issue of the *Journal of Black Studies* devoted to Sea Island culture, edited by Twining and Baird (1980), is a collection of articles which had their first appearance in that publication.

This selected bibliography is intended to be a useful reference guide for continued interest in the Sea Island area and African American family life. Some of the books have bibliographies of their own which lead to further studies. The information is still very scattered, and few definitive modern works on the Sea Islands are in circulation. We look forward to the publication of such works as Herman Blake's tome on Daufuskie Island and other volumes promising to increase our knowledge from reliable sources.

BIBLIOGRAPHY
ABRAHAMS, R. and SZWED, J. (1978) *Afro-American Folk Culture.* Philadelphia: ISHI.

ALBANESE, A.G. (1970) *The Plantation as a School. The Sea Islands of Georgia and South Carolina: A Test Case 1800-1860.* Ed.D. Dissertation, Rutgers University.

ALLEN, W.F., WARE, C.P., GARRISON, L.A. eds. (1867) *Slave Songs of the United States.* New York: A. Simpson and Co., Reprinted Books for Library Press (1971) Freeport, New York.

ALLSTON, E. (1923) *Chronicles of Chicora Wood.* New York.

AMES, M. (1906) from *A New England Woman's Diary in Dixie in 1865.* New York: Negro University Press.

ANONYMOUS (1948) "Note on Gullah." *South Carolina Historical and Genealogical Magazine,* Vol. 50: pp. 56-57.

ARROWWOOD, M.D., HAMILTON, T.F. (1928) "Nine Negro Spirituals (1850-1861) from Lower South Carolina." *Journal of American Folklore,* Vol. 41: pp. 579-584.

BAIRD, K.E. (1980) Guy B. Johnson Revisited: Another Look at Gullah. *Journal of Black Studies* 19/4: 425-435.

BALLANTA-TAYLOR, N.G.J. (1925) *St. Helena Island Spirituals.* New York: Schirmer.

BAMBARA, T.C., ed. (1968) *The Black Woman.* N.Y.: New American Library.

BASCOM, W. (1941) "Acculturation Among Gullah Negroes." *American Anthropologist*, Vol. 43: pp. 43-50.

BASCOM, W. (Dec. 1941) "Gullah Folk Beliefs Concerning Childbirth." Andover, Mass. Paper at American Folklore Society.

"THE BASKET WEAVERS OF CHARLESTON." (Oct. 1970) *Southern Living*. pp. 22-26.

BASS, J. (1972) *Porgy Comes Home: South Carolina After 300 Years*. Columbia (South Carolina): R.L. Bryan.

BENJAMIN, S.G. (Nov. 1878) "The Sea Islands." *Harper's*. p. 255.

BENNETT, J. (Oct. 1908) "Gullah: A Negro Patois." *South Atlantic Quarterly*. pp. 332-347. See also (Jan. 1909) pp. 39-62.

BILLINGSLEY, A.C. (1968) *Black Families in White America*. Englewood Cliffs, N.J.: Prentice Hall.

BLACKING, J. (1967) *Venda Children's Songs*. Johannesburg: Witwatersrand University Press.

BLACKMAN, J.K. (April 22, 1880) "The Sea Islands of South Carolina 1865-1880." *Charleston News and Courier*.

BLOK, H.P. (Sept. 1959) "Annotations to Mr. Turner's 'Africanisms in the Gullah Dialect.' " *Lingua*, 8: pp. 306-321.

BOTUME, E.A. (1893) *First Days Among the Contrabands*. Boston: Lee and Shepard, reprint N.Y.: Arno, 1968.

BOYLE, V.F. (1900) *Devil Tales*. New York and London: Harper Brothers.

BRADLEY, F.W. (1937) "Southern Carolina Proverbs." *Southern Folklore Quarterly*, Vol. 1: pp. 57-101.

BRADLEY, F.W. (1937) "Gullah Proverbs." *Southern Folklore Quarterly*, Vol. 1: pp. 99-101.

BRADLEY, F.W. (Apr. 1948-Nov. 1951) "A Word-List from South Carolina." *American Dialect Society*, Vol. 9-16: pp. 10-73.

BREMER, F. (1860) *The Homes of the New World. Impressions of America*. 2 vols. N.Y.: Harper Brothers.

CARAWAN, G. and C. (1967) *Ain't You Got a Right to the Tree of Life?* New York: Simon and Schuster.

CARAWAN, G. (1964) "The Living Folk Heritage of the Sea Islands." *Sing Out!* 14: 29-32.

CARAWAN, G. (June-July, 1960) "Spiritual Singing in the South Carolina Sea Islands." *Caravan*, Vol. 19-20: pp. 20-25.

CARAWAN, G. and C., compilers. (1963) *We Shall Overcome*. New York: Oak Publications.

CARAWAN, G. and C., compilers. (1968) *Freedom is a Constant Struggle*. N.Y.: Oak Publications.

CARTER, H. (1978) "Kongo Survivals in U.S. Gullah: An Examination of Turner's Material." Paper at 2nd Biennial Conference of the Society of Caribbean Linguistics at Cave Hill Campus University of the West Indies, Barbados, W.I. July 17-20.

CARUTHERS, W. (1867) *The Kentuckians*. N.Y.: Harpers.

CATE, M.D. (1930) *Our Todays and Yesterdays, A Story of Brunswick and the Coastal Islands.* Brunswick, Georgia: Glover Brothers. (1972) Reprinted Spartanburg, South Carolina, Reprint Co.

CATE, M.D. and WIGHTMAN, O.S. (1955) *Early Days of Coastal Georgia.* St. Simon Island, Georgia: Fort Frederica Historical Association.

CHAMBERLAIN, A.F. (1890) "Negro Creation Legend." *Journal of American Folklore,* Vol. 3: p. 302.

CHANDLER, A.D. (May 1946-Nov. 1946) "The Expansion of Barbados." *Journal of the Barbados Museum and Historical Society,* Vol. 13: pp. 3-4, pp. 106-135.

CHASE, J.W. (1971) *Afro-American Art and Craft.* New York: Van Nostrand and Reinhold.

CHATELAIN, H. (1895) "Some Causes of the Retardation of Negro Progress." *Journal of American Folklore,* Vol. 8: pp. 177-184.

CHILDS, J.R. (1940) *Malaria and the Colonization of the Carolina Low Country, 1526-1696.* Baltimore: Johns Hopkins University Press.

CHRISTENSEN, A.M.H. (1892) *Afro-American Folklore Told Round the Cabin Fires on the Sea Islands of South Carolina.* Boston: Cupples. (1969) Reprinted, New York: Negro University Press.

CHRISTENSEN, A.M.H. (1894) "Spirituals and Shouts of Southern Negroes." *Journal of American Folklore,* Vol. 7: pp. 154-155.

CLARKE, J.H. (1975) "The Black Family in Historical Perspective." *Journal of Afro-American Issues,* Nos. 3 and 4.

COHEN, H. (1958) "Burial of the Drowned Among the Gullah Negroes." *Southern Folklore Quarterly,* 22: 93-97.

COHEN, H. (1957) "Caroline Gilman and the Negro Boatman's Songs." *Southern Folklore Quarterly,* Vol. 21: pp. 116-117.

COLSON, E. (1962) "Family Change in Contemporary Africa." *Annals of the New York Academy of Sciences,* 96 (Jan.): 641-652.

CONROY, P. (1972) *The Water is Wide.* Boston: Houghton Mifflin.

CONROY, P. (1972) "Conrack You're Crazy." *Life* 72, 21 (June 2): 49-72.

COOLEY, R. (1926) *Homes of the Freed.* New York: New Republic Inc.

CRAM, M. (1917) *Old Seaport Towns of the South.* New York.

CRUM, M. (1940) *Gullah: Negro Life in the Carolina Sea Islands.* Durham, North Carolina: Duke University Press.

CUNNINGHAM, I.A.E. (1979) *A Syntactic Analysis of Sea Island Creole (Gullah).* Ph.D. University of Michigan.

DABBS, E.M. (1971) *Face of an Island.* New York: Grossman.

DARBY, L. (1917) "Ring Games from Georgia." *Journal of American Folklore.* Vol. 30: pp. 218-221.

DAVIS, G. (1976) "African-American Coil Basketry in Charleston County, S.C.: Affective Characteristics of an Artistic Craft in a Social Context." *American Folklife.* Austin: University of Texas Press.

DRUMS AND SHADOWS. (1940) Georgia Writers Project, Athens: University of Georgia Press. (1972) Reprint, Spartanburg, South Carolina: The Reprint Co. (1972) New York: Doubleday, paper.

. EPSTEIN, D.J. "Slave Music in the United States Before 1860." *The Quarterly Journal of the Music Librarians Association* Summer II.

FANCHER, B. (1971) *The Lost Legacy of Georgia's Golden Isles.* New York: Doubleday. Photos.

FAUSET, A.H. (1925) "Folk Tales from St. Helena, South Carolina." *Journal of American Folklore,* Vol. 38: pp. 217-238.

FORTEN, C. (1864) "Life on the Sea Islands." *Atlantic Monthly.* (1941) Reprint, BROWN, S., et al eds.

FORTES, M. (1949) *The Web of Kinship Among the Tallensi.* London: Oxford University Press.

FORTES, M. (1950) "Kinship and Marriage Among the Ashanti." pp. 252-284 in A.R. Radcliffe-Brown and D. Forde (eds.) *African Systems of Kinship and Marriage.* London: Oxford University Press.

FOSTER, H. (1983) "African Patterns in the Afro-American Family." *Journal of Black Studies.* Dec. 14: 2, pp. 201-232.

FRAZIER, E.F. (1957) *The Negro in the United States.* New York: Macmillan.

FREEMAN, L.C. (1957) "The Changing Functions of a Folksong." *Journal of American Folklore,* Vol. 70: pp. 215-220.

GIBSON, C.D. (1948) *Sea Islands of Georgia: Their Geological History.* Athens, Georgia: University of Georgia Press.

GIBSON, H.E. (1962) "African Legacy: Folk Medicine Among the Gullahs." *Negro Digest* (August), XI: 10 pp. 77-80.

GOLD, P. (Autumn 1972) Reverend W.T. Goodwin from Easter Sunrise Sermon. *Alcheringa,* Vol. 4: pp. 1-14.

GONZALES, A. (1922) *Black Border.* Columbia, South Carolina: The State Co.

GONZALES, A. (1924) *The Captain: Stories of the Black Border.* Columbia, South Carolina: The State Co.

GONZALES, A. (1924) *Laguerre: A Gascon of the Black Border.* Columbia, South Carolina: The State Co.

GONZALES, A. (1924) *With Aesop Along the Black Border.* Columbia, South Carolina: The State Co.

GOODWIN, W.T. (Sept. 1970) "I've Been in the Storm So Long." *New World Outlook,* pp. 17-24.

GRAYDON, N.S. (1960) *Tales of Edisto.* Atlanta: Tupper and Love.

GREENBERG, J.H. (1940) "The Decipherment of the 'Benali Diary': A Preliminary Statement." *Journal of Negro History.* 25: 372-375.

GRIMKE, C. (FORTEN). (1953) *The Journal of Charlotte Forten,* with notes and intro. by R.A. Billington. New York: Dryden Press.

GRISWOLD, F. (1939) *A Sea Island Lady.* New York: William Morrow.

GUTHRIE, P. (1977) *Catching Sense: The Meaning of Plantation Membership Among Blacks on St. Helena Island, South Carolina.* Ph.D. Dissertation, University of Rochester.

GUTMAN, H.G. (1976) *The Black Family in Slavery and Freedom.* N.Y.: Random House.

HAIR, P.E.H. (1965) "Sierra Leone Idioms in the Gullah Dialect of American English." *Sierra Leone Language Review,* Vol. 4: pp. 79-84.

172   Sea Island Roots

HALL, R.A., Jr. (1950) "The African Substratum in Negro English." *American Speech*, Vol. 25: pp. 51-54.

HALL, R.A., Jr. (1952) "Pidgin English and Linguistic Change." *Lingua*, Vol. 3: p. 138.

· HALL, R.A., Jr. (1966) *Pidgin and Creole Languages*. Ithaca, New York: Cornell University Press.

HARRIS, J. (1896) *Story of Aaron Son of Ben Ali*. Boston: Houghton Mifflin.

HASKELL, J.A. (1891) "Sacrificial Offerings Among North Carolina Negroes." *Journal of American Folklore*, Vol. 4: pp. 267-269.

HAWKINS, J. (1896) "An Old Mauma's Folklore." *Journal of American Folklore*. 9: 129-131.

HERSKOVITS, M.J. (1941) *The Myth of the Negro Past*. Boston: Beacon Press. (1964) Reprinted, Boston: Beacon Press.

HEYWARD, D. (1925) *Porgy*. New York: The Literary Guild.

HEYWARD, D. (1929) *Mamba's Daughters*. New York: The Literary Guild.

HEYWARD, J., MRS. SEVERN (1923) *Brown Jacket*. Columbia, South Carolina: The State Co.

HIBBARD, A. (June 1926) "Aesop in Negro Dialect." *American Speech*, Vol. 2: p. 495.

HIGGINSON, T.W. (1869) *Army Life in a Black Regiment*. Boston: Beacon Press.

HIGGINSON, T.W. (June 1867) "Negro Spirituals." *Atlantic Monthly*, Vol. 19: pp. 685-694.

HILL, R.B. (1971) *The Strengths of Black Families*. New York: Emerson Hall.

HOLLAND, R.S., ed. (1912) *Letters and Diary of Laura M. Towne, Written from the Sea Islands of South Carolina, 1862-1884*. Cambridge, Massachusetts: Harvard University Press.

HUBBELL, J.B. (1954) "Negro Boatman's Song." *Southern Folklore Quarterly*, Vol. 18: pp. 244-245.

HUNT, C.M. (1979) *Oyotunji Village: The Yoruba Movement in America*. Washington: University Press of America.

JACKSON, B. (1967) *The Negro and His Folklore in 19th Century Periodicals*. Publications of the American Folklore Society, Biographical and Special Series. Austin, Texas and London: University of Texas Press.

JOHNSON, G.G. (1930) *A Social History of the Sea Islands*. Chapel Hill: University of North Carolina Press.

JOHNSON, G.B. (1930) *Folk Culture on St. Helena Island, South Carolina*. Chapel Hill: University of North Carolina Press.

JOHNSON, G.B. (1931) "The Negro Spiritual—A Problem of Anthropology." *American Anthropologist*, Vol. 33: pp. 157-171.

JOHNSON, G.B. (1949-50) "A Review of Africanisms in Gullah Dialect by Lorenzo Dow Turner." *Social Forces*, Vol. 28: pp. 458-459.

JOHNSON, G.B. (1967) "Gullah Dialect Revisited: 30 years Later." Given as a paper to the Annual Meeting of the American Anthropological Association, Washington, D.C.

JOHNSON, B.G. (1968) "The Gullah Dialect Revisited: A Note on Linguistic Acculturation." Whitten and Szwed, eds. *New World Negroes*, New York.

JONES, B. and HAWES, B.L. (1972) *Step it Down*. New York: Harper and Row.

JONES, C.C. (1888) *Negro Myths from the Georgia Coast*. Cambridge: Houghton Mifflin. (1969) Reprint Detroit: Singing Tree Press.

JONES, K.M. (1960) *Port Royal Under Six Flags*. Indianapolis: Bobbs-Merrill.

JONES-JACKSON, P.A. (1977) "Alive: African Tradition on the Sea Islands." *Negro Historical Bulletin* 46: 3 (Sept.): pp. 95-96, 106.

JONES-JACKSON, P.A. (1978) *The Status of Gullah: An Investigation of Convergent Processes*. Ann Arbor: University of Michigan.

JONES-JACKSON, P.A. (1978) "The Prayer Tradition in Gullah." *Journal of Religious Thought* 39: 1 (Spr-Summer) pp. 21-23.

JONES-JACKSON, P.A. (1983) "Contemporary Gullah Speech." *Journal of Black Studies*, 13: 3 March.

JOYNER, C.W. (1971) *Folksong in South Carolina*. Columbia: University of South Carolina Press.

JULIEN, C. and MARTIN, C. (1954) *Sea Islands to Sand Hills*. Columbia, S.C., University of South Carolina.

KEMBLE, F.A. (1961) *Journal of a Residence on a Georgia Plantation*. J.A. Scott, ed. New York: Alfred Knopf. Orig. (1835) Philadelphia: Carey, Lea and Blanchard.

KERRI, J.N. (1979) "Understanding the African Family: Persistence, Continuity and Change." *Western Journal of Black Studies* 3 (Spr.): 14-17.

KISER, C. (1932) *Sea Island to City*. New York: Columbia University Press.

KLOE, D.R. (1974) "Buddy Qwow: An Anonymous Poem Written in Gullah-Jamaican Dialect Written Circa 1800." *Southern Folklore Quarterly* 38: 2, pp. 81-90.

KOCHMAN, T. (1972) *Rappin' and Stylin' Out*. Urbana: University of Illinois Press.

KRAPP, C.P. (1924) "The English of the American Negro." *American Mercury*, Vol. 2: pp. 190-195.

LADNER, J. (1971) *Tomorrow's Tomorrow: The Black Woman*. Garden City, Doubleday.

LEIDING, H.K. (1910) *Street Cries of an Old Southern City*. Charleston, S.C.

LEIGH, F.B. (1883) *Ten Years on a Georgia Plantation (1886-1876)*. London: R. Bentley and Son. (1969) Reprint, New York: Negro Universities Press.

LINDSAY, N. (1974) *An Oral History of Edisto Island: Sam Gadsden Tells the Story*. Goshen, Indiana: Pinchpenny Press.

LIVINGSTONE, F.B. (1958) "Anthropological Implications of Sickle Cell Gene Distribution in West Africa." *American Anthropologist*, Vol. 60: pp. 533-562.

LOCKWOOD, J.P. (1925) *Darkey Sermons from Charleston County*. Columbia, South Carolina: The State Co.

LORING, E.N. (1976) *Charles C. Jones Missionary to Plantation Slaves, 1835-1847*. Ph.D. Dissertation, Vanderbilt University.

MAC MILLAN, D. (1926) "John Kuners." *Journal of American Folklore* 39: pp. 51-53.

MASON, J. (Fall 1960) "Etymology of Buckaroo." *American Speech*, Vol. 35: pp. 51-55.

MC ADOO, H.P. ed. (1981) *Black Families*. Beverly Hills, California: Sage Publications.

MC DAVID, R.I. (1964) "Post-vocalic -r in South Carolina—A Social Analysis." *Language in Culture and Society*, Hymes, D., ed., New York and London: Harper and Row, pp. 473-482.

MC DAVID, R.I. (Feb. 1951) "The Relation of the Speech of American Negroes to the Speech of Whites." *American Speech*, Vol. 26: pp. 3-17.

MC KIM, J.M. (Aug. 9, 1962) "Negro Songs." *Dwight's Journal of Music*, Vol. 19: pp. 148-149; also, in Jackson, B., ed., *The Negro and His Folklore in Nineteenth Century Periodicals*, pp. 57-60.

MEDNICK, L. and ORANS, M. (1956) "The Sickle Cell Gene: Migration vs. Selection." *American Anthropologist*, Vol. 58: pp. 293-395.

MILLER, M.E. (N.D.) *Slavery Days in Georgia*. Richland, Georgia.

MITCHELL, F. (1978) *Hoodoo Medicine*. Berkeley: Reed, Cannon and Johnson.

MORRIS, J.A. (1947) "Gullah in the Stories and Novels of W.G. Simms." *American Speech*, Vol. 22: pp. 46-53.

NEUFFER, C.H. (Winter 1955) "Some Edisto Island Names." *Names in South Carolina*, Vol. 2: p. 2.

NICHOLS, P.C. (1975) *Linguistic Change in Gullah: Sex, Age and Mobility*. Ph.D. Dissertation, Stanford University.

NIXON, N.M. (1971) *Gullah and Backwoods Dialect in Selected Works by William Gilmore Simms*. Ph.D. Dissertation, University of South Carolina.

NOBLES, W. (1974) "African Root and American Fruit: The Black Family." *Journal of Social and Behavioral Sciences*, 20: 52-64.

ODUM, H.W. (1911) "Folk Song and Folk Poetry as Found in the Secular Songs of the Southern Negroes." *Journal of American Folklore*, Vol. 24: pp. 255-294.

OTTENBERG, S. (1968) *Double Descent in an African Society: The Afikpo Village-Group*. Seattle: University of Washington.

PARRISH, L. (1942) *Slave Songs of the Georgia Sea Islands*. New York: Farrar and Strauss. (1965) Reprint, Hatboro, Pennsylvania.

PARSONS, E.C. (1923) *Folklore of the Sea Islands, South Carolina*. New York: American Folklore Society.

PARSONS, E.C. (1917) "Riddles from Andros I., Bahamas." *Journal of American Folklore*, Vol. 30: p. 275.

PERDUE, R.E., Jr. (1968) "African Baskets in South Carolina." *Economic Botany*, Vol. 22: pp. 289-292.

PETERKIN, J. (1924) *Green Thursday*. New York: Alfred Knopf.

PETERKIN, J. (1927) *Black April*. New York: Grosset and Dunlap.

PETERKIN, J. (1927) "Gullah." *Ebony and Topaz: A Collectanea*, ed., Johnson,

C.S., New York: National Urban League. Reprint, (1971) Freeport, New York: Reprint Books for Libraries Press.

PETERKIN, J. (1928) *Scarlet Sister Mary*. Indianapolis: Bobbs-Merrill.

PETERKIN, J. (1932) *Bright Skin*. Indianapolis: Bobbs-Merrill.

PETERKIN, J. (1933) *Roll Jordan, Roll*. New York: Robert O. Ballou.

PETERKIN, J. (1934) *A Plantation Christmas*. Boston: Houghton Mifflin.

PETERKIN, J. (1970) *Collected Short Stories of Julia Peterkin*. Durham, F., ed. Columbia, South Carolina: University of South Carolina Press.

PHILLIPS, U.B. (1929) *Life and Labor in the Old South*. Boston: Little, Brown.

PIERCE, E.L. (Sept. 1863) "The Freedom at Port Royal." *Atlantic Monthly*, Vol. 12: pp. 291-315.

PLAIR, S. (1972) *Something to Shout About: Reflections on the Gullah Spiritual*. Mt. Pleasant, S.C.: Molasses Lane Publishers.

POLLITZER, W.S. (1931) "The Negroes of Charleston: A Study of Hemoglobin, Types, Serology and Morphology." *American Journal of Physical Anthropology*, Vol. 16: pp. 241-263.

POLLITZER, W.S. et al. (1964) "Blood Factors and Morphology of the Negroes of James Island, Charleston (County), South Carolina." *American Journal of Physical Anthropology* (December) 22: 4.

POPKIN, Z.F. (1931) " Heaven Bound': An Authentic Negro Folk Drama out of Old Savannah." *Theatre Guild Magazine* Aug. 8, 1931: 14-17.

PRINGLE, E.W. (1913) *Patience Pennington, A Woman Rice Planter*. New York: Macmillan Co.

PUCKETT, N.N. (1926) *Folk Beliefs of the Southern Negro*. Chapel Hill: University of North Carolina Press.

PUCKETTE, C.C. (1944) *Old Mitt Laughs Last*. New York and Indianapolis: Bobbs-Merrill.

RAYMOND, J. (Sunday, Feb. 7, 1971) "Past, Present Meet in Georgia's Island." Review of Fancher in *Atlanta Journal and Constitution*.

RHAME, J.M. (1933) "Flaming Youth: A Story in Gullah Dialect." *American Speech*, Vol. 8: pp. 39-43.

RICE, J.H. (1936) *Glories of the Carolina Coast*. Columbus, South Carolina: R.L. Bryan Co.

RITTER, M. (1974) "South Carolina's Gullah Blacks." *The Great Escape*. New York/Toronto/London: p. 202.

ROSE, W.L. (1964) *Rehearsal for Reconstruction*. Indianapolis: Bobbs-Merrill.

SALE, J. (1929) *A Tree Named John*. Chapel Hill: University of North Carolina Press.

SALTER, P. (April 1968) "Changing Agricultural Patterns on the Sea Islands." *Journal of Geography*, Vol. 67: pp. 223-228.

"SEA ISLANDS: THE SOUTH'S SURPRISING COAST." (March 1971) *National Geographic.*

SIMMS, W.G. (1843) *The Geography of South Carolina*. Charleston: Babcock.

SIMMS, W.G. (1859) *The Cassique of Kiawah*. New York: Redfield.

SIMMS, W.G. (1944) *The Yemassee*. London: Bruce and Wyld.

SMILEY, P. (July-Sept. 1919) "Folklore from Virginia, South Carolina, Georgia, Alabama and Florida." *Journal of American Folklore*, Vol. 32: pp. 363-370.

SMITH, P. (Feb. 1966) "Buckaroo (Vaquero)." *Negro History Bulletin*, Vol. 30: p. 107.

SMITH, R. (Nov. 1, 1926) *Gullah*. Bulletin of the University of South Carolina, Columbia, South Carolina: No. 190.

SMITH, R. (1928) *South Carolina Ballads*. Cambridge: Harvard University Press.

SMYTHE, A.T. (1931) *The Carolina Low Country*. New York: Macmillan.

SMYTHE, A.T. (1959) "Preface." *Society for the Preservation of Spirituals*, 2nd Series, a record, Charleston, South Carolina.

SOUTH CAROLINA FOLKTALES: STORIES OF ANIMALS AND SUPERNATURAL BEINGS. (1940) Works of the Writer's Program of the Works Project Administration, Columbia, South Carolina: Bulletin of the University of South Carolina.

SPAULDING, H.G. (1863) "Under the Palmetto." *Continental Monthly*, New York, Vol. 4: pp. 188-203; also in JACKSON, B., ed., *The Negro and His Folklore in 19th Century Periodicals*. pp. 64-73.

STACK, C. (1974) *All Our Kin: Strategies for Survival in a Black Community*. N.Y.: Harper Row.

STAPLES, R., ed. (1978) *The Black Family: Essays and Studies*. Belmont, California: Wadsworth.

STEWART, S.E. (1919) "Seven Folktales from the Sea Islands, South Carolina." *Journal of American Folklore*, Vol. 32: pp. 394-396.

STODDARD, A.H. (Sept. 1944) "Origin, Dialect, Beliefs and Characteristics of the Negroes of the South Carolina and Georgia Coasts." *Georgia Historical Quarterly*, Vol. 28: pp. 186-195.

STONEY, P.K. (1950) "The Incidence of the Sickle Cell Trait in the Negroes from the Sea Island Area of South Carolina." *Southern Medical Journal*, Vol. 43: p. 48.

SUDARKASA, N. (1981) "Interpreting the African Heritage in Afro-American Family Organization." pp. 37-53 in Harriette Pipes McAdoo, ed. *Black Families*. Beverly Hills: SAGE.

SZWED, J.F. (Oct. 1970) "Africa Lies Just Off Georgia." *Africa Report*: pp. 29-31.

SZWED, J.F. (N.D.) "The Gullah: A Heritage Remembered." *Topic*, Vol. 18: pp. 9-11.

THOMAS, J.S. (1977) *Blacks on the South Carolina Sea Islands: Planning for Tourist and Land Development*. Ph.D. Dissertation, University of Michigan.

THOMPSON, R.F. (1969) "African Influence on the Art of the U.S." *Black Studies in the University: A Symposium*. New Haven: Yale University Press: p. 127 (baskets), pp. 130-154 (Sea Island Crafts).

THOMPSON, R.F. (Nov. 1970) "From Africa." *Yale Review*, Vol. 60: pp. 16-20.

THROWER, S.S. (1954) *The Spiritual of the Gullah Negro in South Carolina*. M.A. Thesis, Cincinnati: College of the Conservatory of Music.

TOWNE, L.H. (1901) "Pioneer Work on the Sea Islands." *Southern Workman*, Vol. 30.

TOWNE, L.M. (1912) *Letters and Diary of Laura M. Towne, Written from the Sea Islands of S. C., 1862-1884.* HOLLAND, R.S., ed. Cambridge: Harvard University Press.

TURNER, L.D. (1949) *Africanisms in the Gullah Dialect.* Chicago: University of Chicago Press.

TURNER, L.D. (1941) "Linguistic Research and African Survivals." *American Council of Learned Societies*, Vol. 32: p. 73.

TURNER, L.D. (1948) "Problems Confronting the Investigator of Gullah." American Dialect Society, Greensboro: p. 74-84.

TURNER, L.D. (1945) "Notes on the Sounds and Vocabulary of Gullah." *Publications of the American Dialect Society*, Vol. 3: pp. 13-28.

TWINING, M.A. and SAUNDERS, W.C. (April 1970) "One of These Days: The Function of Two Singers in the Sea Island Community." *Studies in the Literary Imagination*, Burrison, J.B., ed., Atlanta, Georgia: Georgia State University, pp. 64-71.

TWINING, M.A. and BAIRD, K.E. (June 1980) "Sea Island Culture." *Journal of Black Studies* 10: 4.

TWINING, M.A. (1982) "Black American Quilts: An Artistic Craft." *Jamaica Journal* 16/1: 66-71.

TWINING, M.A. (1983) "Harvesting and Heritage: A Comparison of Afro-American and African Basketry in W. Ferris, ed., *Afro-American Folk Art and Crafts.* Boston: G.K. Hall.

TWINING, M.A. (1980) "Sea Island Basketry: Reaffirmations of West Africa" in *The First National African American Crafts Conference: Select Writings.* Memphis: Shelby State Community College, pp. 35-39.

TWINING, M.A. (June 1985) "Movement and Dance on the Sea Islands." *Journal of Black Studies* 15: 4.

TWINING, M.A. (Sept. 1967) "Review of Carawan's *Ain't You Got A Right to the Tree of Life?*" *Ethnomusicology*, Vols. 2-3: pp. 421-422.

UCHENDU, V. (1965) *The Igbo of Southeastern Nigeria.* New York: Holt Rinehart and Winston.

ULMANN, D. (1974) *The Darkness and the Light.* Millerton, N.Y.: Aperture.

VASS, W.K. (1980) *The Bantu-Speaking Heritage of the United States.* M.A. Thesis, University of Florida Gainesville, 1971; also published by CAAS University of California at Los Angeles.

WATSON, J.M. (1940) *Negro Folk Music in Eastern South Carolina.* M.A. Thesis, University of South Carolina.

WHALEY, M.S. (1925) *The Old Types Pass: Gullah Sketches of the Carolina Sea Islands.* Boston: Christopher Publishing House.

WIGHTMAN, O.S. and CATE, M.D. (1955) *Early Days of Coastal Georgia.* St. Simon Island, Georgia: Fort Frederica Association.

WINKOOP, A.P. (Sept. 1970) "The Crafting of Sea Island Baskets." "Contemporary Corner" of the *National Antiques Review*, pp. 28-31.

WOOD, P.H. (1974) *Black Majority.* New York: Knopf.

WOOFTER, T.J. (1930) *Black Yeomanry*. New York: Henry Holt.

WORK, M.H. (1905) "Some Geechee Folklore." *Southern Workman*, Vol. 35: pp. 633-635.

WYLLY, C.S. (1910) *The Seed That Was Sown in the State of Georgia*. New York and Washington: The Neale Co.

YATES, I. (1947) "A Collection of Proverbs and Proverbial Sayings from South Carolina Literature." *Southern Folklore Quarterly*, Vol. 11: pp. 187-199.

YATES, I. (1946) "Conjures and Cures in the Novels of Julia Peterkin." *Southern Folklore Quarterly*, Vol. 10: pp. 137-149.

ZINSSER, W. (June 13, 1967) *The Tree of Life. Look* pp. 18-19.

Contributors

Bamidele Agbasegbe Demerson is a Doctoral candidate in Sociology at the University of Michigan, and has published a number of articles on the African American family.

Keith E. Baird, Professor Emeritus of Anthropology, State University College at Buffalo, New York, has a Ph.D. degree from Union Graduate School. He is a linguist with a special interest in sociolinguistics and creole languages. He edited and co-authored *Names From Africa* with Ogonna Chuks-Orji, Chicago: Johnson Publishing Co., Inc. (1972).

The late William Bascom was a scholar of note in the field of African Studies. His *Continuity and Change in African Societies* co-edited with Melville J. Herskovits has been a stock-in-trade for African Studies courses for many years. He was a senior scholar and faculty member in the Anthropology Department as well as the director of the Lowie Museum at the University of California, Berkeley.

Herman Blake, himself a Sea Islander, is presently President of Tougaloo College, Tougaloo, Mississippi.

Guy Carawan has a Master's degree in Sociology, but perhaps is best known for his role in spreading the song, "We Shall Overcome" through the Civil Rights Movement in the early 1960s. He is the author of several articles and co-editor of *Freedom is a Constant Struggle*, New York: Oak Publications (1968) and author with Candie Anderson Carawan

179

of *Ain't You Got a Right to the Tree of Life*, New York: Simon & Schuster (1967).

John Henrik Clarke, born in Union Springs, Alabama, is a well-known figure in American scholarship. He has published many articles and edited books on the history of Africans and African Americans. He is Professor Emeritus of African History at Hunter College of the City University of New York.

Janie Gilliard Moore, who holds a Master of Sacred Theology degree from Interdenominational Theological Seminary, is from Yonges Island, South Carolina.

Simon Ottenberg, author of anthropology texts and books on the Igbo of Nigeria, is a well-known and extensively-published scholar of African anthropology. He is a senior faculty member at the University of Washington.

Paul Salter is a geographer presently teaching in the graduate school at Washburn University.

William C. Saunders has long played the role of arbitrator between the African American and European American communities of Charleston, South Carolina. A lifetime resident of Johns Island, South Carolina, he is presently Director of the Committee of Better Racial Assurance which handles problems of community relations, Sickle Cell Anemia Counselling and numerous other social and economic issues. He is also the chair of the Democratic Party of Charleston County and part owner of WPAL radio station in Charleston.

George Starks, Jr., is on the faculty of the Performing Arts Department at Drexel University. Dr. Starks has a Ph.D. degree from the University of North Carolia in music and has done extensive research in the music of the Sea Island area.

Mary Arnold Twining has a Ph.D. degree from Indiana University in Folklore and has done a great deal of research and a number of articles on the Sea Island region. Her doctoral dissertation was entitled "An Examinations of Africanisms on the Sea Islands of Georgia and South Carolina." Indiana, 1977.

Index

Acculturation: factors in, 10; civil rights legislation as factor in, 13; agricultural basis of society as factor in, 13; naming practices affected by, 41; basket names fewer due to, 53

African American family: Sea Island cuture as matrix of, 1-18; Billingsley's classificatory scheme of, 4

African American history: folktales, language, polygynous mating, religion as sources in, 2

African American landholders: measures for creation of, 61

African American scholars: responsibilities of, as researchers in African American communities, 161

African cultural continuities: patterns of Sea Island family life as evidence of, 2; naming practices show examples of, 42; theories of, 108-110

African cultural continuum: Sea Island culture in relation to, VII; "superstitutions" part of, X.

African cultural heritage: kinship values reflective of, 59

African culture: Sea Island culture compared with, 107-117

African family: effects of divorce limited in, 60

African languages: names taken from, 38-50

African majority in Sea Island population: social-psychological consequences of, 160

African peoples: cultural memories drawn specifically from, 76

African traditions: durability of mental bonding fostered and secondary marriages sanctioned by, 60

African practices on Sea Island: survival of, 115-116

African World: cultural patterns common throughout, 2

Afrish ("Black English"): relationship of Gullah language to, 12; of Barbados, 12; of Jamaica, 12; of Sierra Leone, 12; of U.S.A., 12

Foot foremost child: belief about, 30. *See also* Childbirth.
Freedman's Bureau: assisted purchasing of land by ex-bondsmen, 15, 61